Psychology in the Trenches

AMS STUDIES IN MODERN SOCIETY

ISSN 0275-8407
SET ISBN-13: 978-0-404-61620-5

No. 25

John A. Corson

Psychology in the Trenches
Stories, Strategies and Outcomes

PSYCHOLOGY IN THE TRENCHES
Stories, Strategies, and Outcomes

***John A. Corson**, Ph.D.*
Dartmouth College
and
Dartmouth Medical School in New Hampshire
Veterans Administration in Vermont

AMS PRESS, INC.
New York

Library of Congress Cataloging-in-Publication Data

Corson, John A.
  Psychology in the trenches: stories, strategies, and outcomes / John A.
  Corson
    p. cm. — (AMS Studies in Modern Society ; no. 25)
  Includes bibliographical references and index.
  ISBN-13: 978-0-404-61632-8 (hardback) (alk. paper)
  ISBN-13: 978-0-404-61633-5 (paperback) (alk. paper)
  1. Stress (Psychology). 2. Self-perception. 3. Violence—Psychological
  aspects—Case studies. 4. Mentally ill—Case studies. I. Title. II. Series.

RC455.4.S87C668 2008
616.85'82—dc22   2003065070
                                                              CIP

All AMS books are printed on acid-free paper that meets the guidelines for
performance and durability of the Committee on Production Guidelines for
Book Longevity of the Council on Library Resources.

AMS Press, Inc.
Brooklyn Navy Yard, 63 Flushing Ave., Unit #221
Brooklyn, New York 11205-1005, U.S.A.
www.amspressinc.com

MANUFACTURED IN THE UNITED STATES OF AMERICA

CONTENTS

Acknowledgments

First, I thank my wife, Mary Schneider for her patient support throughout this project. The work was made possible by the help I have received from many friends and colleagues, and by the participation of hundreds of clients. I am grateful to the parent of a Dartmouth graduate who anonymously established a fund for my research on stress.

I am deeply indebted to Carolyn Mercer-McFadden and Donald Doehring for editorial assistance. I thank Fred Elliott and Debra Scott, who also helped with this book, and who work with me on a daily basis in the trenches.

Both my 1989 book and the present book reflect work with troubled clients, most of whom, since 1974, have been military veterans. Many of these clients have collaborated with me in this work, and I am very grateful to them all.

Introduction

This book elaborates on a theory and related strategies that were first touched on in my 1989 book. This new book updates the status of the violent clients I described in the 1989 book, and describes work with other clients who have no history or apparent tendencies toward violence. It also details my still-deepening appreciation of individual differences, and the resulting shifts and innovations in method that I have come to favor since 1989. Finally, the changes in clinical practices outlined in this new book were partly driven by the attempts of a very small staff (myself and two others) to cope with a large number of clients, and increasingly large numbers of referrals, which forced us to use group strategies for both assessment and treatment whenever possible.

The 1989 book described work that made use of physiological monitoring systems combined with strategies of assessment and treatment that had both behavioral and cognitive behavioral elements. Use of these various modalities revealed vast differences between clients who had very similar backgrounds and had received identical diagnoses from other practitioners. These differences emerged as I came to know each individual better, and had considerable impact on the choice of therapeutic methods and on the eventual outcomes of therapy. Since 1989 I have frequently been surprised by even more remarkable differences between clients, and I have been even more seriously challenged to match treatment strategies to the needs of individual clients. Attending to the individual differences while making increased use of group assessment and treatment strategies has been particularly difficult.

Anyone who is "in the trenches," without a large support staff, and with new clients being referred each week, will appreciate the value of standardized diagnosis and treatments. Clinicians who make individualized diagnoses and attempt to match subtleties of treatments to the needs of each client may be slowed to a crawl, and be unable to meet the demands of their caseload. This new book is intended to be a guide to working quickly and effectively between these two extremes.

For two reasons, much of this book is presented in the form of stories about individual clients. First, the differences between individuals cry out for an ideographic, i.e., individual storytelling format. Second, even with many hundreds of clients having been assessed and treated since 1989, we have not had the time or resources to do the controlled nomothetic, i.e., group studies. However, we have been conducting repeated case studies by using both standardized and individually-tailored methods of gathering data on each client. For intake we have generally used a group psychological screening format combined with an interview. On the basis of this information we have developed a case formulation and selected both treatment methods and specific data-gathering procedures for use throughout treatment. In some instances we have aggregated data from all clients presenting with a similar problem. Such an aggregation of data, from many dozens of violent clients, was presented in the 1989 book. Several sets of data are presented in the present book. The following is a listing. Data are presented on a family optimization program used with normal families, used with disorganized families, used with child abusing families, and a variation used with infant abusing families; data from group testing are presented; data are presented on outcomes of work with violent clients; data are presented on outcomes from application of a 10-session group format based on Linehan's dialectical behavior therapy model, as well as on a 4-session adaptation of the model; finally, data are presented on outcome of work with sex offenders. However, in the present book there is much more focus on strategies and outcomes with individual clients than on aggregation of data.

Some personal history will show how I came to be fascinated with psychology, particularly with the relationship between stressful experiences and something to do with a sense of self as an entity isolated from all other entities (in the 1989 book I called this self-concept).

Self-Concept and Stress

When I was three, my father died. In the late afternoon I saw him collapse. Sometime in the night he died. This began one of the most stressful experiences in my life. My mother was distraught. She was also attempting to deal with my younger brother, who was then only a few months old. My world came apart. I had been evolving a self-concept, developed in the context of a supportive and admiring family system. I was put into a foster home for almost two years, and then was shuttled back and forth among summer camps, boarding schools and various relatives until I was about 10 years old. The salient memories of those years include a desperate struggle to survive, a sense of extreme and increasing isolation, and stunned gratitude whenever someone seemed to care about me.

Positive Expectancies and Failure Signals

Around the age of 7 I became interested in the demerit system that was used in my grade school. I brought it home to my aunt, who was struggling to help me grow up. She and I worked out our own version of the demerit system. Our system implied an expectation of good behavior, listed unacceptable behaviors as well as the consequences for them, and ensured 30-60 minutes of individual adult attention each day. It worked very well for us. That system persists for me today, with only minor alterations. It serves as a format (described later in this book) for optimizing the management of parental attention to children. The basic notions have also been adapted for managing the behavior of difficult clients.

Individual Differences

An important watershed occurred in high school. My homeroom teacher asked us to write a page about what we wanted to do with our lives. Instead of giving what had been my stock answer, wanting to be a surgeon like my father, after a few seconds of thought I realized that I wanted to study individual differences. I was fascinated by the differences between people. It was most clear that everyone else was very different from me. I felt isolated and odd, seeing others as more at ease and more connected to their friends and families. However, I also noticed that they were very different from each other. I assumed that many of the differences among people had been caused by differences in experience and learning, along with differences in genetic makeup, which would create the conscious and unconscious dispositions that we see as individual differences. In that one page, I boiled it all down, perhaps too simplistically, to finding out more about the processes of learning and memory.

My reading of Adler in college convinced me that the self-concept is a central issue in psychology—a key to understanding individual differences. My undergraduate research in psychology was a cumbersome attempt to examine the role of self-concept in determining how different individuals cope with failure signals.

Learning and Memory, Mathematics and Neuropsychology

Shortly after completing the undergraduate research project, I decided to go to graduate school to find out what Adlerian psychology had to offer in the study of individual differences. Heinz Ansbacher, an expert on Adler, was at the University of Vermont. I applied there. By a stroke of luck the only person there who was able to provide funds to support a graduate student was Norman Slamecka, who was studying the learning process. Thus I was also able to pursue my high school plans and examine individual differences by way of studying the process of learning and memory. While working in Slamecka's laboratory, I came up with some notions about the early stages of memory formation. In particular, I had ideas about what happens in serial learning when one attempts and fails to retrieve a specific item of information. I developed a simple neurological model and a testable mathematical version. Eventually I found that the model only worked for serial learning and not for paired-associate learning. This limitation was a bit disappointing, but I was thrilled that I had been able to develop a model that could be tested

Around the time I was finishing my master's thesis, I came across Donald Hebb's presidential address to the American Psychological Association (1960), which was reprinted in the *American Psychologist* under the title "The American Revolution." In this magnificent piece, Hebb described his attempts as a psychologist to understand neurological ideas and to make them work as part of a model or theory that would cast light on human behavior. Again I was hooked. I acquired his book *The Organization of Behavior* (1949) and quickly read it from cover to cover. At about the same time I also read a statistics text by George Ferguson (1959) and a book on motivation by Dalbir Bindra (1959). A very important moment came when I realized that Hebb, Ferguson, and Bindra were all at McGill University. I applied for admission to the graduate psychology program at McGill and was accepted as one of Hebb's students.

Nomothetic Research

Both Slamecka and Hebb tried to shift my attention away from individual differences and guide me to a more careful consideration of a nomothetic quest, carrying out group studies and searching for possible generalizations. I complied with their urging and focused my doctoral thesis on the acquisition and retention of discrimination habits in rats. Some of that data led me back circuitously to consider individual differences. Specifically, I had gathered some data which suggested that during the learning process the emotional state or mood of the subject is very important. When the emotional state or mood that pertained during learning was reinstated at the time of the attempt to retrieve the memory, the retrieval was facilitated. All of this led me into a post-doctoral fellowship with an eminent psychiatrist cum physiologist, R.A. Cleghorn.

Biological Variables

My association with Cleghorn exposed me to his research, clinical interests, and experience. One paper in particular had a profound influence. Cleghorn and Pattee (1954) observed opposite emotional and cognitive effects of steroid injections on two adult subjects. One person became manic and the other became deeply depressed. This finding provided a possible insight into some of the odd results I had obtained with laboratory animals.

Stress and Individual Differences

During this period, with Hans Selye, a leading pioneer in research on stress only a few hundred yards away, I became more deeply interested in reading and thinking about individual differences in responses to stress. Eventually I came to see that although most studies involved nomothetic hypotheses, the conclusion often acknowledged the existence of individual differences.

Since those days I have kept a foot in each camp, but always the group (nomothetic) work has been less intriguing to me than the individual (ideographic) work. Through a combination of circumstances, I went from being primarily a postdoctoral researcher at the Psychiatry Department of McGill University in 1964, to being a research adviser to the Psychiatry Department's Behavior Therapy Unit. Then, when Medicare came into Quebec and some physicians left the Province, I became codirector of that behavior therapy unit. By 1974 I was supervising 22 people. Three of these people were doing basic research and the rest were involved in the clinical work. I had become more of an administrator and grant writer than either a researcher or a clinician. When I received an offer to move to Dartmouth College, I saw it as an opportunity to return to a more simple existence, where I could resume my neurologizing, modeling, and testing of models. However I had become much less interested in research with college sophomores and laboratory animals, and much more interested in clinical research with troubled adults. Fortunately, the position offered by Dartmouth College included the Chief of Psychology position at a Veterans Administration Hospital across the river from the college. This position came with two funded technicians, allowing me to avoid the burden of constant grant writing. It also gave me access to a large sample of troubled adults that in 1974 included the returning veterans of the Vietnam War as well as the aging veterans of the Korean War and World War II. Since then all of my work, with one client after another, has been a series of research projects, each done in collaboration with a unique individual.

This book is about those research projects.

Overview

As my work has gone on, I have developed a multilevel, flexible theory of human behavior, and my colleagues and I have paid a lot of attention to tactics of assessment and treatment that involve psychophysiological, behavioral, and cognitive-behavioral procedures.

Part 1 presents this theory as it pertains to stress, self-concept, and personality. Chapter 1 briefly introduces an individualistic strategy for thinking about stress and self-concept. Chapter 2 integrates this system into a "shifting" or "shifty" theory of personality. Chapter 3 continues the consideration of the personality theory, but focuses on biological variables.

Part 2 contains four chapters about families, personality development, and behavioral problems. Chapter 4 considers developmental influences on personality. Chapter 5 presents a program for optimizing these developmental influences and presents data on the use of this system with normal families and with troubled families. Chapter 6 describes a program for working with families who have preverbal children. Chapter 7 focuses again on the development of the individual personality and specifically considers what happens "when things go wrong."

Part 3 contains three chapters dealing with technique. Chapter 8 describes our recently developed group psychological assessment program. Chapter 9 describes approaches to case formulation. This begins with examination of the client's self-concept, their view of how they are seen by others, and events in their lives (past and present) that have produced powerful emotional responses. This chapter then describes a simple approach to focusing on single episodes of problematic behavior. Finally, this chapter presents a format—the flow diagram—for organizing thoughts and data on the self-concept, stressors, and plans for treatment. Chapter 10 reviews the present status of biofeedback, and includes a few comments on clinical psychophysiology.

Part 4 consists of four chapters about violent behavior and my work with violent adults. Chapter 11 is a selective review of literature on violent adults. Chapters 12 and 13 present theory, methods, data and case histories (with very long-term follow-up) of patients referred for violent behavior. Chapter 14 provides some reflections on the violent personality and some practical observations and suggestions. Chapter 15 is a conclusion to my work with violent clients in individual sessions. This chapter reviews key points from the earlier chapters and emphasizes the importance of continuing attention to the evolving reciprocal relationship between stressors and self-concept.

Part 5 consists of four chapters describing our work with other populations. This work focuses on self-regulation strategies and is done in both individual and group sessions. Chapter 16 focuses on working with male clients in groups. Chapter 17 is a brief description of our weekly psychoeducational group. This group is modeled loosely after Linehan's DBT program, and is used with individuals with a very wide range of diagnoses. Many clients with a history of violent explosions now attend this group. Chapter 18 presents detailed examples of strategies we use in groups to train clients in self-regulation. This chapter focuses on strategies used with urges to do violence or express hostile feelings, and transient problems with attention deficit that often accompany extreme agitation. Chapter 19 presents detailed examples of self-regulation strategies we use in individual sessions. This chapter focuses on two problem areas, panic attacks and sex offenses.

Part 6 includes two chapters on work with life stories, self-concept and available selves. Chapter 20 presents the basics of our approach to brief narrative therapy. Chapter 21 is entitled "Putting It Altogether and Making It Last: Working with Life Stories and Optimizing Available Selves." This chapter updates and expands on the theory spelled out in chapter 2, and pulls together threads that have appeared in other chapters.

You will probably notice as you read through these chapters that sometimes I speak in the voice of an academic, and other times I speak in the voice that I would use with my clients. The choice of words is different, and there are other differences that you may notice. As you reflect on what I write about "available selves" you will see that my writing fits the ideas I am dealing with now. The shifts between voices are shifts between two of my available selves. They are both really me, but they are very different from each other in many ways.

Part One

Theory and Strategy

1: An Ideographic Approach to Theory

The focus of this book can be characterized as follows: "Here is a troubled individual. What can we do to help understand that individual and help him or her improve the quality of life?"

Even with this focus, we still have to deal with many variables. I will describe a theory that seems to help. This theory treats self-concept as the superordinate variable. It spells out developmental relationships among parental attention, sense of self, and the selection of incentive stimuli. Finally, it traces these relationships to their manifestations in the behavior of the adult.

The focal point in attempting to understand our clients is their sense of self or self-concept. Consistent with this approach, my colleagues and I have developed treatment strategies and procedures that have helped our clients manage better. This book describes the theory, strategies, and procedures, and describes some data, as well as discussing some remaining problems and possibilities. The case histories of specific people in extremely stressful situations provide much of the context of this book.

Systems Theory and Modeling Applied to Individuals

Until recently, most systems theorizing and modeling attempts in psychology were conducted in the nomothetic (group) arena. In our clinical setting, however, it seems more fruitful to work at the ideographic (individual) level, using systems thinking and modeling to deal with individuals and with the behavior of specific individuals.

My formal introduction to systems thinking and modeling was in the mid-sixties in a course offered to graduate students and faculty members at McGill University by John Milsum, a pioneer in systems theory, modeling, and biomedical engineering. Much of the course focused on modeling systems of regional temperature regulation in living organisms. However, it was clear that these strategies could be put to work in the analysis of other systems, including systems involved in human behavior.

A Blueprint

The term "biopsychosocial" (e.g., see Engel, 1980) expresses the idea that human biological, psychological and social variables are organized in a reciprocally-determined system. According to this model, everything that a human being experiences and does is influenced by and influences everything else that he or she experiences and does.

A few years ago, a summer symposium at Dartmouth College was considering the topic of reciprocal determinism (i.e., everything influences and is influenced by everything else) among biological, psychological, and social variables in alcoholism. We were attempting to develop models of alcoholism using strategies of systems dynamics. I was in a minority, which advocated modeling an individual alcoholic rather than modeling alcoholism in general. As a result of this symposium, one student produced a master's thesis that did indeed focus on modeling the biological, psychological, and social variables in the life of a single alcoholic, who was one of my clients. The model dealt with the phenomenon of multiple and reciprocal influences bearing on a single outcome. This attempt at modeling involved a hierarchical system with sense of self, or self-concept, as a superordinate variable.

In the past twenty-five years, my colleagues and I have applied such modeling strategies to individual clients with other problems, often to clients referred to us for outbursts of violent behavior. We have learned that large and formal models are not as useful in assessing and treating an individual's problems as are a variety of mini-models regarding specific behaviors in specific situations. In fact, the utility of these mini-models is much greater than we had originally anticipated.

Mini-Models

We have found that our general theory and modeling strategy can quite easily be explained to most clients. Many clients are able to grasp the ideas of reciprocal determination and biopsychosocial modeling best if we select a single episode in their lives and work out a tentative mini-model around this episode. The procedure will be detailed later, but a brief example may be helpful at this point.

With numerous clients we have been able to use physiological monitoring, television feedback of facial expression and verbal behavior, and role-playing. Along with these tactics we have used various strategies for assessing the interaction of self-satisfaction with specific life situations. These procedures are used to create a multilevel model of a specific episode from real life. Figure 1.1 shows the set-up and equipment for using all aspects of this strategy. Table 1.1 shows the format for gathering data and generating ideas in preparation for using the strategy. (We generally use only a part of this format, and, as will be seen, we also use many other ways of gathering data and developing ideas.)

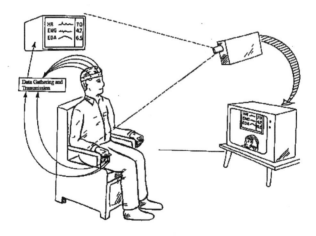

Figure 1.1. *Physiological monitoring system combined with TV system to provide feedback to the client of both biological and behavioral variables. This is used both for simultaneous feedback (e.g., during a role-playing situation) and for later playback.*

Table 1.1

Format for Gathering Information About a Behavioral Episode

PERSONAL SCIENCE – FORMAT FOR DEVELOPING A MULTILEVEL **ABC** DIAGRAM

Use this format to describe the most recent (or most memorable) occurrence of your problem and fill in as many of the spaces you can.

ANTECENDENTS: Ask yourself what was going on in yourself and your environment just before the problem occurred;

BEHAVIORS: Ask yourself what behavior did you show and what was going on in yourself and environment during the behavioral episode;

CONSEQUENCES: Ask yourself what happened after the behavioral episode ended.

		ANTECEDENTS	BEHAVIORS	CONSEQUENCES
THINGS OTHER PEOPLE	DO			
	SAY			
OTHER ENVIRONMENTAL EVENTS				
MY OVERT BEHAVIOR				
MY COVERT BEHAVIOR				
	THOUGHTS			
	MOODS, EMOTIONS & FEELINGS			
LABELS I USE FOR MYSELF				
THE LEVEL OF MY SELF-ESTEEM	HIGH			
	MEDIUM			
	LOW			
THE LEVEL OF MY EXCITEMENT	HIGH			
	MEDIUM			
	LOW			

This format has been applied successfully with a number of violent clients. An example follows. We were able to use this format with Mr. C., a violent client (who is described in some detail in chapter 13) to help him develop insight into the following processes:

(1) How a cumulative biological priming influences his behavioral dispositions in certain social situations.

(2) How his own stimulus value (his face and posture) is likely to have a "feed forward" effect in a social situation. Specifically, before he says anything, or interacts with anyone in a social situation, he influences other people by his menacing facial expression and his threatening posture. Thus, the first response that anyone makes to him is already influenced by the other person's responses to a certain perceived level of threat resulting from his presence and presentation.

(3) Realization of how his facial expressions and posture influenced others led this client to describe his expectations that others are very likely to try to humiliate him, and his unwillingness to permit this to happen.

This simple reenactment of a real-life experience helped us develop a mini-biopsychosocial model that depicted a complex, multifaceted system of influences. The model facilitated insight for the client, and this insight brought about eventual dramatic improvement in his behavior.

Definitions and Postulates

Stress

Defining stress has long been considered problematic.[1] Definitions are often relative, and frequently tautological. When I consider stress from an individual point of view in association with self-concept, the relativism and the tautology become functional rather than problematic.

In the late 1930s, Selye proposed a distinction between the cause of bodily disturbance and its effect. He referred to the external

---

[1] Everly and Sobelman (1987) have carefully addressed the issues of definition and assessment of stress.

cause, or the stimulus, as a "stressor," and to the state of bodily disequilibrium, or the response, as "stress." This simple definition has been widely accepted, but it does not address several important issues. For example, it does not consider the extent to which stress responses are nonspecific and the extent to which stress is good or bad.

Selye (1974, 1976) summarized some of his views in the following way:

(1) Stress is nonspecific, although each stressor has both specific effects (sweating during heat) and nonspecific effects (the adrenal enlargement, the thymus involution, and the development of ulcers that may occur if a stress continues for a long enough period of time).

(2) A stressor is whatever produces these nonspecific effects (admittedly a circular definition).

(3) Psychological events can produce the same stress responses as physical stressors.

(4) Some stressors produce good stress. Selye (1978) called this "eustress," a mixture of the words euphoria and stress. Other stressors produce bad stress, which he called "distress."

(5) Stress is always a matter of degree.

(6) Stress in human beings can be moderated by various treatment techniques.

In current usage, we do not consistently distinguish between eustress and distress. In fact, we typically use the word "stress" to denote both the stimulus and its effects, including internal (psychological, emotional, and physiological) and behavioral responses.

As Selye pointed out, the stressor, or stimulus, can have many sources: bright lights, loud noises, social interactions, anticipation of an examination, a disturbing thought, a threat, a sore throat. The list is endless. Clearly, the stimulus can be internal or external to the individual experiencing stress.

The nature of the stress response also varies widely. Stress responses may include changes in respiration, changes in perspiration, diarrhea, disturbing thoughts, dry mouth, crying, swearing, fatigue. Again, the list is very long.

As noted by Holms and Rahe (1967), even a pleasant stimulus such as getting married or giving birth to a child can produce a wide variety of responses, reflecting both pleasure and displeasure.

To cope with this complexity, I will identify the stimulus and its effects as specifically as possible, and place the concept of stress within an individual framework and a systems theory.

Self-Concept

As mentioned before, to make any sense of the idea of multiple causality interacting with individual differences we need a flexible multilevel theory. A key role in this theory must be played by something like the individual's self-concept. (Along with many others, I have struggled with ideas about, and various terminologies that refer to, the self-concept, sense or awareness of self, or sense of agency. Some of these struggles will be described in more detail later.)

Just as stressor and stress are redefined for each individual and for each new situation that the person interacts with, so is self-concept. Self-concept can change with each instance in which an individual interacts with a particular stressor and experiences a stress response. It also appears that the functions of certain physiological systems co-vary with these changes in self-concept (more about this later).

Such complexity could easily become overwhelming. However, I have developed strategies, specific formats, mnemonic devices and other simple routines that help me and may help you to think quickly and flexibly about the shifting complexities. They make it easier to follow the strategies and evaluate the ideas.

The most compelling reasons for using this approach are that (a) the important clinical data are variable, and (b) within non-clinical, or "normal," samples, intraindividual variations are significant.

Shifting Variables

When I began to do clinical work in the 1960s I realized that many important variables (mood, agitation, self-satisfaction etc.) were in constant flux. This realization led me to develop a very simple method (described in detail later) to keep track of the relationships between different situations and different levels of self-satisfaction, or status of self-concept in individual clients. During each session, I used a format that quickly determined the client's highest and lowest levels of self-satisfaction in the preceding 24 hours, and in what situations the client experienced these high and low levels. The results demonstrated that intraindividual variations, even within a single day, are so wide that any of the existing theories of personality would simply not suffice. Furthermore, any existing assessment procedure, whether it be a complicated personality test or a psychophysiological profile, taken at any specific time, would not do a good job of predicting the relationships between situations and behavior patterns for any particular client. Rather, the predictive ability increased as I saw the client over time, and gathered data about relationships concerning specific interactions between situations and behavior.

As I met and consulted with more and more clients, I became convinced that this highly individualized approach to the person and the situation is essential. I also saw that such an approach was a prerequisite for eventually developing some rules about the organization of behavior and some general concepts regarding individual differences.

A more recent experience that convinced me of the need for this approach to stress, self-concept, and situations was a study I conducted in collaboration with 22 Dartmouth College students in the fall of 1978. These students were registered in my course on individual differences, and served as both co-experimenters and subjects. For 14 consecutive days during the term, they monitored daily their highest and their lowest levels of self-satisfaction, or self-concept, on 21 bipolar continua (e.g., attractive–unattractive; smart–stupid; interesting–boring). They made notes regarding the situations that corresponded with the three highest and the three lowest ratings on each of the 14 days. They analyzed and reported on their own patterns of behavior in a wide variety of situations. They carefully noted how the interactions between themselves and the situations were reflected in, and, to varying degrees driven by, the status of their own self-concept at the time of experiencing each particular situation. The students also completed a variety of tests[2]: Rotter's locus-of-control scale; Rathus's assertiveness scale; Eysenck's introvert-extrovert scale, Jenkins's activity scale; the Adjective

---

[2] References to all published tests mentioned in the book are provided in the three following sources: Buros (1974), Newmark (1985), Sweetland and Keyser (1983).

Check List; the Tennessee Self-Concept Scale; a "personal constructs" test modified from work done by Kelly (1955); and a physiological stress profile that monitored biological variables (skin conductance and temperature) during a period of relaxation, a period of stress, and a final period of relaxation (see Chapter 10).

This project resulted in a massive and multifaceted database. At the end of the course we developed a collective synthesis and overview. The fundamental conclusion was that while some general consistencies did appear, the intra-individual variability in this sample of healthy and intelligent young people was truly remarkable. No existing personality theory can encompass these variations adequately, although some have tried, e.g., Epstein (1980) and Mischel (1976).

Another observation, made by almost every student, is reflected in the following feedback. "Professor Corson, thanks for what turned out to be a very worthwhile experience. The course opened my eyes to a lot of issues I would never have considered otherwise, and working on the incentive survey gave me more satisfaction than any other project." One student told me that his experience with the course had led him to think of himself and his likes and dislikes in a totally new way and to dramatically alter his career plans.

Such feedback suggests that the outlines of a stable sense of self, and stabilities in likes and dislikes regarding situations, can indeed be distilled by a well-informed observer from a mass of data gathered over a long enough time. Such experiences have led me to work with each individual client, as the sessions go by, to develop an understanding of the range of their problems in thought, feeling, and behavior, and the range and types of situations in which these problems are experienced. These experiences also emphasize that it is important to work to determine the range of the client's positive feelings, thoughts and behavior, as well as the situations that put the client at ease. This approach has enabled me to gather the data that now provide the basis of what I like to call a "shifting theory of personality."

2: A Shifting Theory of Personality

Human behavior is remarkably complex and variable. A general theory of personality, particularly one that attends to person-situation relationships in proper detail, can prevent the scientist or clinician from being overwhelmed by human diversity and by the intraindividual differences as a person passes through time and through various life situations.

Shifting Definition

When I am asked about personality by psychology students, or when I hear them attempting to describe someone's personality, I ask them to consider how they are defining personality. "Tell me what behavior makes you say this person has personality X, and then tell me what situation is most likely to cause that person to show this X-type behavior." And that's it! I can only see personality as a description of specific behavior patterns in specific situations.

To go any further toward understanding personality, we must focus on a single person. We must perform a microanalysis of the various domains or aspects of this person's behavior patterns and their relationships to a range of specific situations. Here we would be using our shifting personality theory, and strategies, to guide us to a highly specific mini-theory. Such a personality theory, by definition, is only good for one person. Some variable aspects of behavior-situation interactions that would contribute to a mini-theory are as follows:

(1) Environmental events,
(2) The subject's overt behavior as time passes and as the behavior is modified by environmental events,
(3) The subject's changes in arousal level and pattern,
(4) The subject's changes in self-concept and self-satisfaction,
(5) Other aspects of the subject's covert behavior, including the wide range of cognitive and emotional states.

This list is not exhaustive, but it gives you an idea about the range of ever-changing variables involved in personality. The list also sets the stage for our further elaboration of this "shifting" approach to personality.

Shifting Biases

The word shifty, shift in adjectival form, is defined by Webster's as 1: resourceful, 2 a: tricky; b: elusive. I use the words shifty and shifting to connote how constantly resourceful we must be in dealing with the multitude of tricky and elusive variables that constitute personality. Theorizing about personality has always been a complex task. In 1937, Allport surveyed the literature on theories and definitions of personality and, more than a half century ago, came up with a vast array of ideas about personality.

Allport found more than 40 different definitions of personality in the literature. One of the problems in this field, as reflected by Allport's observations, is the remarkable range of values and points of view among those who have attempted to observe, explore, and define personality. The differences among the theorists in their biases concerning personality seem largely related to differences in their samples of subjects or clients. Freud, for example, was exposed to many troubled people. Cattell, on the other hand, was an experimental psychologist who spent more time studying relatively normal subjects. Thus Freud's theory and definitions include different aspects from Cattell's.

My own values and biases about personality theory have evolved largely from my clinical experience. I had the good fortune of working with a famous gastroenterologist, Thomas Almy. While Almy would not call himself a personality theorist, I learned many things from him about personality theory. Almy carried an implicit personality theory and strategy into each new clinical interaction. He developed, years ago, the strategy of using a "life chart" (Almy &,

Corson, 1987). This life chart relates the events in a person's life to various gastrointestinal and other medical symptoms. The life chart allowed Almy to simplify and to relate various physical symptoms, behavior patterns, and experiential events to each other so that the complex symphony of the life of a person in various situations would become clearer. Almy's life-chart strategy also confirmed my bias toward microanalysis, mini-models, and an individualistic approach.

Violent Clients as Examples for Theorizing

My initial approach in theory development draws heavily on a narrow database from a small sample of violent people. There are several reasons for choosing this sample.

One very good reason is that people who have violent outbursts scare us. They often scare me. My general theory and the activity of developing a mini-theory for the individual client not only reduces the complexities that face me as a clinician, but also reduces my fear, as it increases my sense of understanding and control of the situation and the client's behavior.

Another important reason I chose violent clients as examples for theorizing is that I have had extensive experience with this group. My sample consists of people who have been referred for assessment and treatment of problems involving violent outbursts over the past 30 or more years. I have dealt with over 500 people with these problems. Between 1964 and 1974, while I was at McGill, approximately 3,000 people were referred to our clinical group, and about 10% of these people were referred for violent outbursts. Between 1974 and 1984, at the White River Junction VA Hospital, 115 violent clients were referred to the Psychology Section for these problems (out of about 1,100 in all referred to the Psychology Section during that period). Since 1984, the rate of referrals has increased, but the percent of violent clients has remained between 10% and 20%. (It is worth noting that not all of these violent clients had been diagnosed with PTSD.) Finally, my reasons for choosing violent clients, as examples for theorizing about psychology are conceptually pragmatic:

(1) The behavior is relatively dramatic and salient.
(2) The behavior is easy to describe and operationalize.
(3) The situations in which the behavior occurs are
      relatively easy to define.
(4) The consequences of the behavior are easy to describe.

(5)   The behavior can be reproduced without too much difficulty by reinstating some or all aspects of the stimulus situation.
(6)   The reproducibility of behavior and situation permits us to study the various levels of interaction between the stimuli and the responses that drive the complex behavior-situation relationship which characterizes the personality.

Self-Concept: Stable Constructs

By definition, the shifting theory contains no static constructs regarding traits or states. At the individual level, however some stability of construct does emerge from a careful analysis of data concerning the self-concept. The relatively stable constructs are as follows:

(1)   The compelling situation.
(2)   The working self.
(3)   The available selves.
(4)   The possible selves.
(5)   The essential audience.
(6)   The personal scientist/theorist.

The Compelling Situation

As I come to know a client, I begin thinking about how they might fit with some of the concepts and definitions proposed by earlier personality theorists. I refrain from using personality labels or trait labels until I have identified some stable features in the client's behavior, by learning about compelling situations in the individual's life. Earlier theorists have also attended to individually-compelling situations. Murray's (1938) concept of "alpha press" and Cattell's (1965) concept of "erg" are based in part on the observation that for some people, certain specifiable environmental events or situations are particularly compelling. For such people, these compelling events or situations reliably result in a specific form of behavior. The particular behavior links up to a reciprocally-determined sequence of interactions with the individual's environment. Such interactions will be examined in subsequent chapters.

Stressors can be intrinsically involved in compelling situations. Some compelling situations, such as being involved in a train wreck, are universally stressful, and others are highly individual, such as seeing a particular sort of facial expression on a man in a barroom. Some compelling situations are imposed on a person, such as getting multiple sclerosis or being injured in an accident, and others are sought after, such as participation in a chess game or an arm-wrestling contest.

A history of having been exposed to some extremely compelling situations, such as combat experience or the experience of being raped, can have a devastating effect on self-concept, and can lead to a long struggle that many of our clients are in the throes of during our work with them. Ulman and Brothers (1988) in a book entitled "The Shattered Self" address these issues.

In the clinical setting universally-compelling situations, often vividly illustrated in the clients' accounts of their previous experiences, can provide a starting point from which one can begin to identify some important aspects of the client's personality. As the clinical work goes on and more individually-compelling situations become evident, we can begin to focus on some relatively stable traits.

In my clinical experience, I have repeatedly dealt with individuals who were coping with the most compelling situations of their lives (e.g., the active man who suffers a spinal injury in a fall and becomes paralyzed at T-2). As mentioned above, the relationship between self and situation is clarified in these tragic conditions.

By putting clients in compelling situations in a test environment, some of the stable aspects of personality can be examined. We have examined thought, behavior, and physiological patterns in response to a variety of moderately stressful, but universally compelling situations. Three such situations in the laboratory are: 1) the pain caused by putting one's hand in ice water for 30 seconds, 2) the excitement caused by being exposed to a fast-paced test of verbal and math skills and 3) the excitement involved in discussing the most recent situation in which one felt anger.

A very interesting approach to the use of compelling situations in the assessment of personality was suggested by Wallace (1966). Rather than using the traditional method of assessing personality, which involves asking a subject to indicate how he or she usually responds to a particular situation, Wallace's paper suggests the use of combinations of situations and challenging instructions. The subject could be asked, for example, to indicate how capable he or she is of responding in a cruel way.

Willerman, Turner, and Peterson (1976) provided some data supporting Wallace's suggestion. More recently, Seligman and his co-workers have developed powerful ideas and methods that examine thoughts and behaviors of individuals in compelling situations (Peterson and Seligman, 1984). Observation of the types, directions, and degrees of shifts in behavior and thought patterns during exposure to compelling conditions can tell us a great deal about an individual's personality.

These ideas about the use of compelling situations can be boiled down to two general statements. 1) The term biopsychosocial implies the existence of three domains, biological, psychological, and social: a compelling situation in any one of these three can be seen to influence the other two domains. 2) Patterns with regard to how the three domains in an individual's life influence each other are helpful in formulating a theory of the individual's personality.

Now, briefly setting aside the shifting aspect of sense of self or self-concept, we must consider the definition of self-concept. In very simple terms, self-concept could be defined in terms of the list of adjectives one would select as self descriptors, e.g., beautiful, handsome, ugly, brilliant, stupid, creative, average, charming, dull, loyal, honest. However, my understanding of self-concept is more complex, and I do not have a satisfactory definition. A preferred definition would include an attempt at self-description, or a description of some aspects of self-awareness. It is worth noting, however, that many people in many situations would be unlikely to come up with anything but a primitive and unsatisfactory self-description, if they came up with any description at all.

The concept of a self has been considered from the earliest writings of philosophers to the present, by religious writers, scientists of various disciplines, and writers of fiction. Over the past 20 years there have appeared a wonderful array of publications considering the self from various points of view (e.g., Detrick and Detrick, 1989; Cheshire and Thomae, 1987; Gergen, 1991; Csikszentmihalyi, 1993; Nurius and Berlin, 1994; Bermudez, Marcel and Eilan, 1998; Tesser, Felson, & Suls, 2000). Accordingly, there have been many definitions of and approaches to self-concept. Some writers have proposed other terms, such as "self theory" (Epstein, 1973), but all formal definitions will probably always miss some of the essential elements that I wish to include. These elements include unverbalized, and perhaps unverbalizable states, traits, processes, images, judgments, hopes, fears, expectancies and dispositions, all of which can shift to other states and processes in the blink of an eye.

In my 1989 book, I introduced self-concept as follows: "To make any sense of the idea of multiple causality interacting with individual differences, we need a multi-level systems theory. I am convinced that the superordinate role in this theory must be played by the individual's self-concept. Just as stressor and stress are redefined for each individual and for each new situation that the person interacts with, self-concept is relative. Self-concept changes with each instance in which an individual interacts with a particular stressor and experiences a stress response."

I went on to explain some assessment strategies, specific case formulation formats, mnemonic devices, and simple routines to help us think quickly and flexibly about the complexities in the shifting manifestations of self-concept and its interaction with environmental situations. I made much use of the work of Markus and Nurius (1986), who have greatly enriched the literature on self-concept. They pointed out that there have been many failures to link self-concept to behavior, and suggested a strategy that does a much better job. Because their strategy represented an economical codification of some important aspects of my thinking, I quoted and paraphrased them extensively. As they saw it, self-concept is not a unitary entity. Self-concept is a system of "salient identities or self-schemas [possible selves] that lend structure and meaning to one's self-relevant experiences (p. 158)." These self-schemas are generalizations about the self-derived from past experience, and they help one to integrate and explain one's own behavior.

The Working Self

Markus and Nurius made an important distinction concerning the self-concept as it operates in ongoing situations:

Self-schema reflects a pervasive concern with a certain domain of behavior ... self-schemas define a past and present self, but even more importantly they define a future, possible self. And it can be argued that this component is in fact the most significant aspect of the self-schema in shaping and fueling behavior (Markus and Nurius, 1986, page 158)... it is the possible self that puts the self into action (page 159)... To examine the potential utility of the notion of possible selves, we have proposed thinking not in terms of the self-concept but instead in terms of the working self-concept. The working self-concept is that set of self-conceptions that are presently accessible in thought and memory. It can be viewed as a continually active, shifting array of available self-knowledge. Not all knowledge is equally accessible for thinking about the self at any one time. The array changes depending on the contents of the prior working self-concept, on what self-conceptions have been activated by the immediate social circumstances, and on those self- conceptions that have been willfully invoked by the person in response to current experience. (163)

Note how Markus and Nurius use the word "shifting." They agree that self-concept shifts, and that it is frequently redefined. As they go on, Markus and Nurius point out that in two different compelling situations, two very different concepts of the working self may be active:

These two sets may well contain the same self-schemas or core self-conceptions. Yet these core self-conceptions may be accompanied by views of the past, current, or future self that derive primarily from the immediate social circumstances. And it is these latter self-conceptions that will often effectively compete with one's core self-conceptions for influence over the individual's prevailing affective and motivational states, current cognitive appraisals, and immediate actions. (164)

Available Selves

From the above we see that the term "working self" is the combination of self-concept and self state that is actually present *in vivo,* while other self states and concepts may merge into the working self at one point and later disappear from use, only to emerge again. There is an expanding literature on variations in self-states (e.g., Horowitz, 1994: Ryle and Marlowe, 1995). However, this literature is primarily concerned with shifts in self-states that are relatively passive, or occur in response to environmental shifts. In addition to these passive and reactive shifts, some attention has been given to shifts in self-states that are consciously self-induced. For example, in the above passages from Markus and Nurius we see "self-conceptions that have been willfully invoked."

In my 1989 book, I presented some examples of such intentional shifts in self-states in my violent clients. For example, Mr. B added a postscript to a letter stating "I might add: self-induction of mania, together with willful intent, was part of my dysfunction for many, many years" (page 174). He was describing induction of a very powerful state of himself (a "working self") that would be clearly dominant and threatening in a social situation. It often seems that such willful inductions of a self-state occur in anticipation of a challenge, in response to a drop in self esteem or sense of efficacy, or in response to a sign of disrespect. Induced self-states in my violent combat veteran clients frequently function as a form of armor. They are often well-practiced responses to fear, which were learned sometime between childhood and military service. I have come to think of these different self-states as "available selves." It appears to me that within each of us there really are at least two parts. One part represents such thoughts, feelings, and behaviors as one might associate with the id, the warrior, the animal, the rude, and the infinitely entitled self-state. The other would represent the more gentle person, the wise, the thoughtful, the caring side of ourselves. As we consider these self-states, at least in some people, as being available for willful induction, the term "available selves" begins to make more sense. Chapters 20 and 21 present ideas about how to work with these concepts regarding available selves in the therapy setting.

The Possible Self

As described above in connection with their comments on the working self, Markus and Nurius (1986) told us that the possible future states of self that a person seriously considers could provide keys to understanding that person. They speculated that the possible selves that are endorsed, along with the probability attached to each possible self during exposure to a compelling situation, provide very powerful indicators of the stable aspects of self-concept. In some ways we can say that personality is a shifting combination of traits and possible states; and that those states repeatedly seen in compelling situations are somewhat trait-like.

An example of this can be taken from our sample of violent clients. The possible selves of violent individuals can best be specified in terms of compelling situations. For the violent client, the compelling situation is the general set of social circumstances in which they become violent. Their behavioral, thought, and biological processes in such circumstances can be analyzed. For these people, the possible self of specific interest is the feared possible self (as opposed to the hoped-for possible self). This possible self is a particularly salient motivational force for violent clients. The subjective probabilities attached to the most-feared self, along with the client's prior history of being in the state represented by that feared self, can also be examined. Finally, during the construction of each client's narrative history regarding fearful events in childhood, adolescence, and in the military, a clear relationship often becomes obvious. This is the relationship between fear, a feared possible self, and the experience of banishment of fear by violent behavior. The feared possible self takes the form of a helpless victim of circumstances. The savior, the hoped-for possible self, takes the form of a powerful and respected warrior.

The Essential Audience

An important force in the development of self-concept is the internalized representation of significant others. I will call this the "essential audience." The essential audience often serves a "critic function." This is the social aspect of the biopsychosocial model, as it pertains to the assumptions one makes regarding the way one looks to other people. Attention to this aspect is not new. For example, Lorr and Wunderlich (1986) describe development of a scale that measures perceived positive appraisal from "significant others." I will refer to these appraisals as the "critic function."

The role of the essential audience can be seen in several domains. It plays a powerful role in the person's compilation of a subjective track record. It also plays a role in the probability a person attributes to various possible selves; for example, if a member of the essential audience predicts that one will end up in jail, this might become a powerfully negative possible self. The role of the essential audience, with its critic function, evolves in early life and represents the internalization of some aspects of parental behavior.

The essential audience also plays an intrinsic role in the formation of possible selves. Markus and Nurius said, "self-schemas are constructed creatively and selectively from an individual's past experience in a particular domain." Some of these past experiences involve relationships, events and processes that can be specified quite clearly, and as will be shown in Chapter 4. The labels given a child by the parents are primary initial sources of possible selves. Also, negative reinforcement (the termination of an aversive event, such as fear, by a behavior, such as a violent outburst)—as reflected in the history of many of our violent clients—is a notable and powerful source of the development of self-schemas.

As indicated above, most violent clients in my sample cite a specific experience (compelling situation) in childhood, adolescence, or the military when they were being terrorized and were suffering, and when they ended this suffering by a sudden outburst of violence. This led to a realization that their repertoire contained a response that had a guaranteed positive outcome. Hence, a new possible self arises, the possible self who is powerful, and violent. Frequently this possible self is emotionally and conceptually attached to, and involved with, memory of the particular individual(s) who precipitated, or were involved in, that first successful violent explosion. Accordingly, individuals reminiscent of those who were present at that first violent explosion can trigger the violent possible self to suddenly become the working self. Such individuals are important members of the essential audience.

The figures in Chapter 14 elaborate on the ideas and observations about essential audience, and show the general sequence of events that leads to the development of the possible or available self with a disposition to be violent. In my experience, it is a fortunate violent client who also has relatively benign members of the essential audience, perhaps composed only of a long deceased grandparent or neighbor. In some cases, activation of this benign essential audience member can lead to emergence of an available self that is not at all violent. In later chapters we will consider tactics for working with the essential audience in order to help in the therapeutic process by increasing the probability that a nonviolent available self will be manifested as the most frequent working self.

The Personal Scientist/Theorist

Kelly (1955) and others have noted that we are all personal scientists, in the sense that we work and even struggle to make sense of the world, of our impact on the world, and of our possible roles within the world. We are all personality theorists in the sense that we strive to develop law like statements about our own and other people's personalities. Important motivations for these activities include the desire to increase our understanding and predictive ability regarding things that are important to us. Increasing our understanding and predictive ability in turn increases our sense of control over things that are important to us.

Personal theorizing takes many forms and serves many purposes. In some situations, when we have a sense of ourselves, and of our values and wishes with regard to particular outcomes, we behave in accordance with relatively describable goals, roles, and so forth. In other situations, our own behavior can be surprising to us, and we can become scientists and theorists and even explainers or interpreters (e.g., see Gazzaniga, 1998), working on the lifelong project of developing (and sometimes defending) a theory about ourselves. Sometimes we provide ourselves with raw data about ourselves, data that our scientist self gathers and that can be processed to develop a more detailed theory about ourselves. The suggestion of shifts in our point of view through this process is intentional. We shift from being an actor and a conscious role-player with defined goals, to being a reactor, merely an observed source of data. We can shift back and forth again, from data source to observer, to scientist, and to theorist, in order to analyze and use new data.

Self-Concept: Shifting Variables

The Binary Switch

The remarkable differences among and within people as time passes represent a monumental challenge to the personal scientist/personality theorist. While some similarities emerge in the behavior of people as time passes, the differences are many and salient. These extend even to the energy available for theorizing about the data from our own behavior. Sometimes we are active and clear-minded. At other times we are passive, lazy, or confused.

Meichenbaum (1980), in agreement with Goldfried et al. (1974) pointed out, "Because of the habitual nature of one's expectations or beliefs it is likely that the thinking processes and images become automatic and seemingly involuntary like most overlearned acts." I have observed that I, like others, often do act and think in ways that ignore data, reduce ambiguity, and reduce the number of opportunities available to make active choices and to act as a scientist or theorist about my own or other people's behaviors. One way to reduce ambiguity is to revert automatically to either-or propositions. The concept of a "binary switch" comes to mind when I think about these seemingly automatic reactions.

This "binary switch" quality is easily observed in my clinical sample of individuals referred for outbursts of violent behavior. It is as if they have an either-or expectation of being insulted or being feared (two possibilities), and an either-or disposition of attacking or not attacking, (only two possible behavioral modes). Certain situations dramatically illuminate this binary quality in expectancy and disposition. This observation of the binary switch with violent clients is elaborated in later chapters (see especially Chapter 14). However, the occasional presence of such binary qualities in the expectations and dispositions can be observed in others as well.

Variability in the quantity of energy available for use in the theorizing endeavor seems to be accompanied by variation in the quality of that energy. At times we seem driven by negative, angry energy, and at other times we seem to express a more positive, happier energy. These quantities and qualities of energy interact with the binary switch in ways that can be quite clearly specified for some individuals. These issues are addressed in Chapter 3.

The Quality of Internal Dialogue

Another area of variability among and within individuals is in the type, frequency, and role of their internal dialogue. In many of my violent clients, the internal dialogue seems (at best) to be monosyllabic and binary. In addition, the internal dialogue—if it does occur—often has the function of an interpreter/explainer and occurs *after* the overt behavior. In other words, environmental stimuli frequently lead directly to overt behavior, without time being taken for internal dialogue.

There are differences in the sorts of violent acts, and probably in internal dialogue, between my clients and those treated by Novaco (1975), and also by most other authors who describe the assessment and treatment of violent individuals. In addition to demographic differences (mine appear to have lower average levels of education and income), the typical violent acts committed by my clients are different from those committed by the clients described by Novaco. For example, public fistfights have been the rule among my clients; more than half of the 115 clients described in my 1989 book had beaten someone into unconsciousness during the year before treatment began. Novaco's clients were more likely to yell or push someone, and seemingly only one of 34 had a fistfight in public. Perhaps the most important difference is in the richness of their internal dialogue and the related opportunity to pause and consider before striking out. With my clients, I had to work hard to move them from the binary switch mode of expectancy and disposition to a different mode, to get them to slow down and process environmental events, to reflect, and to consider a variety of possible expectations, dispositions, responses and possible outcomes. As we go along you will see that the issue of slowing down a very fast process is a crucial key in the work I have done with violent clients.

My own thinking on internal dialogue, and indeed on the issue of all people being personal scientists/theorists, has been influenced by a number of others in addition to Hebb. These include William James, George Kelly, and Joseph Rychlak. Writings by active investigators show some similar influences. For example, Meichenbaum (1980) said:

> *Imagine yourself attending your junior-high-school reunion twenty years after graduation. Could you guess what your classmates are like? Why else do we attend such reunions? Perhaps we are all personologists at heart! As Block (1971) stated in describing such a hypothetical reunion: "In the passage of almost a generation, the capriciousness of adolescence has been left and lives have taken their essential form and direction. There are the usual indicators of the passage of time—the formerly lissome and lithe may now be pudgy and stiff; the great adolescent dreams of glamour and omnipotence largely have been deflated by reality; for most, money, comfort, and status have become the order of the day" (pages 306 and 307)...*

> *How you observe and describe the behavioral changes and constancies in your fellow classmates at that 20-year junior-high-school reunion will be influenced by the implicit theory of personality you hold. (page 309)*

These engaging quotes raise two subtle issues that deserve comment. First, note that the data being processed by the personal scientist/theorist are provided both by behavior of self and by behavior of others. Second, not only does the point of view thereby shift, but a continuing transaction among data sources is considered. While other personality theorists have examined these two issues, the examination has generally been cumbersome and long-winded. Meichenbaum's and Block's words provide a reference point to help bring such subtle and complex considerations into a clearer focus.

Summary

At this stage, we need all the clarity of focus we can manage. This chapter on a shifting personality theory has made the point that certainty and stability are elusive in this work. To clarify this focus, here is a summary of what has been covered so far with regard to the shifting personality theory:

(1)   A good personality theory will help prevent the clinician and client from being overwhelmed by behavioral and situational diversity.

(2)   Personality is a description of specific behavior patterns in specific situations.

(3)   A shifting personality theory is, by definition, a theory of one person's behavior.

(4)   A shifting personality theory can be developed, over time, as one gains experience with a particular individual. It is built up from mini-theories developed by observing interactions, or from hearing stories about interactions between that person and certain specific environmental events.

(5)   A good approach to shifty personality theorizing is to make use of a "life chart" that relates important events in a person's life to the various biological, psychological, and social experiences of that person's life.

(6)   Careful attention to naturally-occurring and universally-compelling situations, such as a trauma or the death of a family member, will help develop a personality theory that encompasses some of the stable aspects of the individual's personality.

(7)   Examination of behavior in replicable, universally-compelling situations (such as evaluation of reactivity to a standardized stressor) will also help clarify aspects of the individual's personality.

(8)   The identification of compelling situations that are idiosyncratic to the client and that interact with reliable patterns of thought (e.g., expectancies and dispositions) and behavior will also help in the development of a personality theory.

(9)   The three facets of the biopsychosocial model can differentially influence the individual's personality; monitoring of the relationships among compelling

situations in each of the three domains provides the data
from which a shifting personality theory is formulated.

(10)   The working self is a key concept, and the shifts in the
working self from day to day and from situation to
situation should be encompassed by a shifting
personality theory.

(11)   The social facet of the biopsychosocial model is
illuminated by the concept of essential audience and its
critic function; these should be carefully considered as
having origins both in early experience and in the
present social circumstance.

(12)   The client should be involved as a personal
scientist/theorist in the formulation of a shifting
personality theory.

(13)   The binary switch concept should be carefully
considered as it applies to the manifestation of problem
behavior.

(14)   Developing, testing and practicing specific forms of
internal dialogue should be considered in the
development of a personality theory, as well as in
therapy for many clients.

(15)   Training the client in the development of conceptual
models, in the use of various points of view, and in
accessing an adaptive and nonviolent available self to
serve as the permanent working self are worthwhile
activities.

(16)   In clinical settings, development of the shifting
personality theory is a joint effort involving client and
therapist. Both the activity and its result facilitate the
processes of assessment and therapy. The client and
therapist should be aware of the continuing transactional
and shifting nature of personality—because a personality
theory is never finished.

3: Biological Variables in Personality

In Meichenbaum's engaging discussion of the quote from Block in the preceding chapter, he noted four major processes that influence the theorizing activity:

(1)   Cognitive structures
(2)   Internal dialogue
(3)   Behavioral acts
(4)   Evaluation of outcomes

Meichenbaum did not mention the biological dimension of personality in his example, but it is essential for developing an understanding of the personality of a violent client in a compelling situation.

In the personality literature, one rarely sees mention of such biological concepts as activation or arousal levels, or hormonal or neural processes or events, perhaps because compelling or stressful situations are not often considered by personality theorists. The interactions among biological variables, a stressful situation, and a relative absence of internal dialogue are illustrated by an event in the life of one of my violence-prone clients. This man attended a class reunion, and after most of the attendees had consumed at least one glass of beer and done some vigorous dancing, one of his classmates greeted my client's fiancé with what my client thought was too much enthusiasm, a long lingering kiss on the cheek. Immediately, while the kiss was still going on, my client punched his classmate in the face and knocked him to the floor. At this point, according to the testimony of the client and his fiancé, the client began to weep uncontrollably. The client's story continued with complications and provided a rich tapestry of interaction between biological variables and the behavior of one who made scant use of internal dialogue.

The eventual reconstruction of this particular scene in a role-playing situation, with biological variables being monitored (in this case both central and autonomic nervous system processes were monitored), permitted the client and therapist to develop some understanding about the relationship among biological variables, expectancies, dispositions, and behavioral acts. This client had a history of sudden and impulsive responding to any form of threat. His sudden response had led to a long series of negative outcomes. By considering in the client's history and the factors underlying the responses to the kiss, the client and therapist were eventually able to lay the foundation for a more adaptive internal dialogue, and for an increase in the client's ability to access a nonviolent working self in future situations of a similar sort.

The Sympathetic Nervous System: An Emotional Fire in the Boiler

A discussion of the sympathetic nervous system helps illustrate the interplay between emotional or arousal processes and cognitive processes such as internal dialogue and expectancy.

Most readers are probably well aware of some aspects of central nervous system function, but perhaps less aware of the functions of the autonomic nervous system. The autonomic nervous system (ANS) innervates heart, viscera, smooth muscles, blood vessels, and glands. Bannister (1982) noted that all organs and processes in the body are influenced by the ANS. Other writers, including Brooks and Lange (1982), have described the modulating and level-setting functions of the ANS.

The ANS has two divisions—the sympathetic nervous system (SNS), which arouses or activates, and the parasympathetic nervous system (PNS), which generally functions to quiet the target organs and actually counteracts many of the SNS functions, but often only after a long time and sometimes very weakly. A number of measures have been used to monitor SNS activity. Two of these reflect activities of the SNS that are not modulated by the PNS—these are skin conductance (or skin resistance) and peripheral blood flow. By 1989 my clinical and research work had convinced me that the level of arousal in the SNS could be seen as an indicator of an emotional storm or an emotional "fire in the boiler."

Accordingly, I argued in my previous book that the autonomic nervous system has a level-setting function for all systems and organs of the body as well as for behavior. It is now clear to me that it would be wiser to say that the autonomic system participates in a multiple component level-setting system. LeDoux, in 1996, summarized the large body of work on the relationship between the nervous system and emotion. He presented a well substantiated argument that an emotionally-important stimulus quickly reaches the amygdala. Next, following propagation through the lateral hypothalamus, it reaches the brainstem structures that control the autonomic nervous system. The autonomic nervous system sends signals to many target organs. Among these is the adrenal medulla. The signal to the adrenal medulla releases adrenaline and leads through several stages to an eventual feedback influence on the amygdala. Ledoux's work led me to think of the amygdala as providing an igniting spark for the autonomic fire in the boiler. At a more complex level it has become clear that we are dealing with a great symphony of interactions, and that much of my work with clients involves the attempt to improve the ability of the conductor—the working self, self-awareness, and the self as an agent—to direct this symphony.

Skin conductance level has proven, in my work with clients, to be the most useful parameter to monitor. We have repeatedly observed that skin conductance provides a real-time index of emotional arousal. It correlates very closely in time course and magnitude with subjective sensations of emotional arousal. For example, in a sample of 50 consecutive clients who were all monitored by the same set of instruments, we observed reliable correlations between skin conductance level and a two-minute discussion of the client's most recent experience of anger. We placed this discussion between two five-minute periods of relaxation. Specifically, the magnitude of skin conductance elevation and the time course of development and recovery of this change corresponded with the period of discussion and with the sensations of emotional arousal. We have not observed this level of correspondence between arousing discussions and other biological variables that we have monitored frequently, such as peripheral blood flow, heart rate, or forehead EMG.

By 1989, in clinical work with more than 100 violent clients (monitored by several types of skin conductance detecting procedures), I had never seen an exception to the following statement:

SNS arousal, as indexed by skin conductance, correlates with descriptions of situations that provoked anger and descriptions of anger-related violent behavior.[1]

The following generalizations have been supported by our observations:

(1)   Descriptions of other arousing experiences (for example, humorous occasions) also correlate with SNS arousal, but less reliably.

(2)   Whenever other indicators of arousal (facial expression, tone of voice) are present, skin conductance is always elevated.

(3)   Even when there are no other objective indications of arousal, but when a subjective report of emotional arousal is given, arousal is tracked reliably by skin conductance level.

For the purposes of this book, I consider that the SNS level reflects the emotional "fire in the boiler." It sets, or at least influences, the levels of many other bodily processes. This level-setting function results in shifting of the probability of perceptual, cognitive, and overt behaviors. The level-setting function also

---

[1] Since 1989, I have seen many more clients. Three of these showed the opposite profile—specifically, they showed a drop in skin conductance when describing a situation that provoked anger and the related behavior. One was an outpatient in our clinic who was tested at 11:15 a.m. and showed this odd pattern. He also showed a much lower skin conductance resting level than he had shown in previous sessions. When questioned, he sheepishly confessed that he had smoked marijuana at 7:30 in the morning. The other two clients were part of a study we did in a local prison. They also confessed to the use of marijuana a few hours prior to participating in the study. It may be worth noting that some investigators believe such a pattern would characterize people with severe antisocial personality disorder, people who have been called "psychopaths." They would argue that psychopaths seem to become calm when pressure is applied. My clients who smoked marijuana in the morning were perhaps behaving like psychopaths when we tested them. I am not sure whether this marijuana effect would hold up, and have no intention of conducting an exploration of it.

appears to influence both the speed and the wisdom of any behavioral response to an emotionally-important stimulus. The specificity of these relationships will be demonstrated in later chapters.

Central Motive State

While some functions of the ANS are actually patterned, or differentiated, and lateralized (Wallin and Fagius, 1986; Lane and Schwartz, 1987; Ekman, 1983), in our work the relatively undifferentiated arousing function is the most important contribution of the SNS.

In order to understand the mechanisms behind the differentiation, direction, quality and blends of mood, we must look for interplay between the ANS and the central nervous system. Bindra's (1974) "central motive state" theory provides a useful summary concept for the interplay between the central and the autonomic nervous systems This concept refers to functions of the central nervous system, and is related to earlier concepts such as "drive," "need," and "press," but the logical consistency and heuristic power of Bindra's central motive state are very appealing. Central motive state is shifting, reciprocally determined, and determining. It is influenced by the ANS (both the SNS and the PNS), by endocrine, digestive, and other internal processes, and by the interaction of these processes with environmental events. In turn, these environmental events take on incentive value as they interact with the central motive state.

In 2002 I feel less lonely when I preach about mixtures and shades of moods and thoughts interacting with shifting levels and qualities of arousal. Many writers have noted that several emotions can be experienced at one time (e.g., Plutchick, 2001), and examination has begun on the complexities of how individual differences in one process can affect the operation of another process (Kosslyn et al., 2002).

This multilevel and multifactorial symphony is what Bindra was referring to with the idea of central motive state. For this discussion therefore, the central motive state can be seen as a central integrator or registry, while the SNS functions as the level-setting "emotional fire in the boiler." The central motive state serves to interpret global ANS, endocrine, and other variables that contribute to psychological entities typically grouped under the heading of "mood," while the SNS emotional fire in the boiler is both a level-indicator and a level-setter. The intensity of the fire in the boiler will thus be accurately reflected by skin conductance, while the particular direction, quality, or mood of the central motive state will be reflected by overt behavior (or by a combination of behavior with several physiological indicators, as was demonstrated by Ekman, 1983).

Central Motive State, Working Self, Personal Theorist, and Point of View

The central motive state is also helpful in considering, or describing the forces in play at any given moment in the behavior of a person. As mentioned above, the construct of the working self refers to the aspects of the self-concept that are in play, or functioning at any specific time. The working self in any specific environment includes several related sets of expectancies. These include expectancies about the particular stimuli or stressors, available responses, and likely outcome of each response. In accordance with the definitions and concepts discussed earlier regarding point of view, I will now define and describe a few ideas about the interfaces between personal theorizing, current working self, and central motive state.

At almost any waking moment, an individual may be said to have available to him or her a sense of existing, of being alive, of being a self in an environment, of being an agent—of being able to shift attention (point of view) to various aspects of the environment. Which particular aspects of the self or the environment attention is shifted to will be partly a function of the central motive state. The central motive state will cause some aspects of the environment that would otherwise have been ignored to become incentive stimuli (i.e., stimuli that are sought after or avoided). The central motive state may be determined in part by aspects of self-concept, including feared future possible selves. As mentioned above, central motive state is also influenced by SNS arousal, and the particular behavioral acts that are selected are also influenced by working self-concept, internal dialogue, past conditioning, and expectancies and response dispositions. These interactions are depicted in Figure 3.1.

An example of how these various features work together is provided by an elaboration of some aspects of the kissing episode at the class reunion described above. My client had a history of being humiliated by older brothers and neighbors, and his first girlfriend had been taken away from him by an older brother. He had developed an expectancy of certain kinds of humiliation. A salient experience with the termination of humiliation (negative reinforcement) coming about as a function of his physically exploding and hitting someone (negatively-reinforced behavior) had led to a very strong disposition to hit or explode whenever he was humiliated. This disposition was more evident when he sensed an emergency, and emergency reactions were more likely when he had consumed some alcohol. Thus the relationship between the amygdala, the emotional fire in the boiler and central motive state, with attendant expectations and dispositions, led to a very rapid response to this incentive event—a response that could have been predicted with some knowledge of this client's background, apparent concepts of self and proclivities. The feared possible self-humiliated loser, unlovable person, someone without a girlfriend—appeared to be a salient motivator. The drama of the kiss, the resultant sensing of an emergency, and the alcohol led to the primitive response.

A more clear delineation of all the aspects and forces at work in this particular situation would be very difficult. However, we often work with clients to develop a mini-model of relationships among a compelling situation, a working self-concept (including possible selves), and biological variables. This allows us to see how various settings of parameters and points of view can influence the behavior of this person. My colleagues and I have occasionally used computer-based, systems-dynamics modeling of the forces acting in a specific situation experienced by a particular client. We have used a format in which the client interacts with the computer to adjust parameters of the situation and his reactions, to describe what happened, and to assist him in thinking through what reactions might have been more sensible. Sometimes this has been helpful in the development of more adaptive internal dialogue, and with the development of a personal theorist point of view. As far as we have been able to determine, the computer-based, systems-dynamics modeling did not seem as helpful for these purposes as the more simple models shown in Chapters 8, 9, and 12. However, a few clients have been able to profit from participation in a long-term exercise involving such complicated modeling activity.

With one client (Mr. B described in Chapter 13), we developed a systems-dynamics model of his responses to a compelling situation, which involved looking out his window and seeing a snowplow hit his car and move it a few feet. His reactions and the events of the next hour were diagrammed. He collaborated with us in every aspect, filling in the various details of events at each level shown in Table 1.1 in Chapter 1. He went on to develop two careful drawings of his own mini-models, depicting the time course and the variables involved in the rise and fall of his fire in the boiler, how these interacted with his working self-concept, his internal dialogue, and the responses of the snowplow driver. It is worth noting here that this particular client is highly intelligent and well-educated, and the outcome of our work with him has been excellent.

To illustrate some of the individual differences involved in this level of processing, consider Mr. D (who will reappear later). While we were developing the data for the systems-dynamics depiction of the episode involving Mr. B., Mr. D, another intelligent violent client, was present and was asked to participate. Mr. D participated only passively and expressed no real interest in the project. He was a client whom we knew well, and we were able to develop a tentative systems-dynamics representation of one of his own episodes of violent behavior. However, it rapidly became clear that the computer-modeling strategy was wasted on this individual. He could understand the complexity, but the theorizing style and point of view were not interesting, motivating, or helpful to him. Furthermore, it became clear that even the first individual was better served by a more simple diagram, such as is shown in the less complex Figures 13.13–13.18 in Chapter 13.

The simple notions of emotional fire in the boiler and mood, or central motive state, were helpful with both clients. The client who was not interested in the modeling activity described above was interested in a one-sentence rationale that summarized the following more elaborate concept:

> *The level of the emotional fire in your boiler, and the reactivity of the emotional fire in your boiler, as well as your mood, is determined by your attitudes toward yourself and toward the situations you find yourself in. Part of your job is to lower the level of the fire in your boiler and to lower the reactivity of the fire to situations that have previously caused you to become violent; another part of your job is to control your attitude. A way to do this is to attend to the level of the fire in your boiler and to early warning signs of a sudden increase in the fire. Whenever the fire is hot—or getting hotter—you must say out loud, "I'm upset," and then you must simultaneously begin the tasks of quieting yourself and working toward developing an attitude of thoughtful*

problem solving, while actively avoiding the old attitudes that have led so often to violent behavior.

While this statement is long and complicated, repeated reminders about and rehearsal of the simple formula embodied in the following short sentence have proved helpful even with many relatively primitive and impaired clients (e.g., clients with a history of numerous head injuries):

When you notice the fire in the boiler say, "Timeout, I'm upset, I need to take a break"; and then quickly start using your relaxation response.

How we use this simple formula illustrates the basic aspects of a wide variety of clinical applications of the shifting personality theory. Clients easily come to understand, and recognize in themselves, the relationships among responses to emergency signals, the fire in the boiler and their various biopsychosocial problems. In fact, if there is a common cornerstone to the shifting personality theory developed for each client this is it: *The fire in the boiler has to be acknowledged and consciously monitored and modulated by the client if he or she is to improve.*

The idea of monitoring and modulating the fire in the boiler actually implies a wide range of activities—depending on the particular client. For those such as Mr. B, who responded well to a complex systems-dynamics model, the whole range of forces can be considered: the level and reactivity of the boiler, or sympathetic nervous system, the registration of mood, or central motive state, and the reciprocal interactions of these with the working self-concept, with overt behavior and with the environment. The rapid shifts in point of view that was possible for this personal theorist made such thinking quite easy. He developed a rich internal dialogue and moved himself quickly away from the binary switch mode of reacting that had characterized his behavior at the time of referral. On the other hand, Mr. D seemed to be stuck at the binary-switch level. His internal dialogue, if it was present, was only monosyllabic, and it was usually so slow to occur that it didn't happen until after he had already become violent. The simple sentence described above worked to move him from the extremely rapid binary switch mode by an external version of internal dialogue (saying out loud "I'm upset" whenever he notices the fire in his boiler at a high level, or notices it rising). This simple formula led to immediate changes in his behavior outside of the treatment setting and laid the foundation for the development of some internal dialogue and some, albeit primitive, alteration in cognitive-perceptual function.

Summary

The constructs and variables considered in this and the previous chapter are depicted in Figure 3.1. While I rarely use figures of this sort in direct work with clients, variations of this figure and sections of it can be helpful. Chapter 13 contains an example of the use of the figure with a violent client; see Figure 13.14. For our current purposes, this figure summarizes this chapter, as well as the previous chapter and the general approach to shifty personality theorizing. Once again, the common foundation of all shifting personality theories for the clients I work with is the emotional fire in the boiler. This fundamental force must be constantly monitored and modulated if the client is to progress.

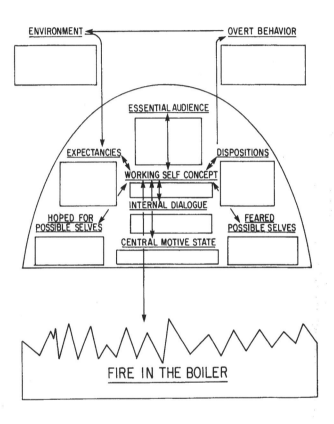

Figure 3.1. *Pictorial summary of constructs and variables involved in shifting personality theory.*

Part Two

Lessons from the Family

4: Families as Mutual Control Systems

In this chapter, I will present some theoretical notions about families. I will emphasize the relationship between parental attention and the development of social incentives. My main assumption is that the way parents give their attention to their children is a key to the children's later sense of themselves (their self-concept), their responsiveness to all incentives, and their general mode of adjustment to the adult world.

In her popular book *For Your Own Good,* Alice Miller (1984) points out many problems and hidden cruelties in childrearing and sees these as the primary roots of violence. She concentrates most on psychological cruelties, but also addresses the issue of physical abuse. She equates any form of physical punishment of children with abuse, and she does not accept the differentiation of spanking from abusive beating. She cites examples of physical and psychological violence being perpetuated from generation to generation, and she makes a very strong case that Adolph Hitler was abused by his parents in ways that had much to do with his devastatingly violent behaviors as an adult.

Parental Attention

Miller emphasizes the power of parental attention and gives numerous examples of parental attention evolving into a very negative "essential audience." For example, she traces the development of parental coercive tactics into a power so great that a brief disapproving glance from the parent causes the child to feel both transparent and guilty. She explains how, in some cases, these tactics of management of parental attention can lead to the eventual development of psychotic paranoid behavior (see especially pages 4–6).

Miller says she values any possible methods of helping children see themselves as agents and as persons to be taken seriously, but she avoids offering specific advice on what methods might be helpful. Instead, she sees it as her task to "expose the roots of hatred" (page 9).

In an afterword to her second edition (1984), Miller says that the knowledge she has offered us "concerns every single one of us, and—if disseminated widely enough—should lead to fundamental changes in society; above all, to a halt in the blind escalation of violence."

Miller's message can be summarized in a few words. The mere use of physical punishment does not itself cause a child to eventually become violent; but the cruel and unpredictable use of parental power, in the form of physical or psychosocial punishment and control, is very likely to lead to later problems, many of which involve violence. While Miller does not specify methods, she does specify objectives: "For their development, children need the respect and protection of adults who take them seriously, love them, and honestly help them to become oriented to the world" (Afterword, 1984).

Miller describes many wrong-minded attempts to specify guidelines, formats, and programs for child-rearing and pedagogy. She scorns them all and illustrates their sometimes subtle abusive features. There are many published programs for child-rearing that Miller did not mention, including my own (1974). This chapter presents that program as a possible means of reaching Miller's objective of producing a fundamental change in society that will help halt the blind escalation of violence.

Mutual Control Systems

Skinner (1961) noted that all social organizations can be characterized as mutual control systems, with control being exercised upon, as well as being exercised by, each member of an organization. Individuals can be seen as members of many mutual control systems, including their families, their work environment, and the various levels of the society in which they live. Within each of these systems, the individual's behavior is controlled by a characteristic set of reinforcers and schedules of reinforcement.[1]

In this context, development from infancy to adulthood can easily be seen as involving a progression through various types of mutual control systems and various levels of participation in each control system. Furthermore, any mutual control system can be characterized by an implied and more-or-less concise contract that sets forth the privileges, responsibilities, and contingencies of reward and punishment for each member of the system. The laws in adult society can be seen as a set of explicit contracts, and in some occupational systems contracts are explicit. But explicit contracts are relatively rare at other levels of society. In fact, most other systems, including family, demand inferences on the part of their members about the nature of an implied contract.

The implied nature of most contracts can be seen as a source of confusion about privilege and responsibility and, in turn, as a source of many developmental problems. The case has been made that some of the problems of adolescence are due to the increasing ambiguity of the adolescent's changing role (privileges and responsibilities) in the family as he or she progresses toward adulthood. I believe that these problems can be minimized, and the eventual transfer into other control systems can be facilitated, if family members develop an explicit contract, instead of relying on the implied (and often inconsistent) contract. The explicit contract will, of course, need to be modified as expectations change.

Reinforcement and Learning

A number of attempts to reach these general objectives have been based on Skinner's plan for the redesign of society (1948, 1971). This plan involves careful management of positive

---

[1] Instead of the term reinforcement, I would have preferred to use the term incentive stimulus throughout; but this theory is not well known, so exclusive use of it would have confused most readers. Incentive theory was described in detail by Bindra (1974) and is used in the present chapter to deal with interactions between parental attention and self-esteem. Following this introduction, I will assume that the reader understands that, in the rest of this book, I equate positive reinforcement with presentation of appetitive or positive incentive stimuli, and punishment with delivery of aversive or negative incentive stimuli. Negative reinforcement will refer to the removal of aversive incentive stimuli.

reinforcement (reward or "good things") and the minimum use of punishment and negative reinforcement (a term typically used to denote termination or removal of an aversive incentive stimulus in order to increase the probability of the behavior that terminated that incentive). We now have a large body of data with which to evaluate the impact of these procedures. Results obtained with the very early phases of development and with regressed and retarded populations are encouraging (Kazdin and Bootzin, 1972, Atthowe, 1973). Results obtained with later phases of development and with subjects who are not retarded or regressed are not as encouraging. Among the problems encountered in the programs involving relatively normal populations (in both therapeutic and communal settings) are:

(1) High administrative costs of positive reinforcement schemes;
(2) Eventual necessity of using powerful aversive incentives to prevent system failure (Kinkade, 1973);
(3) Mismatch problems (or sequencing failure) when a person leaving such a program reenters the real world as it now is.

An essential aspect of the mismatch problem is the difference between the reinforcement schedules of Skinner's programs and those of the real world. The Skinnerian system carefully manages and makes maximum use of rapid positive reinforcement and attempts to make minimal use of punishment and negative reinforcement. On the other hand, the schedules of reinforcement in the real adult world, as it is now, can be characterized as follows:

(1) Salient positive reinforcement events are often unreliable and/or separated from salient positively reinforceable behavior by long intervals (that is, it is on variable low-ratio [e.g., 30:1] or long-interval schedules). Another way to say this is that "the experience of being rewarded (positively reinforced) is often unreliable and/or separated from good (or positively reinforceable) behavior by long intervals."
(2) Salient punishment events are usually reliable and/or separated from salient negatively sanctioned behavior by short intervals, (that is, it is on fixed high-ratio [e.g., 1:1] or short-interval schedules). Another way to say this is "the experience of being punished is usually reliable and

occurs during or almost immediately after bad (or punishable) behavior."

(3) Salient negative reinforcement events (removal of aversive incentives) are similarly reliable and/or separated from the appropriate behavior by short intervals. Another way to say this is "the experience of having an aversive stimulus terminated is usually reliable and fairly close to the behavior that terminates it."

Certain of Skinner's remarks suggest that he would agree with this characterization of the present real-world reinforcement schedules (1961, page 542; 1971, page 57).

Additional support for this point of view comes from a classic paper by White (1976), who summarized data from a number of studies concerning the presentation to students, in grades 1 through 12, of signals that can be categorized as "positive reinforcers" and "aversive or negative incentives." Results showed a shift toward an increasing percentage of aversive or negative incentives after the second grade. Further support comes from an article (Tharp and Gallimore, 1976) describing the coaching behavior of the famous and extremely successful basketball coach, John Wooden, at UCLA. Their results showed that the coach was giving his players about twice as much negative-incentive information as positive-incentive information. If these characterizations of the reinforcement schedules in the real world were accurate, I would argue that it is a mistake not to organize educational and remedial systems to facilitate the individual's transition to this state of affairs.

The Development of Self-Concept

Another important objective of these educational and remedial systems should be the development in the individual of the concept of self as an agent capable of contracting with other agents for the operation of mutual control systems. The basic idea underlying this objective has been put forth by Skinner and others, including Miller (1984), who uses different terminology to make this same general point. The optimal level of participation in a mutual control system ranges from informed and consenting participation in system operation to active participation in system design and evolution. To reach this level, a person must develop:

(1)   A sense of self;
(2)   Some understanding of the mutuality of control in the systems in which one participates;
(3)   A concept of the examinable, negotiable, and relatively arbitrary nature of contracts (or of the objectives and operational details of the control systems);
(4)   An impression of oneself as an active and respected agent in examining and negotiating the contracts for the mutual control systems in which one participates.

An additional objective of educational and remedial systems should be the development of self-esteem, or a positive self-concept or "self-theory" (Epstein, 1973, 1980). (While this objective relates closely to the development of the concept of the self as a contracting agent [point 4 above], it also relates to broader concepts such as "self efficacy.") All of these notions touch on many important issues, such as questions regarding determinism versus freedom of choice and the presumed existential states of "object" and "being." However, I will not deal with these in order to focus on the operational details of my position and proposals.

As discussed in earlier chapters, *self-concept* is a term for summarizing many effects of an individual's reinforcement history and for his or her current self-labeling and self-reinforcing behavior (Bandura, 1969). In terms of incentive theory (Bindra, 1974), the development of self-esteem or self-concept has several major stages. In the first stage, parental attention becomes a strong conditioned incentive stimulus. This happens when the infant learns the correlation between parental attention and various unconditioned incentive stimuli like food and warmth. In earliest infancy, deviations from a homeostatic, balanced, comfortable state are the primary unconditioned aversive incentive stimuli; reinstatement of homeostasis involves the primary unconditioned appetitive incentive stimuli. The repeated pairing of parental presence with the return to the homeostatic state attaches, or conditions, appetitive incentive stimulus power to parental presence (see Figure 4.1). This notion can easily be supported; for example, Fitzgerald and Brackbill (1976) described a number of remarkable examples of conditioning in human beings at very early ages. Additional confirmation, admittedly of a tangential nature, comes from an observation I made (1964) of a cat that had learned to press a wheel in order to obtain milk. During extinction (i.e., a period during which milk was not available) this cat pressed more when I was in the room than when I was

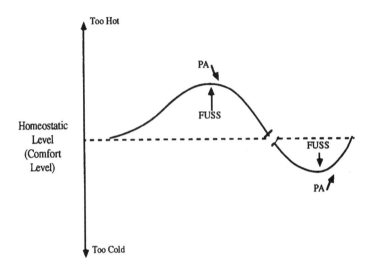

Repeated Pairing of PA with the Return to a Comfortable Level is the first case of pairing a previously neutral stimulus PA with a positive incentive or "Reward"

Figure 4.1. *Parental attention becomes the first conditioned incentive stimulus.*

out of the room, suggesting that I had become a conditioned appetitive incentive stimulus. From such evidence, I concurred with the conclusion of other investigators that the very young infant may be able to form the same sort of association between parental presence and homeostasis.

The conditioned incentive power of parental attention is, as stated above, observable very early in life and is sometimes awe-inspiring (Kolata, 1987). In fact, I have often likened this power to an overwhelming addiction (see Figure 4.2). I expect that the data and examples presented below will support this analogy. (A story about the amazing power of attention in the life a troubled adult is presented in an appendix.) The power of the essential audience (as discussed in Chapters 2 and 3) comes from the conditioned incentive power of parental attention, and the critic function of the essential audience depends for its development on subtleties of the management of parental attention. These features are spelled out in the following paragraphs.

The relationship between parental presence and various unconditioned incentive stimuli becomes more complex as the child grows older (see Figure 4.3). For the fortunate infant, somewhere between the ages of 3 and 12 months, appetitive and aversive qualities of parental behavior and related variables become clearly distinguishable and easily predictable (see Figure 4.4). For example, messages in the "You're OK" category become conditioned appetitive incentive stimuli because they are so frequently correlated with delivery of unconditioned appetitive incentive stimuli. (See Harris, 1967, for an elaboration of the "OK" terminology and Bandura, 1969, for a discussion of social learning theory.) Messages in the "You're not OK" category become conditioned aversive incentive stimuli because they are correlated with unconditioned aversive incentive stimuli (such as pain, or deprivation). The developmental course of the conditioned incentive power of parental attention determines the success or failure of its later subdivision (or discrimination) into positive and negative qualities (see Figure 4.5). This course also determines the success or failure of the eventual transfer to nonparents of the conditioned incentive power of various qualities of attention. In other words, this course lays the foundation for later responses to social reinforcement. And this foundation constitutes the general self-concept or self-theory (see Figures 4.6 and 4.7), including the associated expectancies and dispositions. (See Figures 4.8a through 4.8c).

By its association with almost all good
experiences in early months of life "PA" gains great
incentive power – one could say that the infant becomes
<u>"ADDICTED" TO PA</u>.

Figure 4.2. *Addiction to parental attention.*

PARENTAL ATTENTION

is often paired with both
<u>verbal and nonverbal behavior of Parents</u> – these
behaviors also become
<u>CONDITIONED INCENTIVE STIMULI</u>

These stimuli include labels of the child and/or
child's behavior as "OK"

Figure 4.3. *Generalization of incentive power of parental attention.*

PARENTAL ATTENTION

is later subdivided into "OK" and "Not OK" categories

Figure 4.4. *Discrimination-subdivision of parental attention.*

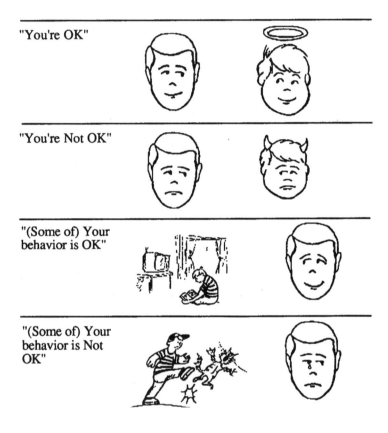

Figure 4.5. *Further discrimination-subdivision of parental attention.*

WHEN PARENTS MANAGE ATTENTION WELL
THE CHILD'S SELF-CONCEPT IS -

"I'm OK

- Even if some of my behavior is Not OK"

Figure 4.6. *Outcome when parents manage attention well.*

WHEN PARENTS MANAGE ATTENTION BADLY
THE CHILD'S SELF-CONCEPT MAY BE -

"I'm Not OK

- No matter if some of my behavior is OK

- everyone still knows I'm Not OK

Figure 4.7. *Outcome when parents manage attention badly.*

A POOR SELF-CONCEPT CAN PRODUCE UNUSUAL RESPONSES – EVEN TO MESSAGES INTENDED AS REWARDS.

Figure 4.8a. *A poor self-concept can produce unusual responses.*

OR

Figure 4.8b. *A poor self-concept can produce unusual responses (guilt).*

OR

Figure 4.8c. *A poor self-concept can produce unusual responses (fear).*

Summary

In summary, I have argued the following points:

(1) Families are mutual control systems;
(2) The family system should be regularly changed so that it is appropriate to the age levels (and changing responsibilities and privileges) the children go through, and so that the older children can transfer successfully to the control systems of the real adult world;
(3) Children should see themselves capable of evaluating and influencing the systems in which they participate;
(4) The development of self-esteem, or a positive self-concept, and of later responses to social reinforcement, are profoundly influenced by children's experiences with parental attention.

5: The Family Optimization Program

With my colleagues, I have developed a program to assist families in optimizing the participation of their verbal children in society's mutual control systems. In this chapter I will describe this program and its application in two kinds of families—families that seem normal and families that are troubled. Procedures involving preverbal children will be discussed in a following chapter.

The family optimization program can be used as a prophylactic, or optimizing, strategy for "normal" families, or it can be used to help troubled families. The overall objective of the program is to promote a wealth-sharing team concept and to give both greater and more explicit control to the children than is typical in North American society. (By wealth sharing I mean sharing some portion of the families' financial resources with the children in the form of an allowance adjusted to each child's age level and reflective of the child's participation in the family's tasks.)

Primary components of the program are:

(1) A specific family-unit contract regarding the duties and privileges of all members;
(2) A method for systematizing parental attention;
(3) A method for systematizing, monitoring, and eventually matching positive and aversive incentives (rewards and punishments in parental language) to real-world schedules.

Application with Normal Families

I will first describe the methods we used and the results we obtained in implementing the program with five normal families. (Many dozens of families have used this program before and after its testing with these five families.) General features of the program will be described, and some data presented, but I will omit the specifics of baseline procedures, operationalization, and parent training, in part because these varied so much from family to family.

The Contract

First, whenever possible, we gathered the family together and discussed the general idea of the family unit as a team. We emphasized the importance of all members knowing their privileges and responsibilities and of refraining from behaviors detrimental to themselves or to other family members. A contract was developed as follows:

(1)   The parents and children listed the responsibilities and privileges of each family member.
(2)   The parents and children listed any behaviors of any family member (including themselves) that bothered them or other family members.
(3)   The parents and the children listed the rewards and punishments currently used in the family.
(4)   We discussed and edited these lists in collaboration with the family.
(5)   The lists were made into a contract (a sample contract for a 9-year-old boy is shown in Table 5.1).

Parents' responsibilities were understood to include earning money, preparing most meals, and being systematic and self-controlled in monitoring behavior and in delivering rewards and punishments. Parents also had the responsibility to be the leaders and primary decision-makers and to be evenhanded in discussing problems and progress, as well as in reconsidering contract details at regular intervals. The children, as developing members of the team, also had responsibilities, and certain of their behaviors were to be monitored by the parents. Children would receive some of their usual rewards and punishments in accord with the contract. (See Table 5.1) Throughout, the complex mutuality of control within the family team was emphasized, as were two obligations of all members: (1) to be aware of the necessity for changes in the contract (such as permitting increases in responsibility and privilege as children grow), and (2) to take an active role in considering and discussing possible changes.

Systematic Parental Attention

We systematized some parental attention by means of a very simple procedure. Every morning at breakfast, for the five days of the working week, one child was in a separate room (such as a den) with the father alone, and without sibling(s) or mother present. This lasted for about 45 minutes, and in a two-child family each child would receive father's attention every other day. On alternate days, the child would be in the kitchen with the mother (receiving some of her attention). This can be seen as programmed parental attention that is not contingent upon bad or good behavior of the children. Parental attention was paired with part of the daily ritual to ensure its occurrence, and was intended to partially satisfy the children's urge for (or even addiction to) individual parental attention.

Our technique for systematizing punishment and reward was more complex. The family taped to the kitchen wall a chart on graph paper with days of the month blocked out on it (sample charts are shown in Table 5.2). Each incident of contractually proscribed detrimental (unacceptable) behavior was immediately entered on the chart in the form of the first letter of the descriptive term (e.g., a tantrum was denoted by a T, hitting by an H). The letter G denoted good behavior. Marks for unacceptable behavior were entered at the time the behavior occurred, and the Gs were entered during a review session the following morning. The maximum possible number of Gs per day was two; two Gs were given when a child had indulged in no unacceptable behaviors on the previous day. Two Gs implied that the child had met all responsibilities. A child who indulged in one unacceptable behavior on the previous day got only one G, and if unacceptable behavior occurred, two or more times he or she got no Gs. The parents were instructed to complete the morning review session quickly after giving praise for Gs and then to have a general discussion with the child over breakfast. This discussion was to be unrelated to unacceptable behavior and was to be used as a specific time for the child to receive individual positive attention.

Table 5.1

Sample Contract for a 9-Year-Old Boy in a Two-Child Family

Tommy's Responsibilities	Unacceptable Behaviors
1. Brush Teeth	1. Hitting sister
2. Make bed	2. Destroying others' belongings
3. Clean up room	3. Teasing sister
4. Feed dog	4. Untidiness
5. Get along well with sister	5. Disobeying
6. Complete homework	6. Arguing
7. Go to bed at 8:00	7. Irritating

Examples of Privileges and Sanctions for Tommy:

1.   If Tommy gets two "G's" on any one day, he may watch two hours of T.V. programs of his choice the following night.

2.   If Tommy gets only one "G" on any day, he may watch one hour of a T.V. program of his choice the following night.

3.   If Tommy gets a total of 14 "G's" in any week, he receives $1.40 that Saturday, he may pick his choice of dessert for two suppers in the following week; he may stay up until 9:00 on Saturday and Sunday nights.

4.   If Tommy gets only 10 "G's" in any week, he receives $1.00 that Saturday and he may pick his choice of dessert for one supper the following week.

5.   If Tommy gets only 7 "G's" in any week, he will not go bowling with Dad on Saturday morning; he may not watch T.V. all of the following week; he may not get to pick his choice of dessert, and he gets one dime for each "G" received in that week.

6.   If Tommy get 5 marks for unacceptable behavior on any one day, he is given a spanking immediately after he receives the 5th mark.

7.   Whenever a mark for unacceptable behavior is entered on the chart, Tommy is notified about it, and whenever possible, this will be the only attention Tommy receives for the unacceptable behavior.

8.   No matter how many marks of any category Tommy gets, he can spend time alone with one of his parents each morning.

Signed and agreed upon by:

_____   _____   _____

Table 5.2

Sample Charts

	Week #	Sat	Sun	Mon	Tues	Wed	Thurs	Fri	# Bad Behaviors/ # Good Behaviors	Weekly Income
Tommy	1	HDD	HG	HG	DG	GG	DH	CG	8/7	.30
	2	TG	HH	UD	UG	CG	CG	DG	7/7	.35
	3									
	4									
	5									
	6									

	Week #	Sat	Sun	Mon	Tues	Wed	Thurs	Fri	# Bad Behaviors/ # Good Behaviors	Weekly Income
Susan	1	TG	GG	TAU	DG	TTDU	TG	UG	11/6	.05
	2	DG	AID	UG	GG	GG	TG	GG	6/9	.60
	3									
	4									
	5									
	6									

Note that the reinforcements were delivered in accord with the real-world schedules mentioned earlier, with punishment on a high-ratio, short-interval schedule and with certain salient positive reinforcers on a low-ratio, long-interval schedule. Note also that this scheme is very different from the typical "token economy" approach (Atthowe, 1973). This family optimization program is in fact opposite to the token approach in some respects. In the family optimization program attention is paid to rapid delivery of aversive incentives and there are frequently long delays of material and non-routine positive incentives.

All the marks together had a long-term consequence. Each Saturday morning, the parents reviewed the previous week's behavior with the children. In all families that had previously used allowance as an incentive, the marks were assigned monetary values to match existing allowance rates. For example, in some families each G earned the child 10 cents (maximum week's total, $1.40), and each unacceptable behavior subtracted 5 cents from the total. In all cases the week's minimum was set at zero rather than having a child incur a debt for a particularly bad week. One family had not previously used monetary incentives, but had instead used family outings; for example, bowling on Saturday afternoons had been withheld when the child had misbehaved. In this family, we systematized the delivery of various types of family outings in a manner similar to that used for money in other families.

Physical Punishment

We superimposed on this system a second system of rewards and punishments. Since all of these families had typically used physical punishments in the form of apparently minor and non-physically damaging spanks, and all but one had used rewards in the form of money or allowance, these features were incorporated into the system. Whether these families were typical of North American families in the 1960s and 70s might be debated. However, some earlier surveys showed that use of some form of physical punishment in the family setting was the rule rather than the exception (Miller, 1984, page 58). In subsequent applications with other families, we have tailored the rewards and punishments to the incentives already being used in the family. Many families do not employ spanking, and most of those that do have eventually been able to eliminate this feature. In all of the families I have seen, I have worked to eliminate physical punishment.[1] I learned very early that it would do no good to preach to parents about right and wrong ways to raise children or about how to use rewards and punishments. In fact, it seemed as if such preaching could do more harm than good: some of the families I worked with early in my career became upset over what they saw as preaching and terminated treatment. I have also learned that many parents still believe in the saying "spare the rod and spoil the child." This belief simply would not yield to direct argument. Accordingly, I developed several strategies to help lessen the severity, duration, and frequency of spankings, as well as to help parents resist sudden angry impulses to hit. The simplest strategy was to contract with the parent to hit him—or herself on the thigh at least three times before hitting the child—in the same manner and as hard as the child was to be hit. This had at least two effects: (1) Parents realized what damage and pain might be inflicted, and (2) The severity and duration of hitting was usually lessened; sometimes the parent refrained from hitting the child at all.

I have also used a more complex method of working toward total cessation of physical punishment. In those families that insisted on continuing to spank "when necessary," we agreed that a spank would be administered only when a child had indulged in three consecutive incidents within the same category of unacceptable behavior, or in five incidents across categories. The spank was administered immediately after the final mark was obtained (three or five); as mentioned above, the chart entries were made when each incident of unacceptable behavior occurred. I stressed to the parents that the child should be told of the mark being put on the chart and that this announcement (or the spank when necessary) should as rule signal the end of the attention gained by the child for the unacceptable behavior. In cases where a child continued to be dangerous, destructive, or intensely disruptive he or she was

---

[1] I was occasionally spanked as a child, and I confess that I spanked each of my four children at least once; I also should note that my wife and I used a form of the program described here to help us avoid such behavior. When my children were young, spanking was not considered by most people to be abusive. However, things have changed. Over the past 20 years I have had many conversations with parents who would not generally be considered abusive. Many of these people still occasionally spank their children, and many are very secretive about it. In fact, some of these parents live in dread of the possibility of their children calling 911 and reporting them for abuse after a spanking.

removed, isolated, and ignored for a "time-out" period of five minutes. This additional step was rarely necessary, since the entry of a mark on the chart generally ended such behavior. Each spank was denoted on the chart with an asterisk. After a spank, the child began anew, in the sense that the next single unacceptable behavior was the beginning of a new series. Children also started with a clean slate each morning, in that no marks for unacceptable behavior from the previous day were counted toward a spank on the subsequent day.

Some Data

Table 5.3 shows some of the data from these five normal families. In all cases, daily occurrences of physical punishment were monitored by the parents for a four-week baseline period prior to the onset of the program, and the table compares this baseline with the frequency of physical punishment during the program. According to this index, the program resulted in a clear improvement, with the frequency of physical punishment at the end approaching zero in all five families. In the three families (numbers 2, 4, and 5) for which we have informal, longer-term follow-up, the frequencies of physical punishment have for 12 more months remained at or below the levels shown in Table 5.3.

Other indications of a more desirable level of function in all five families varied from family to family. One of the most notable changes was the realization that each child thrived on undivided attention from a single parent (i.e., one-to-one interaction). Each family devised some format for indefinitely maintaining this feature, and this outlasted the formal monitoring of behavior and programming of incentives.

Table 5.3. *Some Effects of the Use of Behavior-Control Technique in Five Normal Families*

Family	Number of boys (ages)	Number of girls (ages)	Mean Weekly Number of Physical Punishments per Child During:			Mean Weekly Number for the Most Recent Month of:		Total duration of chart use	Modification to chart procedure described in text
			the month before the start of chart use	the last week of the second month of chart use	the most recent month of chart use	Bad marks	Good marks		
1	2 (9,8)	1 (5)	2	1	.1	6	7	31 mo.	Maximum number of G = 1 per day.
2	2 (10,7)	1 (4)	2	0	.1	6	7	10 mo.	maximum number of G = 1 per day.
3	1 (5 1/2)		7	1	.25	6	14	8 mo.	G is given at the time of occurrence of certain target behaviors (maximum of 5 G's per day) if child gets more G's than bad marks he earns a family outing (e.g., bowling).
4	1 (8)	1 (6)	4	1	.5	10	9	4 mo.	G = 5 cents, bad marks = 2 cents
5	2 (4 1/2) Twins	1 (5 1/2)	21	0	.25	10	9	4mo.	Chart is discussed in evening befoire prayers; G = 5 cents, bad marks = 1 cents

Handout Description of This Program

We have recently developed a description of this program for handing out to parents. This has helped us to decrease staff time and seems to be effective in getting the ideas behind the program across. This simplified version is presented in an addendum at the end of this chapter.

Application with Troubled Families

We have also applied the program with dozens of families that would not be considered normal. I will present three such families as illustrations. The second and third of these families were clinically judged to be abusive.

A Boy with Problems

One troubled but not clinically abusive (by the standards of the late 1960s), family came to us complaining about the behavioral problems of their seven-year-old boy. This boy was the older of two children, residing with his family in a suburban middle-class home. He was doing average work in school, although his intelligence was superior. His behavior in the home showed long periods of normal behavior, with daily shorter periods of intensely disruptive behavior (see Figure 5.1). His disruptive behavior included the following: severe tantrums in which he would destroy furniture, draperies, and belongings; incidents of apparently unprovoked verbal and physical abuse (some of which was very dangerous) toward his younger sister; and incidents of making very loud noises and creating various disturbances when others preferred quiet (in church and in the middle of the night). The parents had tried to deal with him in various ways before bringing him to us with their tearful plea for help.

Conversation with the parents and child suggested the following:

(1)   The child's self-esteem was low or "Not OK" as reflected in word counts, in good and bad categories, and in response to the request "tell me about yourself."
(2)   The child felt guilty about his behavior.
(3)   The parents confessed that they had frequently resorted to spankings (apparently more severe than those used in

the families described in the preceding section) and to guilt-producing statements in an attempt to control the child's behavior.

(4)　　Reports from both the parents and the child on what happened before and after his misbehaviors indicated that he was reinforced by parental attention and that he very rarely received parental attention that was not contingent on bad behavior.

Figure 5.1. *Disruptive behavior of a seven-year-old boy over a 16-week period.*

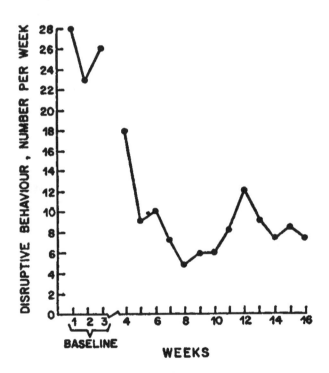

We implemented the family optimization program. Some of the results are shown in Figure 5.1. The parents reported that the disruptive behaviors occurring after approximately the sixth week were much less prolonged and less disturbing to the other members of the family. A follow-up evaluation 15 months after instituting the program showed that the boy's frequency of disruptive behavior remained at the level shown in the final four weeks covered in Figure 5.1. However, his parents reported that certain disruptive behaviors no longer occurred (such as tantrums involving destruction of furniture and his sister's belongings and physical abuse of his sister) and that the remaining disruptive behaviors were relatively mild and brief.

According to the parents' reports, this boy's behavior outside of the home and with his schoolmates, while not a target problem, was improved markedly after the institution of the program. This suggests that his new style of behavior became generalized since his new style showed up in other settings even without a targeted and programmed scheme of rewards and punishments. His school grades also improved.

Finally, his self-esteem, as reflected by self-references, shifted to the point where bad references were hardly ever present and where neutral and good references predominated (a standardized self-esteem measure for children was not used here).

Abusive Parents

The program has also been used with numerous abusive parents. These family settings are unsafe and often highly disorganized. In these cases, we always involve the appropriate civil authorities.[2]

In one abusive family, the average number of episodes of hitting per child (there were three boys, aged three to seven) was about 19 per week during the baseline period.[3] One of the boys was

---

[2] Great caution must be exercised in all aspects of dealing with cases of abuse. Civil authorities, such as state social service department employees, generally seem well equipped to deal with these cases. They understand the legal options and are trained to make a correct clinical judgment about the degree of danger to the child.

[3] Baseline periods when abuse is confessed are usually retrospective estimates. In this case I did not know that abuse was occurring until after the last baseline week. In this family both parents made separate counts that corresponded well; also, the oldest boy corroborated the counts given by his parents.

brain-damaged; this may have resulted from hitting. The parents admitted that some of their previous hits had been closed-fist assaults above the neck. By the time the program had been in effect for six weeks, the frequency of physical intervention had dropped to one per week per child, and the severity had decreased to a far less dangerous level (according to reports from both parents). The family remained in the program for at least five years, and we received periodic reports over the five-year period indicating that the lower frequency and severity had been stabilized. No further damage to any of the children could be detected by our evaluation (see Figure 5.2).

In a second abusive family (two girls, aged two and five, and one boy, aged three and a half), the mother was hitting the oldest daughter from 6 to 16 times per week during the baseline period. By the time the program had been in effect for six weeks, the average frequency of physical intervention had dropped to less than one hit per week, and again, according to the mother, the severity of these interventions was reduced to a far less dangerous level (see Figure 5.3).

Both of these abusive families (and all other abusive families I've seen) required long-term family therapy. The adults and the children received various forms of individual counseling and therapy. These services were provided by other caregivers who occasionally consulted with me.

Figure 5.2. *Median (range shown in brackets) number of physical interventions (father or mother to three sons) over a 34-week period.*

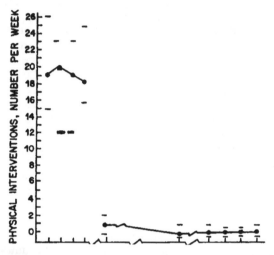

Figure 5.3. *Physical interventions (mother to five-year-old daughter) over a 12-week period.*

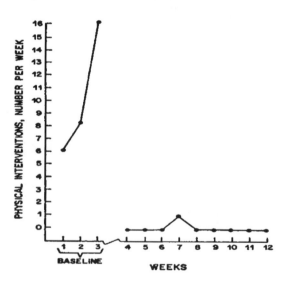

From the information I have gathered in my work with abusive families, I am left with the following impressions:

(1)   The abusive families profited from the long-term use of the optimization program;

(2)   The families needed frequent reminding and prodding to maintain systematic use of the program;

(3)   The families had greatest difficulty in
[a] making proper use of the program when they suddenly became upset and had the urge to hit and in
[b] scheduling and giving non-contingent (or clock contingent) positive attention each day;

(4)   The families and the individual members had many problems that required long-term attention from well-trained, talented, creative and tenacious caregivers;

(5)   The most successful caregivers were those who maintained the optimization program as a low-cost and humane background condition, and who went on to attend to remaining problems using other methods.

Advantages

In all but the final case described in this chapter, the basic method of assessment was the entry of letters on the chart. In the first abusive family, where each parent was abusive, the parents reported separately on each other's behavior. In the final case, the family with the single abusive parent, two methods of record keeping were used, which permitted a cross-check. All data, from families making any use of physical punishment, demonstrated a rapid reduction in physical punishment soon after implementation of the program.

As mentioned earlier, we have some evidence that the program effect outlasts its formal application. One of the normal families (the second shown in Table 5.1) was periodically observed before, during, and after the use of the program. These observations suggested that the behavior patterns developed in all family members during use of the program (for 11 months) continued for more than 10 years after its termination. For example, while the mean weekly average of physical punishments per child prior to the program was two, no physical punishments occurred during the post-program observation period.

A very important aspect of the program was control of parental behavior beyond the demonstrated reduction in use of physical punishment. For example, systematizing and ensuring the parental attention given to the disruptive seven-year-old boy may well have been the basis for the change found in that case. In many less-troubled families we have observed significant positive change as a result only of ensuring the daily period of parental attention (with no control over other behaviors or incentives). In the abusive families, uncoupling the parental mood swings from the parental delivery of aversive incentives was an important result of the use of this program. The most important force in this uncoupling may have been the prescription of a specific parental response to a child's misbehavior.

There was some indication that the program effects generalize to other settings and to changes in behaviors outside the home (such as the dramatic improvement in school behavior and in grades shown by the seven-year-old boy). We also have some evidence of program effects on self-esteem, or self-concept, and sense of agency. For example, in addition to the improvement in one child's self-esteem in the second abusive family, the mother reported that she also experienced dramatic improvement in her self-concept and her sense of self-control during the use of the program. In some subsequent applications, we did a careful assessment of the self-concept of all members of the families being treated, and we occasionally assessed other dependent variables (such as contracting skills). In all cases, the data supported the observations described above.

This program differs markedly from the most popular format in which Skinner's plan has been applied. The most important difference is that we match the reinforcement schedules and contingencies to those that apparently prevail in the real world.[4]

The objective of matching and sequencing the details of a program to promote generalization to the outside adult world has received attention from workers concerned with therapeutic applications of programs based on Skinner's plan. Numerous reviews of progress in this area (e.g., Kazdin and Bootzin, 1972) suggest the need for continuing work on this problem. Furthermore, in a non-clinical application, Feallock and Miller (1976) examined the high failure rate of experimental group living arrangements that were

---

[4] This program also answers some of Skinner's complaints about punishment in that it (1) depersonalizes punishment and (2) makes punishment events "informationally strong."

based on Skinner's ideas. The data they present demonstrate that the living arrangements become more stable when both aversive and positive incentives are included and when contingencies more closely approximate those prevailing in the real world.

In addition to the advantages already cited, the family optimization program has the following values:

(1) Low cost in time required for administration;
(2) A team approach to negotiating contracts;
(3) A boilerplate strategy that implies the expectation of good behavior and removes the necessity of rewarding each episode of good behavior;
(4) The control of parental attention, which in some cases is very difficult to manage properly, and which in many cases can provide the solution to many problems.

6: Troubled Families with Preverbal Children

Procedures for preventing the abuse of preverbal children have received little attention in the literature. The procedures that have been documented are generally more appropriate for families whose children are verbal and are over one year old.

In one published report, Sanders (1978) described the use of systematic desensitization with an infant-abusing parent. This effective treatment stemmed from Sanders's observation:

> *An infant's crying can cause the parent to become*
> *anxious and frustrated, and this in turn may lead*
> *to an episode of abuse.*

His observation is supported by data on the physiological and emotional effects of an infant's crying on adults (Frodi and Lamb, 1980; Frodi, 1985, 1990; Tyson, 1996). Our experiences with many anxious couples who had preverbal children, and with three parents who severely abused their infants, further support Sanders's observation.

In fact, some parents report feeling that the crying infant is intentionally tormenting them (Bauer and Twentyman, 1985). The interaction thus becomes an unequal power struggle. Parents have also confessed to me that they feel the presence of a judgmental entity (a "critic function") in the infant, or in their own minds; the infant's crying translates into an accusation that the parent is a failure.

Many children spend a lot of time crying, and even the very young infant will fuss or cry for parental attention. Crying usually does lead to either positive or neutral parental attention, but it can also lead to negative parental attention. The parent's negative attention may begin and end with a minor physical intervention such as a pat on the fanny. With an abusing parent, though, the negative attention often escalates rapidly to a level at which tissue damage occurs (an abusive episode).

Christopherson and colleagues (1976) have emphasized the value of using time-out procedures in conjunction with written protocols in order to help parents avoid using corporal punishment. We have combined these methods in a specific format for coping with the fussing of preverbal infants. This treatment format aims to break the connection between the infant's fussing and the negative parental attention, while guiding and supporting the parents as they learn to give positive attention when the infant is not fussing.

The Time-Out Procedure

For breaking the connection between fussing and negative attention, we have successfully used a simple behavioral procedure involving a time-out technique. The procedure consists of a checking routine, a time-out period, record keeping, instructions on positive attention (all presented in Table 6.1), and therapist support. A key element in the procedure is for the parent to leave the child shortly after the start of an episode of fussing and after a routine check for problems. In about half of the cases we have seen, the infant initially showed an increase in the intensity, duration, or frequency of crying.[1] Since this increase in crying may last from three to seven days, the therapist should try to make frequent supportive contacts by phone or in person, at least every third day, with one or both of the parents. In the ideal circumstance these contacts should continue at a frequency of twice a week for at least two weeks and can then be phased out gradually over the next two to four weeks. Support helps the parents (and the infants) to persist long enough to realize the benefits of the strategy, and also seems necessary to help parents take seriously and abide by the instructions for giving daily positive attention. (You will see, in Tables 6.2 and 6.3 that many entries are "estimates." I have consistently urged parents to keep data carefully, but I have not been very successful in combining support with data gathering.)

---

[1] Drabman and Jarvie, working with older, verbal children also noted an increase in misbehavior and crying in the early stages of using a time-out procedure (Pediatrics, 1977, 59, pages 78-85).

Table 6.1
Time-Out Procedure for Baby's Crying Episodes

INSTRUCTIONS
When baby starts crying: 1) write down time; 2) go through prescribed routine and enter finishing time below; 3) wait 30 minutes (if possible go for a walk, or somehow occupy yourself); 4) if baby is still crying, repeat first three steps.

Date	Time when crying started	Time when you finish the "check" routine? (Check diapers, pins, sheets, blankets, gas, and for possible hunger.)	After finishing the "check" routine, what did you do in the 30 minute waiting period?	Was baby crying at end of the 30 min.? (If so, repeat "check" routine and 30 minute cycle. Record this new cycle as a new episode on this page.)

Remember: 1) During "check" routine, do not yell or show any emotions. Make it as mechanical as possible. B) Give the baby attention when he/she is not crying; schedule at least half an hour in the morning and half an hour in the evening to play with the baby; this will help the baby learn to cry only when he/she is in need of help.

Table 6.2

Crying and abuse of Preverbal Children

Family	Measure	Preprogram Week	During program		Follow-up Duration
			Week 1	Week 2	
1 (Mr. D)	Number of cries	20	17 [0,5,3,1,5,2,1]	8 [0,3,1,1,1,1]	10 Years
	Duration of cries	(30 min.)	(5 min.)	(5 min.)	
	Number of physical interventions	14	0	0	
2 (Mrs. S)	Number of cries	(100+)	(35) [12,7](5 estimates of less than 5)	23 [4,1,0,6,4,7,1]	1 1/2 Years
	Duration of cries	(5 min.)	(5 Min. +)	(2 min. ±)	
	Number of physical interventions	(1-2)	0	0	
3 (Dr. G)	Number of cries	(14)	(35) [5](6 estimates of 5)	22 [3,2,6,2,3,4,2]	2 Years
	Duration of cries	(60 min.)	(10 min. +)	(10 min. ±)	
	Number of physical interventions	(5)	0	0	

Note: Estimates are in parentheses. Daily numbers from charts are in brackets. In Family 3, Dr. G's mother was present for the first program week. In Family 1, the subsequent frequency of physical intervention varies – see text.

Table 6.3
Crying of Preverbal Children

Family	Measure	Preprogram	
		Week 1	Week 2
4	Number of Cries	(24 times per day)	(24 times per day)
	Duration	(15 minutes)	(15 minutes)
5	Number of Cries	(28 times per day)	(28 times per day)
	Duration	(1 to 30 minutes)	(1 to 30 minutes)
6	Number of Cries	(7 to 10 times per day)	(7 to 10 times per day)
	Duration	(15 minutes +)	(15 minutes)
7	Number of Cries	[7 (6 estimates of 5 + times)]	[(5 estimates of 5+ times) 2,6]
	Duration	(20 minutes)	(20 minutes)
8	Number of Cries	(7 estimates of 2 times)	[1,3,2,0,2,1,1]
	Duration	(1 hour each time)	(fluctuating-range 5hrs to 2hrs)
9	Number of Cries	(7 estimates of 2 times per night)	(2 times per night)
	Duration	(15+ minutes)	(15 minutes each time)
10	Number of Cries	(7 estimates of at least 1)	(7 estimates of 1 time per night)
	Duration	(30 minutes)	(30 minutes)
11	Number of Cries	(7 estimates of 1 or 2)	[(6 estimates of 1 or 2) 1]
	Duration	(at least 30 minutes)	(30 minutes)
12	Number of Cries	(7 estimates of 3 to 5)	[(6 estimates of 3 to 5) 4]
	Duration	(at least 15 minutes)	(15 minutes each)

Note: Estimates are in parentheses. Daily numbers from charts are in brackets.

Table 6.3 (continued)

Family	During Program	
	Week 1	Week 2
4	[15,10,18,12,7,(7),10] (15 minutes +)	[(10) (20) 10, 17, 4, 7, 5] (10 minutes)
5	[10] (6 estimates of "more than 10") (15 minutes)	(7 estimates of 5 times per day) (25 minutes)
6	[6 (16)(12)(12) 9,15 (5)] (15 to 30 minutes)	[(4 estimates of 5) 5, (3), 3] (15 minutes +)
7	[2, 0, 1, 3, 2, 1, 1] (30 to 60 minutes)	[(6 estimates 1-2 times) 2] (less than 10 minutes)
8	[2 (2) 3, 3, 3, 0, 1] (decreasing from 1 hour to 5 minutes)	(7 estimates of 0-2 times) (none more than 15 minutes)
9	[3, 1, 2, (2) 0, 1, 0] (30 minutes each time)	("He sleeps through most nights, maybe outgrew it".)
10	[1 (3), 2] (4 estimates of 1 each night) (10-20 minutes)	[1,2, (1), 1, 3, (3), 1] (5 minutes)
11	(7 estimates of 1) (more than 30 minutes for 1 or 2 nights then less)	[(6 estimates of 1) 1] (less than 2 minutes)
12	[2, 5, 1, 2, 1, 0, 1] (fluctuating-range 15 minutes to 1.5 hours)	[0, 2, 3, 2, 0, 1, 1] (15 to 5 minutes)

Table 6.3 (continued)

Family	Follow-up Duration	Comments
4	None	Both parents are nurses; work different shifts.
5	3 months	Single parent & sitter did estimates; child cried 1 time in the day before last follow-up visit, 15 minutes.
6	2 years	Physician husband, nurse wife, & sitter did counting.
7	None	Parents and several sitters did counting.
8	None	Counted only cries at night.
9	None	Counted only cries at night.
10	1 Month	Counted only cries at night; follow-up at 1 month-"He cries 1 time most nights-but only for a couple of minutes."
11	10 Days	Counted only cries at night.
12	6 Months	Counted only cries at night; 6 month follow-up "1 cry for 5 minutes or less."

As mentioned above, we have used the procedure with three infant-abusing parents (see Table 6.2) and with many couples who did not report abusing their infants but who reported feeling extremely anxious when their infants cried (data for nine families are presented in Table 6.3). The following paragraphs illustrate the use of this procedure with a particularly troubled abusive parent (Mr. D reappears later, especially in Chapter 13).

Mr. D

Mr. D was a 27-year-old Vietnam veteran who was married and unemployed. He had a high-school education. Initially, Mr. D was referred to the Psychology Section at the White River Junction, Vermont, Veterans Hospital for treatment of serious generalized anxiety. A detailed psychological and neurological assessment indicated that Mr. D had some organic impairment resulting from a head injury, was experiencing difficulty with impulse control, was mildly depressed, and was fearful of social situations. During the assessment phase, Mr. D assured us that his family life, with his wife and his preverbal 11-month-old stepdaughter, was not a source of difficulty.

Following the psychological assessment, we conducted four sessions of progressive-relaxation training with Mr. D over a 10-day period. At the last of these sessions, Mr. D reported that he was feeling much less anxious and depressed. He then mentioned, for the first time, that he was having a persistent problem with his stepdaughter. He said, "She cries all the time, and I think she knows what it does to us." Although Mr. D admitted to spanking his stepdaughter, he did not at the time mention using excessive force. Nonetheless, considering the client's own obvious concern, we decided to attend to this issue.

Mr. D agreed to record the time of each incident of anger toward his stepdaughter, what caused him to become angry, and what he did about it. At the end of the first week, Mr. D's record showed that he had become angry with the child 20 times (each time she cried) and that he had hit her 14 times. Discussion revealed that some of these blows were severe enough to cause physical injury, and that such episodes had been occurring since the child was about 5 months old. Our subsequent conversations with the mother corroborated Mr. D's statements, and examination of the daughter revealed multiple bruises and scars. (At this time, Mr. D also revealed that he had been abused as a child and that he was ashamed that he was doing "the same thing" to his child.)

We then instituted the time-out procedure. (State social services were also notified,[2] and they made weekly visits for several months and occasional visits over the next six years.) Mr. D was given a page of instructions, along with a record-keeping format (see Table 6.1). This page was taped to the wall of the child's room. Mr. D and his wife were instructed to use the format and to keep a record of what happened whenever a crying episode occurred. Mr. D was instructed to bring the completed record for the week to each session.

After using this procedure for two weeks, Mr. D had reduced his frequency of hitting the child to zero, and the frequency of the child's crying had gone from more than two episodes per day in the first week to about one per day in the second week. During an initial 18-month follow-up period for this problem[3], we had ten meetings, most of which involved a discussion with both parents and an examination of the child. These sessions also involved systematic desensitization and biofeedback for control of autonomic arousal and cognitive treatments for anger. We found no evidence of further physical abuse that extended to causing tissue damage. However, Mr. D and his wife did occasionally resort to physical interventions. They classified these interventions as "normal spankings" or "pats on the fanny." The state social service personnel and I had many discussions with Mr. and Mrs. D about this issue. The repeated debates over "spare the rod and spoil the child" seemed to get us nowhere. However, Mr. and Mrs. D used this program with fair consistency for five years and four months. They also apparently abided by my rule regarding hitting their own thigh before hitting the child (see Chapter 5). However, they were not consistently able to incorporate other components of the mutual control strategy described in Chapter 5. The data and our own experiences with physical intervention in the D family are summarized in the following paragraphs.

---

[2] Again, great caution must be exercised in all aspects of dealing with cases of abuse; state social service employees have training which improves their chances of making a correct judgment about the degree of danger to a child.

[3] We later saw Mr. D for problems with violent behavior toward other adults; details of this treatment are presented in subsequent chapters.

The last detected tissue damage was that observed immediately prior to onset of the program. The only known episodes that appeared to be outside of the "pat on the fanny" range occurred in a four-day period five weeks after the start of the program—these did not result in detectable tissue damage and the social service representative decided to leave the child in the home. The number of spankings each week was four or less for the first year, and two or less for the next four years. In the five years after termination of the formal program, there were no occasions on which physical intervention occurred more than once per week.

Throughout the follow-up period, prior to 1989, Mr. D maintained most of the gains he had realized in the first four sessions of progressive relaxation. He showed better impulse control and a steady decrease in his fear of social situations. He also reported an increase in his ability to prevent and control feelings of anger and a decrease in the anxiety and frustration he felt when his stepdaughter cried.

Advantages

Our time-out procedure has proved effective both in reducing an infant's crying and in stopping abuse of the infant. Used alongside the program described in Chapter 5, the procedure has helped to stabilize several large and highly-disorganized families with two or more children ranging from infancy to late adolescence. It has also been used successfully with families of various socioeconomic levels. Mr. D's family was the least well-educated and the most disadvantaged of our small clinical sample of three families who abused preverbal infants. In the other two infant-abusing families, the parents were both college-educated and one was a practicing physician.

The procedure is quite simply applied using the framework and instructions in Table 6.1. The use of this procedure dissociates parental attention from behavioral episodes that elicit negative attention. It not only decreases the likelihood of abuse, but it also lays the foundation for a positive parent-child relationship. With less pressure for the child to misbehave in order to get attention, the child is free to learn new ways of getting attention, and the parent can practice new ways of giving it. In all of the families treated, use of the routine has increased the frequency of positive interaction and has apparently aided in the formation of a positive relationship between parent and child.

Beyond the advantage of its apparently wide applicability, the procedure has two significant technical advantages. First, the procedure is easy to teach and learn and thus can be instituted rapidly. Second, the parents' use of the system can be easily monitored. Both of these features are of obvious importance when we are intervening in so serious a problem as infant abuse.

The procedure and our system for its use can also have certain operational efficiencies. The probability of negative parental attention is decreased as the parent follows a prescribed routine that specifies both an appropriate direct response to the infant's crying (the neutral checking routine) and a method for coping with negative reactions (the 30-minute waiting, or time-out routine). The parent is thus separated from the infant during the period when abuse is most likely to occur. Positive episodes of parental attention are programmed, and these episodes are clearly separated from the infant's crying behavior.

Positive parental attention has not been carefully programmed in many published procedures for dealing with abuse. Parents often need to be reminded regularly of this aspect of the program in order for them to take it seriously. Many parents act as if it were best to leave the infant alone when he or she is quiet. Doing so they put the infant in a bind; specifically, the infant is addicted to attention and if enough is not given he or she will be forced to work for it—that is, to cry. Those published procedures (e.g., Drabman and Jarvie, 1977) that do attend to the management of positive attention generally try to arrange for it to be contingent upon positive behavior of the child. While the child should frequently be rewarded for good behavior, it is also crucially important that the child not be forced to "earn" all positive attention. As emphasized earlier, it is the non-behavior-contingent (or clock-contingent) positive attention from the parents that will help develop the self-concept in the child that he or she is loved. One who must get attention by doing tricks—or "polishing apples"—does not necessarily develop the good self-concept.

Sanders (1978) combined systematic desensitization with various other procedures, including medication, counseling, and supportive psychotherapy. His program took more than 13 months, including 12 sessions of systematic desensitization, and it required considerable cooperation from the patient. It is worth noting that, in our sample, Mr. D was the only client for whom we used systematic desensitization, biofeedback, or anger-management training. Many abusing parents do, of course, require long-term treatment. In the meantime, our time-out procedure can be instituted at the first or second visit so that risk of further abuse can be reduced while the other parts of the intervention (including the involvement of appropriate social services) are getting underway.

7: Troubled Adults

Having considered some ideas and methods pertaining to families and the development of individual personalities, let us reconsider what happens when things go wrong. One matter at least should be obvious by now: I believe that most behavioral problems can be traced to problems with the impact of incentives, and, in turn, to self-concept. I also believe that many behavioral problems can be traced all the way back to how parents manage the attention they give to their children.

Mismanaged Parental Attention

The power and effect of mismanagement of parental attention can be illustrated in various ways. One of the most frequent problems arises when the child learns that misbehavior is the only reliable method of getting parental attention. Misbehaving in order to get attention usually has a number of effects, of which the following five are quite frequent:

(1)   Misbehavior usually results in further fogging or confusion of the boundaries between positive and negative attention, or between the intended positive affective messages and the intended negative affective messages from the parent.

(2)   This fogging usually causes both the child and the parent to expect misbehavior.

(3)   Once they expect misbehavior, the parents are less likely to spontaneously give attention to the child, and they may even begin to avoid the child.
(4)   The child will begin to perceive the essential audience, or significant others, as having a negative and critical attitude toward him or her (see Figure 4.8 in Chapter 4).
(5)   The child's general self-concept develops in the "I am not OK" direction (see Figure 4.7 and 4.10 in Chapter 4).

Thus, the child who learns to misbehave in order to get attention will eventually come to feel not "OK," will have difficulty differentiating intended positive social incentives from negative social incentives, and may well develop unusual responses to other forms of incentives if this pattern continues.

Some evidence supports the notion that a reversal in the impact of incentives can develop. This reversal may be associated with environmental factors in addition to the fogging that can occur during early learning. J. McV. Hunt (1972) and a number of other investigators have examined the relationship between self-esteem and preferred incentives, with socioeconomic level as a related variable. Children at lower socioeconomic levels, who show lowered self-esteem (Coleman, 1966; Keller, 1963; Long and Henderson, 1967), show greater preference for concrete rewards such as M&M candies than they do for symbolic incentives such as praise or knowledge of results (Teffel, Durkin, and Weisley, 1959; Zigler and DeLabry, 1962). Children at lower socioeconomic levels also tend to prefer immediate delivery of incentives over delayed delivery of incentives, even when the incentive to be obtained later would be greater. On the other hand, children of higher socioeconomic levels prefer to wait for the larger, but delayed, incentive (Maitland, 1966; Mischel, 1961; Mischel and Metzner, 1962; Steen, 1966).

In depressed adults (who generally show lower self-esteem) investigators (Lewinsohn, Weinstein, and Shaw, 1969; Miller and Seligman, 1976) have observed alterations in incentive responsiveness. Rehm and Plakosh (1975) demonstrated that the higher a person's depression score (measured by a multiple-adjective checklist), the greater the person's preference for immediate delivery of incentive would be.

Incentive Stimuli Inverted

Taken together, these ideas and findings might lead one to believe that a complete inversion, or reversal, of the impact of an incentive stimulus could take place in certain circumstances. In fact, as I think about some of the depressed adults and adults with low self-esteem that I have known, I quickly recall examples of apparent reversal of the impact of intended positive social incentives. There are various mechanisms by which this might happen. Consider the following five possibilities:

(1) An intended positive incentive may carry a conditioned negative component. For example, a child who is repeatedly told, "That's nice, but why can't you do it every time?" may experience both positive and negative incentives. The child may hear, "The behavior is nice, but you are not expected to show that nice behavior on a regular basis." It seems that the repeated experiencing of such communications could fit the classical conditioning model such that the receiver experiences a negative incentive, even when the message seems totally positive to the sender.

(2) The occurrence of a positive incentive may sharpen the expectancy of a negative incentive. This may happen because the individual is functioning as if he or she were on a schedule for incentive delivery. (One of my clients recently said, "whenever something good happens I get worried, because I know something really bad is going to happen next.")

(3) A positive incentive may signal "time out" from future positive incentives. Again, this may happen because the individual is functioning as if he or she were on a schedule for incentive delivery (e.g., low ratio). The comment, "Well, that's my good luck for today," seems to fit this model.

(4) The delivery of an intended positive incentive may increase or sharpen feelings of unworthiness or guilt (see Figure 4.9 in Chapter 4). This is a dynamic explanation of a phenomenon epitomized by the person who is unable to accept a compliment. For example, if one attempts to compliment such a person on a painting, he or she might say, "Well, thank you, but that was just a

lucky one, and really not much good; if you look closely, you'll see that the good effect is produced by the cat getting into my paint and dragging its tail across the picture." Some such people actually seem afraid to enjoy compliments. Perhaps they fear that the omnipresent essential audience will criticize them for rejoicing in their own accomplishments.

(5)   The occurrence of a positive incentive may be seen as a random event, or as an event that was not produced or controlled by the individual. Even though the individual may show some signs of pleasure at the occurrence of the positive incentive, he or she may experience an increase in the sense of helplessness, or even in the sense that he or she is being controlled by someone else. Thus the positive incentive can again be seen as having a negative component.

A large body of research by Seligman and his colleagues provides support for such notions (e.g., Miller and Seligman, 1976).

Tracing Back

Such mechanisms and examples of the relationship between incentives, depression, and self-esteem can be taken to great lengths. They can sometimes be clarified in an individual so that a specific behavioral problem will be traceable to problems in incentive impact, and in turn to self-concept, and finally all the way back to delivery of attention by parents.

One of the best-known examples of tracing an adult behavioral problem back to the parents' strategies of managing their attention is that of the paranoid German man described by Schatzman (1973) in a book appropriately entitled, *Soul Murder*. The man's father had developed and published a general program for raising children and had described his tactics in great detail. The concepts of the essential audience and the critic function are starkly illustrated by Schatzman's descriptions of relentless and structured use of an array of punitive signals, such as disapproving glances eventually coming to have a very large effect on a child's behavior.

Goleman (1985) considered the same case and juxtaposed with it the consideration of some children who were in therapy because they had been abused by their parents. These latter children also showed features of paranoia and the critic function in their self-labeling behavior (e.g., "bad," "stupid"), and in other areas of their behavior as well. Goleman says,

> *In these tragic children denial and displacement—*
> *key mechanisms of the paranoid style—are already*
> *in place. These paranoid predispositions need not*
> *come from such explosive events as abuse; these*
> *same tendencies can be imprinted on the mind by*
> *less obvious forms of tyranny. Violence can come in*
> *subtler forms—as disapproving looks, silent rebuffs,*
> *humiliation, or love withdrawn. The net effect can be*
> *the same, provided the implicit injunction is*
> *instilled: that the parent is blameless for the feelings*
> *of hurt and anger that the child feels (page 153).*

The critic function established by the parents can lead to criticism of both self and others and to related expectancies and dispositions that become involved in a reciprocally determined tangle of relationships between the working self-concept and the behavior of other people.

> *A child who expects rejection from his parents may*
> *become hyper-alert to signs of it in his playmates.*
> *Such a child is likely to distort innocuous comments,*
> *seeing them as hostile. In anticipation of such*
> *hostility, a child prepares to counter it by meeting*
> *his playmates with a cold, rigid stare and some*
> *aggressive words. This in turn evokes the very*
> *response it was meant to anticipate—the child*
> *becomes the target of his playmates' real rather*
> *than imagined hostility (Goleman, 1985, page 153).*

Goleman has thus provided an excellent description of what appears to be going on in the interactions of my violent clients with other people, including what goes on with their own infants.

Part Three

Technique

8: Group Assessment

In 1989 I described a general set of methods for individual assessment and treatment of violent clients that took an average of 17 sessions. Almost all of this work was done in individual sessions. Since then we have turned more to group work, including initial assessment with a group neuropsychological screening battery. Now many of the clients referred to us meet with us for the first time at our Monday morning group assessment meetings. The following is a brief description of the group assessment procedures.

Our small psychology section (two full-time employees and one part-time employee) receives testing referrals from all clinical departments of the Veterans Administration Hospital, in White River Junction, Vermont. After the first year of this program we also began receiving referrals for testing from other hospitals, including another VA Hospital. The most frequent referrals involve compensation and pension examinations; evaluating the possibility of dementia or organic impairment; assessing the severity of depression, anxiety or pain; and, where appropriate, providing suggestions for case formulation and treatment planning. These referrals are generally urgent and we are often asked to respond very quickly. In the past, the section chief, a PhD. psychologist, received the referral and selected the instruments for individual testing. A Master's level psychology technician conducted the testing, scored the tests and drafted a report. The section chief then collaborated with the technician to produce the final report.

Five years ago, increasing numbers of clients were being referred for assessment. There was usually a three-week delay from receipt of referral to beginning of testing, and another two-week delay before the report was ready for filing. From conversations with psychologists at other hospitals (including hospitals with large psychology departments) we learned that their delays were about as long as ours, but that provided little comfort in the face of an occasional complaint from those who referred clients. In an attempt to improve this situation, we developed a group testing strategy. (A large share of the burden for the fundamental creative work was taken on by one of our team members, R. Fred Elliott MA.) Our aims were to reduce the delay in testing, the time spent in testing, and the time from testing to final report. We also aimed to do this without additional staff or money and to maintain or improve the clinical usefulness of the assessment results.

We had to start almost from scratch in selecting tests for the battery. The previous literature on group testing did not provide much guidance. Our groups included no more than 12 clients (usually between 2 and 6) and would be carefully monitored by three staff members. Standardized tests were used wherever possible. We used those tests from our existing collection of individual tests that could be adapted to group use. Where we have modified procedures or used only selected items from tests, local norms are used to evaluate the results. (The tests are described in an appendix.)

During testing there are two or three of us in the room. We carefully observe the behavior of each test taker. At any sign of confusion we intervene quickly. As each data sheet is completed, two of us examine it and note problems that may require individual attention when the group session has been completed.

The group battery serves as a first-pass or screening examination of all clients referred to us. Since assessment goals and client characteristics are diverse, we knew at the outset that further assessment of some clients would be required. When the group battery does fail to answer the referral question (e.g., when the referral requests differentiation of depression from dementia and we see inconsistent signs of both) or reveals indications of possible pathology requiring further examination (e.g., when there are many blank spaces on an answer sheet, or when there is a marked discrepancy—such as when the person has excellent executive function on the calculation test, but poor performance in abstract reasoning or digits reversed) an additional session of individual testing is scheduled. About two in ten clients require additional assessment, the same rate of additional evaluation that we have found with our previous individual testing work. Assessment tools for additional sessions are selected on the basis of information from the referral source and from the group testing behavior and results.

It is generally quite easy to form and support clinical judgments on the basis of the group testing results. Referral questions, usually in the form of a few sentences describing problems that have been observed, are typically answerable on the basis of the results of a sub sample of tests. The remaining test results then provide a more complete description of the client's strengths and weaknesses.

Between 1997 and 2001 we used the group-testing strategy for 534 clients, ranging in age from 21 to 87 and in education from third-grade to 20 years. This sample included 26 females. Diagnoses of referred clients have included the majority of diagnoses represented in the ICD 9 and DSM IV. The most frequent diagnoses have been depression, anxiety, PTSD, chronic pain and dementia.

All of our aims have been achieved. We previously spent about 25 person hours to test and write reports on five clients; we now spend about 14.5 hours to do this work. Group testing sessions are held once per week and last for two hours. The time from referral to testing was reduced from three weeks to one week during the first several years of this program. Currently, due to continuing increases in numbers of clients referred the delay from referral to testing ranges between one and three weeks. The time from testing to filing a report is down from two weeks to six working days. The clinical usefulness has not been degraded as we went from individual to group testing. A survey of the clinicians who most frequently refer clients to us indicated that they rate our group testing reports as equal to, or somewhat better than, our earlier individual testing reports. Referring clinicians also indicated unanimous appreciation of the rapidity of our testing and reporting.

Client acceptance of group testing has not been a problem. In general, the difficulties occurring with group testing have been the same as those encountered in individual testing. No more than five percent of our clients balk at testing, whether individual or group. Furthermore, the quality of the data gathered in group sessions appears equal to that gathered in individual sessions.

There are several indicators that information from our assessment battery is useful in predicting future events (e.g., treatment outcome and later measures of psychopathology). Among these are the following: (1) In group cognitive therapy, those with higher verbal intelligence and abstract reasoning ability are clearly more successful. Those who fall below normal limits for these measures tend to drop out or fail to show much improvement; (2) High levels of remaining function on the Dartmouth Pain Questionnaire predict greater success in a pain management program; (3) When a client shows serious impairment in one or more of our memory tests, later individual memory tests corroborate the original finding, and allow greater specification of areas of difficulty; (4) Clients who perform poorly on the measures of abstract reasoning, executive function and working memory in the group testing battery show clear signs of impairment on later individual tests, such as the Wisconsin Card Sort test, the Mattis Dementia Rating Scale and the Wechsler Memory Scale.

As mentioned above, our testing strategy is fully approved by those who refer clients to us. Other indications of the usefulness of our group-testing strategy are that clients are referred to us from a veteran's hospital in another state when a rapid compensation and pension examination is required; and professionals from a second, even larger hospital have observed our group testing procedures and have subsequently initiated these procedures at their hospital. Follow-up indicates that they are pleased with the results. We hope that our success will encourage other clinicians faced with assessment bottlenecks to adopt similar strategies.

The cost-effectiveness of this group-testing strategy, when used as a first pass or screening system, has financial and perhaps ethical implications for the continued exclusive use of first pass individual testing. In this era of managed care, requests for the funding of testing are often turned down, and thus a needed service is not available. If assessment involves a battery such as we describe here, it may be possible to convince managed-care companies to provide the necessary funding.

9: Case Formulation: Tools and Strategies

In our attempts to understand individual clients and the problems they face, my colleagues and I have used a variety of assessment procedures and modeling strategies. As mentioned in Chapter 8, we usually start with group assessment. If the results from the group assessment indicate that our team should be working with a particular client, then we will either meet with the client individually, or invite him/her to attend one of the groups we run.

Examination of Self-Concept and Incentive Events

We have assessed self-concept using various formats for self-description (such as that used in the Dartmouth Pain Questionnaire, Corson and Schneider, 1984), and we have observed self-labeling behavior, expectancies and dispositions in response to several behavioral assessment procedures. We have also used the following: (1) asking clients to underline words that describe themselves from a long list of possible self-labels; (2) asking clients to write descriptions of themselves that might be written by their best friend, their worst enemy, and by themselves; (3) asking clients to keep records on their best and worst social experiences each day; (4) asking clients to write—for 30 minutes—on one of the most traumatic or stressful experiences of their lives (regarding this last tactic see Pennebaker, 1997); and (5) conducting a brief narrative therapy interview (along the lines of some elements to be described in chapter 20).

For the exploration of incentive responsiveness, we have used behavioral interviews and procedures such as behavioral-avoidance tests, role-playing, and naturalistic observation.

A combination of techniques generally gives us some idea of the development and status of our clients' self-concepts and of various important social incentives. Over the years, though, we have come to favor a simple four-part query, and for the past several years we have been using it with every client on almost every visit. This technique consists of asking the client four questions about self-satisfaction:

1. What has been your highest level of self-satisfaction in the past 24 hours (on a 0-to-5 scale, where 0 is no satisfaction, I is just noticeable, and 5 is as high a level as is realistically possible, given the constraints of your life)?
2. What was happening, or what were you doing, when you felt this high level of self-satisfaction?
3. What has been your lowest level of self-satisfaction in the past 24 hours (on the same scale)?
4. What was happening, or what were you doing, when you felt this low level of self-satisfaction?

The ABC Chart

The following paragraphs go into detail on the formats and modeling routines we use in the attempt to relate incentive events to self-concept and behavior. The results of single episode, or "mini-modeling" for four clients will be presented at first to illustrate some of the complexity we face in dealing with individual clients. Figures 9.1 and 9.2 depict differences among individuals who were referred for the same behavioral problems. Figure 9.1 shows the ABC chart (for Antecedents, Behaviors, and Consequences) for two people with bulimia (persons who overeat and then induce vomiting). They showed marked differences in incentive responsiveness; for example, while the first client never vomited when alone, the second client (Ms. N, who is also depicted in other figures using more complex models shown later in this section) made a serious suicide attempt when her vomiting was discovered. Figure 9.2 depicts antecedents, behaviors, and consequences for two exhibitionists who responded to very different incentive events. (The ABC chart itself was briefly introduced in Chapter 1; see Table 1.1 for a blank chart with instructions. Chapter 13 contains many more examples of uses of the ABC chart.)

The self-labeling or self-concept aspects reflected in these figures were most helpful clinically in specifying the details of important incentive events, as well as in specifying important subjective and objective antecedent events. In turn, the clarification of these issues was helpful in selecting appropriate assessment and treatment regimes.

The Flow Diagram

The complexity shown in Figures 9.1 and 9.2 could easily become overwhelming if one did not have some sort of organizing format. We have developed such a format and call it the flow diagram (Corson and Heseltine, 1971). This is a modeling strategy that provides structure, and it forces us and our clients to hypothesize about cause-effect relationships, to speculate about treatments that might follow from our hypotheses, and to develop ways to evaluate these treatments. Some aspects of the diagram are frequently developed in close collaboration with the client.

Procedure

A blank flow diagram is shown in Figure 9.3. We start with the column marked Target Problems and list the various problems for which the client is seeking help. Next, we use the Stimuli column to list the important historical events and possible causes or triggers or current stressors that might set off these target problems. Then the Presumed Internal Processes column is used to list the guesses or hypotheses regarding internal (psychodynamic?) variables that might link the Stimuli to the Target Problems. Following this, we use the Treatment Methods column to list and sequence the possible appropriate treatment procedures for each Target Problem. Finally, we use the Evaluation Methods column to specify procedures by which we will monitor the client's status and eventually measure the impact of treatment. The last column is crucial in the development of a personal scientist/theorist attitude. We must develop ways to assess the effects of our interventions in order to keep pace with the inevitable shifts in the client's behavior, thoughts, feelings and "personality," and in order to continue refining our theory and treatment strategy for this individual.

Figure 9.1. *ABC diagrams for two bulimic clients.*

	Antecedents	Behaviors	Consequences (short term)
Client #1 (Social)	Stressful social situation – in a conflict – has a request denied. (Working self-concept: NOT IN CONTROL. NOT DOMINANT.)	Client eats a few bites of something (e.g., potato salad) and induces vomiting IN PRESENCE OF PERSON(S) TO BE CONTROLLED.	Pity → Client gets her way. (Working self-concept: IN CONTROL. DOMINANT)
Client #2 (Alone, Ms. N)	Client has no date – is alone – feels lonely – frustrated. (Working self-concept: UNLOVED. GETTING FAT? REJECTED AND GUILTY DUE TO PRIOR SEX EXPERIENCE. PRIOR OVEREATING.)	Client overeats and induces vomiting – ALONE.	Client relieved of full feeling from overeating. (Working self-concept: (1) FEELS LESS GUILTY (PERHAPS BECAUSE SHE HAS NOW SUFFERED FOR HER SINS: (2) KNOWS SHE WILL NOT GAIN WEIGHT FROM THE OVEREATING.)

Figure 9.2. *ABC diagrams for two exhibitionists.*

	Antecedents	Behaviors	Consequences (short term)
Client #1 (confronting)	LONG TERM Social stress (e.g., client is humiliated by his boss (who is a female). (Working self-concept: LOWER SELF-ESTEEM, "NOT DOMINANT", "CONTROLLED.") SHORT TERM Woman isolated-where her screams will not bring immediate attention (Client sees her as a "victim").	Exposure of genitals (while facing woman, three to ten feet away, obstructing her escape route).	(IDEAL) Woman screams [orgasm not necessary] (working self-concept: Client FEELS HIGHER SELF-ESTEEM, "DOMINANT", "ASSERTIVE".)
Client #2 (peripheral)	Woman in park or library (often where screams would bring immediate attention). (Working self-concept: UNNOTICED, UNLOVED, UNWANTED.)	Exposure of genitals (not in line of sight, usually in peripheral field, where woman might notice; 10 to 40 feet away, not obstructing an escape route).	(IDEAL) Woman does not scream (may notice but pretends to ignore client). Client masturbates to orgasm. (Working self-concept: CLIENT FEELS RELIEVED, A BIT ASHAMED, BUT FEELS THAT HE HAS "DONE SOMETHING" AND BEEN NOTICED.)

Applications

Figure 9.4 shows an initial flow diagram for Ms. N, drawn after the first intake interview. (Ms. N was the second person with bulimia whose ABC chart appeared in Figure 9.1.) Notice how quickly you get a feeling from the first two columns for the salient aspects that influence Ms. N's bulimia. Notice also that already some systematic evaluation is planned for the events surrounding her bulimia. You also see two other problems noted, but little understood after the first hour—Ms. N's apparent lack of social skills and her suicide attempt.

As treatment continues, the flow diagram is updated whenever new ideas or data can be added. As it always does, the picture gradually becomes more complex (Figure 9.5). We learned by the fourth session that Ms. N was severely troubled by complex developmental and psychodynamic issues. Most important was her relationship with a judgmental and controlling mother, with a resulting matrix of issues involving anger and control. Figure 9.5 depicts our hypotheses about the relationships among these psychodynamic issues and between these issues and other problems. Notice that even this more complex flow diagram gives an easy overview of the salient issues. Take, for example, the column entitled Treatment Methods. A team approach has evolved, with a therapist doing the behavioral work, coordinating it with an exercise coach, with those doing medical and dietary work, and, in this case, with another therapist who treats intrapsychic problems. (It is worth noting here that in most of our current work the behavioral and cognitive/emotional/intrapsychic work is done by a single clinician.)

I have omitted some details from Figures 9.3 through 9.5 in order to present the format more clearly. For example, we include a general Self-Concept section in the "Presumed Internal Processes" column. Here we list the client's descriptions of his or her interests, strengths, weaknesses, and other salient characteristics. In the Treatment Method column, we often indicate the sequence of the different treatments we are planning, estimate the number of sessions for each treatment procedure, and indicate the evaluation criteria that will determine whether a particular procedure should be continued beyond the estimated number of sessions.

Ms. N's flow diagrams—and flow diagrams in general—do not address all aspects of the shifty/shifting theory of personality (described earlier in this book and as shown in Figure 3.1); they do address the aspects of Ms. N's life that seemed the most important and the most in need of attention. As Ms. N improved, we composed new versions of her diagram.

By now it should come as no surprise that our flow diagrams for other clients with bulimia are very different from Ms. N's. Many of the others include a sizable role for the interplay of SNS activity and central motive state.

Other Uses

The flow diagram is compatible with the ABC approach to understanding clients (as shown in Figures 9.1 and 9.2). The ABC can be used to develop separate initial descriptions for each of the problems presented by the client, along with the descriptions of various aspects of the biopsychosocial dynamics involved in an episode of each of the problem behaviors (examples are given in other chapters). When there are multiple problems I will generally attempt to interest the client in focusing first on a problem that will be likely to yield rapidly to a specific technique that I have experience with. I have found that progress toward a specific goal usually increases the client's sense of self-efficacy, frequently leads to a lessening of severity of other problems, and generally produces positive shifts in self-concept. It is also worth noting that there is some convincing literature indicating that progress toward a specific goal, such as coping with panic disorder, can have helpful effects on comorbid conditions, such as depression (e.g. Tsao et al., 2002). The ABC strategy can also be used in the initial interview and in preliminary communications with consultants and referring agents. The basic ABC diagram does not permit inclusion of general descriptions of internal processes or the matching of assessment and treatment procedures to the various problems. But the obvious temporal sequence ("flow") of the ABC diagram can easily be incorporated into the flow diagram format; the arrows in Figure 9.5 indicate some of our hypotheses about temporal sequences.

Finally, the flow diagram format facilitates communication with consultants and collaborators from outside the mental health professions. The various medical procedures of assessment and treatment are conveniently described and scheduled on the same page with the psychotropic medications and psychotherapy or behavioral therapy. The flow diagram has proven to be particularly valuable when an individual is discharged from an inpatient facility to the care of a practitioner in the community, and when one practitioner turns a client over to another practitioner. The flow diagram is also very useful when I make presentations at case conferences. Chapter 13 contains many other examples of flow diagrams.

Client as Coinvestigator

I have found that the relationship between the therapist and the client, as well as the client's attitude toward the therapeutic effort, are often fostered and supported by enlisting the client as a personal scientist/theorist, or coinvestigator. For example, at the end of the first session, most clients can be given a record-keeping assignment tailored to their particular presenting problem. At the very least, the client might be asked to log the status of his or her presenting complaint once per day, between suppertime and bedtime. Or, a phobic client might log the number of panic attacks that had occurred since the previous meal; this could be done before each meal. For each panic attack, he or she would note the situation and the severity of the panic on a scale of 1 to 5. (Tying these record-keeping activities to a specific, routine behavior such as eating increases the chance that the forms are filled out.) Or one might ask that the client record only a description of the most anxiety-provoking, most emotionally powerful, or most enjoyable experience of the day. Whatever the schedule for recording, the client brings the record-keeping sheet to each session for discussion. Becoming a co-investigator in this manner can enhance the client's sense of self-control and responsibility. (It is worth noting that I have found a highly significant relationship between compliance with record-keeping requests and progress in therapy. This is spelled out in Chapter 12.)

Putting It All Together

The group assessment method touches on some of the issues addressed by other well-known case formulation strategies (e.g. Lazarus, 1987 and Frisch, 1992). However, it is worth noting that this group assessment exercise gives us really helpful guidance in developing a case formulation only when combined with our initial conversation with the client.

In that first conversation we are usually able to understand more clearly the client' s presenting defense system, and how they see the problems that they would like to have worked on, or goals they would like to work toward. The development of the flow diagram, and the eventual sharing of the flow diagram with the client, is an additional important step in case formulation that can often be completed during this initial conversation.

The flow diagram, when well done, gently sketches out the initial defenses, pinpoints specific targets, selects goals for each target, specifies methods for approaching each goal, and specifies a measurement system for determining progress toward each goal. The client is asked to consider the work involved, and the losses, as well as the gains that will be realized as they move toward a goal. During this conversation it sometimes becomes clear that the client will be reluctant to let go of their problem and present defense system. Some clients will see a change as stepping out into the terrifying unknown —perhaps risking a return to the dreaded feared possible self. It is as if they imagine that they will risk losing the armor/protection of the warrior role, thus returning the underdog role, or possibly losing the comfort of the established dependency role in their particular system. Fruitful negotiation can be stimulated by this activity. Once targets, goals etc. are agreed-upon the work can begin. As the work goes along, occasional reference to the updated flow diagram, with its suggestions of time/session number limits for application of each method, is a valuable activity, particularly when daily crisis management becomes an impediment to movement. Daily crisis management demands and other forms of resistance to taking small steps in the unknown can be expected. The negotiation of the small steps toward treatment goals, which generally involve simple homework routines and daily record keeping, often is a form of negotiation regarding which specific small steps will be taken into the unknown.

Evaluation Issues

We often encounter the need for baseline data against which to judge therapeutic interventions, whereas the client's clinical needs may demand that treatment (and record keeping) be started immediately. In such cases we have used the "retrospective baseline" method proposed by Houtler and Rosenberg (1985). During a very early interview we collect as much information as possible concerning the variables in question (such as severity of symptoms, number of incidents of maladaptive behavior) during, for example, the previous four weeks. We solicit this information very carefully, often not only from the client, but also from significant others or from previously written critical incident reports. At regular intervals throughout treatment, or at least at the end of treatment, we then obtain similar retrospective information, using exactly the same procedures as we used during the collection of the retrospective baseline. While bias cannot be eliminated in this way, at least the data points are more or less compatible, and the client is spared a possibly unethical delay in needed treatment.

The flow-diagram format described in this chapter is easy to use and easy to adapt as shifts occur. Without it, we would be less effective.

Figure 9.3. *Flow Diagram Format*

Name _____ Education _____ Marital Status _____ Referred by _____

Date _____ Age _____ Occupation _____ Presenting Problems _____

STIMULI	PRESUMED INTERNAL PROCESSES	TARGET PROBLEMS	TREATMENT METHODS	EVALUATION METHODS

Figure 9.4. *Preliminary Flow Diagram for a Self-Inducing Vomiter at Intake.*

Name ___F.N.___ Education ___University Graduate___ Marital Status _Single_ Referred by _Dr. S. John_
Date ___3/4/74___ Age ___21___ Occupation ___Social Work (internship)___ Presenting Problems ___Self-induced vomiting and stomach pain.___

STIMULI	PRESUMED INTERNAL PROCESSES	TARGET PROBLEMS	TREATMENT METHODS	EVALUATION METHODS
Being alone	Self-concept: "unattractive, fat, guilty, angry, depressed"	Overeat (feels full)	Continue assessment	Record keeping of urges to eat beyond scheduled amount or outside scheduled times.
Memories of first sex partner	"punished enough; won't get fat"	Vomit	Systematize food purchase and consumption	Miles and times (set up schedule for running).
		Possible social skills problems		
		Suicide attempt	Systematize exercise	Do record keeping on best and worst social experience each day.

Figure 9.5. *Flow Diagram for vomiter after four sessions.*

Name __F.N.__ Education __University Graduate__ Marital Status _Single_ Referred by _Dr. S. John_
Date ___3/14/74___ Age __21__ Occupation ___Social Work (internship)___ Presenting Problems _Self-induced vomiting and stomach pain._

STIMULI	PRESUMED INTERNAL PROCESSES	TARGET PROBLEMS	TREATMENT METHODS	EVALUATION METHODS
Being alone (not being asked for a date). Social situations. Memories of a series of enjoyable but secret and socially unacceptable sex experiences with a married man who has moved across the continent. Any unpleasant experience. Vomiting discovered on 2/25/74	Self-concept: "Large: I tend to get fat; I'm not attractive to most men; I have sinned; I am "soiled goods" and probably unworthy of true love; I am a good runner and would like to run in marathons; I think I could be a good wife and mother; I want to be in control of my life." "Lonely, unloved; rejected because I'm too fat; angry." "Tense; guilty, unworthy; soiled goods." After vomiting client feels less likely to get fat (the calories are gone) and less uncomfortable and guilty ("somehow the suffering of vomiting atones for my sins"); "I don't want anyone to know I've sinned or that I vomit." Depression Anxiety	Overeating and self-induced vomiting Client is alone – usually on Friday or Saturday evenings; urge to eat Purchases and eats large quantities of doughnuts, cake, bread Feels full and uncomfortable (feels even more fat) Induces vomiting with finger Stomach pains (for the last 6 months; most intense in social situations) Social Behavior (seems agitated and curt; avoids close relationships by being rude when she feels attracted to someone) Suicide attempt on 2/27/74	Systematize food purchase and consumption Daily exercise (marathon training with the club coach) in late afternoon Medical management, dietary management (exercise has been approved) Progressive relaxation Biofeedback (SCI, temp) for control of autonomic functioning Social skills training Individual psychotherapy	Keep records of urges (+ occasions) to eat beyond the scheduled amount and record vomiting episodes. Keep daily records on weight, food purchase, eating and exercising (miles and times, refer to schedule set up by coach). Medical reassessment in 3 months. Use pain questionnaire for keeping records of stomach pain episodes, and pain medication taken. Weekly Rathus and daily record keeping of best and worst social experiences Weekly Zung index of depression.

Figure 9.6. *The flow diagram format used in 2003.*

Name ________ Age ____ Education ____ Date ____ Marital Status ____ Children: ____ Occupation ____
Referred by ____________ Treated by ____________

History/Current Stressors	Presumed Internal processes	Problems	Treatment Methods	Measures and Notes
	Self concept		Strengths assets; Hopes hobbies, heroes	

10: Psychophysiology and Biofeedback

"Psychophysiology" is a term that refers to the interface, connections, correlations, relationships, etc., between the level of analysis typical of psychology and that typical of physiology. This field of inquiry has been called "mind/body science." In a simple sense it refers to the interface between the biological and psychological components of the biopsychosocial universe. The editors of the Handbook of Psychophysiology (Cacioppo et al., 2000) write "Psychophysiological methods, paradigms, and theories offer entry into a biological cosmos that does not stop at the skin's edge."

I use psychophysiological monitoring systems with many of the clients with whom I work individually. Over the years, psychophysiological monitoring systems have improved dramatically. A recent survey of available devices, systems and methods (Stern et al., 2001) includes many sophisticated devices with which I have no experience. I refer to psychophysiological observations made with relatively simple devices in many parts of this book. For example, a treatment procedure for sex offenders, based on several lines of psychophysiological evidence is described in chapter 16.

"Biofeedback" is a catchy descriptive term for employment of a psychophysiological monitoring device to teach a person to gain control over previously automatic biological function. Biofeedback has been used by generations of psychophysiologists to explore the interface between psychological and biological functions.

As early as 1898, Allan M. Cleghorn (the father of Robert Cleghorn, my postdoctoral advisor) described a blood-pressure feedback device. Cleghorn's device was the size of a fire hydrant and was used to give blood pressure information back to the patient being monitored. Many others in the century since then have described various feedback devices and methods. As far as I can determine, however, the term biofeedback did not begin to enter the language until about 1970. In 1973, some colleagues and I published an article we entitled, "Instrumental Control of Autonomic Responses with the Use of a Cognitive Strategy" (Corson et al., 1973). I cannot remember if we had heard the term biofeedback by then. In any event, the expression has since come into common use, and is certainly more memorable than the terminology used in our 1973 article.

Indeed, part of the problem with biofeedback is that the term is catchy and that the concept can be oversimplified. It is important to recognize that there are problems and limitations—as well as possibilities—in the application of biofeedback procedures.

General Method

Biofeedback operates by detecting, amplifying, and translating an aspect of biological function into a form that can be interpreted by the individual whose biological processes are being monitored. The process of biofeedback thus involves three operations, as shown in Figure 10.1:

(1)   Detection of a biological process that would otherwise be difficult or impossible for the subject to perceive;

(2)   Transduction of the targeted biological process to a signal, which is amplified and modulated;

(3)   Feedback of the signal to the subject, who uses the signal to perceive and control the biological process producing the signal.

The subject can learn not only to sense the targeted biological process (or its correlates), but also to control it—if the signal being fed back is meaningful and corresponds to changes in the underlying biological process.

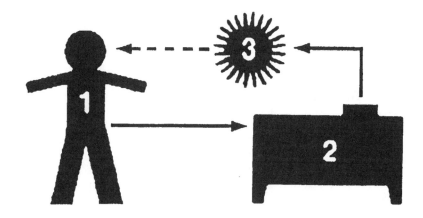

Figure 10.1. *The Biofeedback Loop.*

The information provided in biofeedback procedures can take many forms. In some applications, biofeedback provides information that the subject can use in much the same way visual feedback is used to control accuracy while throwing a ball or shooting an arrow. In other applications, the focus is on the timing of the activity, such as when a musician learns to play within the rhythmic constraints of an unfamiliar musical group. In still other applications, biofeedback can help achieve the integration of complex processes, such as coordination of the respiratory and skeletal musculature in order to learn to swim.

In addition, biofeedback can make different uses of the information being fed back. In some applications, the biofeedback is the equivalent of reward; in others, it is the equivalent of an error signal. In some cases, biofeedback acts as a continuous information source, providing guidance for the honing of a skill; in other situations, biofeedback functions more as a discrete incentive event that occurs only when a successful response is made.

Control of the underlying biological process may also take several forms. In electromyography, or measurement of the electrical activity of skeletal muscle, for instance, the goal may be to change the absolute level of muscle tension. In treating some forms of hypertension, on the other hand, the goal may be to minimize variations in the blood pressure. The following clinical examples will clarify the importance of distinguishing between levels in the biological process and episodes of change in the biological process being studied.

An Application with Pain and Spasms

The first clinical example involves using clinical psychophysiology[1] and biofeedback to relieve chronic pain and muscle spasm. A 48-year-old man with total paralysis below the mid chest, resulting from an injury four years prior to admission, was referred to the Psychology Section at the White River Junction Veterans Hospital for treatment of chronic pain and severe muscle spasms. He was interviewed and administered the Dartmouth Pain Questionnaire (Corson and Schneider, 1984), a brief, six-part questionnaire. This work-up served to identify the locations of his chronic pain and to establish the fact that severe muscle spasms occurred in response to unexpected noises—sometimes as little as a click from a ballpoint pen. The spasms began in areas where the client said he was in constant pain. Psychophysiological assessment using electromyography (EMG) showed that his spasms could be traced from muscle groups that were involved early (two to six seconds after auditory stimulus) to those involved later (seven to fourteen seconds after auditory stimulus). We were also able to identify an electrodermal orienting response—a slight increase in electrical conductance of the skin, which indicates autonomic arousal—that reliably preceded the EMG activation and spasm.

On the basis of these observations, we designed a biofeedback treatment that "uncoupled" the skeletal from the autonomic responses. The treatment took 15 sessions and involved two phases. The first phase took nine sessions of 45 minutes each in which the client lowered his EMG and electrodermal activity levels while monitoring analog, or dial-type, feedback.

The second phase of the treatment took six sessions, in which a combination of analog and binary feedback was used. For the first three minutes in these sessions, the client attempted to lower his EMG using analog feedback once again. Following this three-minute

---

[1] Clinical psychophysiology is a large and active field that is only narrowly addressed here. This chapter focuses on biofeedback—and touches on non-biofeedback applications of clinical psychophysiology only insofar as they are related to the biofeedback applications discussed here.

period, a binary—or simple on-off readout—EMG threshold was set just above the lowest point attained during the period of analog feedback. The client was then instructed to keep his muscles relaxed enough not to trigger the binary EMG signal (a tone). In other words, following the three minutes of unidirectional EMG training a binary threshold was set; then bidirectional electrodermal training was begun. Now the client was asked to first raise the electrodermal tone (using arousing imagery) for 90 seconds, and then to lower the tone for 90 seconds (using relaxation strategies and strategies developed during the previous biofeedback training). In the event that the EMG tone was triggered, the electrodermal feedback was terminated until 20 seconds after the client had relaxed enough to turn the EMG tone off.

A short test—with no biofeedback—was conducted at the beginning and end of each of these 15 sessions. The instructions for this test were as follows: "Now please raise arousal (electrodermal activity) to a point just below that which would trigger a spasm." By the 10th session, the number of spasms during test periods had dropped to zero. The client's overall daily spasm frequency followed a similar pattern: spasm frequency dropped from over 100 per day (a rate documented by EMG monitoring) to zero. Follow-up five years later showed that this effect persisted.

Other Applications

There are many other applications for biofeedback techniques. In medical situations, biofeedback may be the treatment of some choice. For instance, a client suffering fecal incontinence may have lost, or failed to develop, properly timed and integrated control of the internal and external sphincter muscles. Clients with this condition fail to integrate the sensation of fullness in the bowel with proper timing of relaxations and contractions of the sphincter muscles.

A balloon inserted in the bowel allows the therapist to vary the pressure in order to teach the client the sensation of having a full bowel. Other balloons or pressure-sensitive devices are inserted in the internal and external sphincters, and feedback traces from these muscles inform the client of the activity of the sphincter muscles. Using these traces as a guide, the client is able to acquire skill at contracting and relaxing these muscles in response to changes in pressure in the bowel.

In this application, biofeedback provides a sensory prosthesis as well as a guide to the acquisition of particular muscle skills. The client is able to integrate the sensory and muscular components required to gain control over an otherwise intractable clinical problem.

Biofeedback has also been used successfully in the treatment of several conditions in which the client learns to gain control of pathophysiological processes not ordinarily under voluntary control. Headache caused by vasospasm or muscle tension, for example, sometimes can be relieved by biofeedback. Raynaud's disease, characterized by vasospasm in response to cold or emotional arousal, has been treated successfully by training the client to maximize blood flow in the peripheral blood vessels (Schwartz et al., 1995). Likewise, biofeedback has been used in the treatment of respiratory problems such as reactive hyperventilation and continuing dependence on a respirator (Corson et al., 1976); in the rehabilitation of stroke victims needing retraining of skeletal muscles; and in control of such autonomic disturbances as hyperhidrosis, or excessive perspiration.

Epileptic seizures have also been treated by biofeedback (now known as "neurofeedback" when used with brain function). This application has aroused a great deal of controversy (e.g., see Hammond et al., 2002) and provides a bit of a lesson regarding concepts of efficacy. Sterman reviewed the literature on neurofeedback treatment for uncontrolled epilepsy and determined that 82 percent of the clients demonstrated a significant reduction in seizure frequency. He also reported that using the surgical procedure that has been considered by many to be the state-of-the-art and treatment of choice for such severe seizure disorders, at least 27 percent of the patients experienced little improvement. This suggests that somewhere around 73 percent of the patients showed considerable improvement—a similar percentage to that demonstrated with neurofeedback.

Biofeedback has also been used with behavioral and psychological problems. It is particularly helpful when symptoms include a clear physiological component. In anxiety-based panic attacks, for example, the underlying pathology may be psychological, but dramatic physiological signs are reliably present—sweating, dizziness, irregular breathing, racing heartbeat, and so forth. These are so distressing to the client that they compound and perpetuate the anxiety, and they can also lead to further physical problems. Biofeedback has been used to alleviate the physiological signs and thereby to reduce the psychological pathology as well (Peper and Tibbets, 1992; McGrady, Bush and Grubb, 1997).

Athletes have been trained to maximize their performance using biofeedback. Members of the Canadian military biathlon team underwent biofeedback training in addition to regular training to maximize their performance in a sport combining cross-country skiing with rifle target shooting. The team members were trained to lower their arousal rapidly after a period of racing and to squeeze the trigger only between heartbeats. As a result, the Canadian biathletes went from being perennial also-rans to world champions.

Evaluation

It is relatively easy to measure improvement in athletic performance as a result of biofeedback training. However, clinical examples in which biofeedback is the only treatment used, and where the target problem is easy to measure, are not common. Generally, the biofeedback trainer relies on (1) measures of pre- and post-treatment skill level, (2) measures of biological function taken during a training session, or (3) client reports of changes in the frequency, amplitude, or duration of the target behavior, feeling, or process as indices of the improvement. The problem of fecal incontinence is one that does have a simple, objective, and measurable outcome. However, problems of general anxiety disorders are not as easy to monitor.

One problem in obtaining a reliable measure of the improvement is that the various domains of measurement do not always correlate. Measured levels of physiological responses may be at variance with the client's subjective report or with overt behavior. In treating the behavioral problem of stuttering, for instance, observed speaking fluency may not correlate well with physiological arousal or subjective report.

The complexities of individual differences and variations in situational triggers of problems likewise confound studies of results in the therapeutic setting. Nonetheless, several avenues are currently being explored, including psychological and psychophysiological profiling, to evaluate clients' responses to standardized situations. However, many problems remain here as well. Remarkable variability in baseline, as well as in response to provocations, has been reported (Arena et al., 1989).

As mentioned above, biofeedback is often only one technique in a package of modalities. The fact that biofeedback may be adjunctive to several other procedures makes it difficult to measure the singular impact of the biofeedback—or of any other single component of the treatment program. For example, as will be described in Chapter 19, I have been using a brief biofeedback procedure along with a shortened version of the behavioral treatment of panic disorder described by Barlow and his colleagues (Barlow et al., 1989; Craske and Barlow, 1990).

To what extent, people often wonder, does biofeedback permanently "rewire" the client—or is continuing practice necessary? Rewiring probably does not occur—but may seem to occur in cases where continuing practice is assured or automatic. For example, continuing practice is assured in cases of fecal incontinence; if the newly acquired skills are not practiced, a clear failure signal results. Similarly, when a partially paralyzed client is weaned from a respirator and taught to breathe independently, failure to perform the necessary maneuvers is clearly signaled to the client by feelings of dizziness and other signs of respiratory insufficiency.

Practice Issues

In other applications of biofeedback, the necessity for continuing practice is not as easily signaled to the client. In these cases, the clinician must maintain contact with the client for months after the skill has been acquired to insure regular practice and proper use of the skill. Two examples illustrate the complexity of this issue.

The first involved healthy college students trained to control their autonomic levels by way of electrodermal biofeedback. No change was noticed in their cardiovascular response to a painful stimulus unless they intended to use the acquired skill. When the subjects were not thinking about using the skill, their heart rate and blood pressure rose to the same levels as prior to training. However, when they intentionally used the acquired skill during the application of a painful stimulus, they were able to significantly reduce their heart rate, blood pressure, and sensation of pain.

The second example involves clinical application of autonomic biofeedback (skin conductance) to the treatment of muscle spasms. In my experience, clients must continue practicing in order to maintain a reduction in the frequency of spasms. If they do not continue to practice, the frequency, amplitude, or duration of episodes of high-level pain or of spasms may regress toward pretreatment baseline levels. The question of skill level is complex. During the days after practice is terminated and spasms, or episodes of high level pain, are returning to the pretreatment level, clients have come back to the treatment setting to have their skills measured. By the best available measures, clients' skills were intact in the laboratory. But the skills were not sufficient to give persisting relief in the real world, unless the client and therapist were able to develop an effective and durable system for ensuring regular practice. Such difficulties and other paradoxes have been addressed in the published literature (for a brief overview see Corson, 1995), but as far as I can tell no resolutions have been identified.

Other Problems

These problems—measurement of skill acquisition and ensuring the maintenance of those skills—are but two difficult issues facing biofeedback researchers and practitioners. Other issues include:

(1) Some disorders readily lend themselves to biofeedback treatment while others do not;

(2) People differ widely in their self-concept and in their sense of themselves as agents capable of controlling important aspects of their lives;

(3) People differ dramatically in their ability to learn and to profit from biofeedback training (the differences between individuals are truly remarkable and this is definitely not a question of differences in intelligence);

(4) People differ in their willingness to learn (perhaps because of a desire to maintain the sick role or to receive disability payments);

(5) Successful treatment with biofeedback is often mistakenly accepted as proof that the problem was "simply psychosomatic" or "all in your head";

(6) Even successfully-treated clients vary in their ability and willingness to practice the skills that brought them relief, and a rusty skill when called upon in an emergency is almost doomed to fail;

(7) Different practitioners—perhaps depending on their training or on the kinds of cases they see—give widely varying emphasis to biofeedback techniques in their treatment programs, so that it is often difficult to determine the effectiveness of a particular technique or intervention;

(8) The manifestation of the clinical problem may sometimes be confusing (for example, it may be reactive

to a baffling array of life situations, and not reliable in its reactivity to any single life situation);

(9)   The problems with which biofeedback must deal are complex human and medical problems, so that failures or partial successes are more likely than dramatic and complete triumphs.

Whether biofeedback is better than other simpler or quicker treatment interventions is a complex question. For problems like some forms of fecal incontinence, in which there are clear physiological or behavioral factors to shape, biofeedback appears to be the treatment of choice. For other problems, such as tension headaches, the answer is not clear. (These issues are reviewed by Hatch et al., 1987.)

As compared with relaxation training alone, biofeedback combined with relaxation training seems to have a higher yield: more clients continue to attend sessions and persist in practicing their skills. Whether this is because of a placebo effect or due to a heightened expectancy of what the high-technology device will do for them is not clear.

At a more basic level the issue of unconditioned effects of any signal used in a biofeedback paradigm has not been carefully addressed. This need is dramatized by the observation of powerful relationships between training objectives and differences in reactivity to success and failure signals and to the particular phrasing of instructions (Brener, 1977; Bouchard and Corson, 1976). It appears that the necessary research is not being conducted.

The general issues involved in sorting out the reward and the information components of the biofeedback signal—as well as the technical issues involved in the modality of feedback and the spacing of feedback signals—also must be addressed for biofeedback to take what I think is its proper place in the array of clinical options.

Profiling

In 1989 I wrote that one of the most exciting prospects for the future of biofeedback and clinical psychophysiology is that of psychophysiological profiling. The evaluation of psychophysiological responses to standardized stimuli can help understand some of the differences between clinically identified groups. Since I wrote those words, profiling has become a very popular technique. We now see studies such as one on the psychophysiological reactivity of aggressive drivers by Malta and colleagues (2001), and psychophysiological monitoring of people doing various activities such as yoga meditation by Arambula and colleagues (2001).

A Technique for Profiling

In clinical settings, profiling may be able to help (1) select a treatment modality, (2) monitor the impact of ongoing treatment, and (3) assess the long-term effect of treatment.

My colleagues and I have developed a 12-minute sequence to move toward this, involving a five-minute period of relaxation, 30 seconds of submersion of the non-dominant hand (up to the wrist) in ice water, a one-minute evaluation of verbal skills, 30 more seconds of submersion of the non-dominant hand in ice water, and five more minutes of relaxation.

Review of results with hundreds of individuals indicates that there are some consistencies and many remarkable differences in physiological and subjective responses to this test. With further progress in sorting out these differential responses (as well as the variability between initial testing and later testing of the same individual), we may be better able to tailor intervention and evaluation techniques to the needs of individual clients and conditions. A version of this procedure was incorporated into the multimodality format for violent clients that I described in 1989. A brief description of that procedure is presented in Chapter 12.

Part Four

Violent Adults

11: A Selective Literature Review

I have organized this selective review of the literature around the dimensions that I use to describe the violent episodes of our clients. Important dimensions of a client's typical violent outbursts are the stressors or triggers that may have provoked the outburst and the working self-concept that was apparently active at the time of the outburst. Table 11.1 operationalizes these and other dimensions into a series of continua.

Initially, I developed these continua to help me and my clients develop an understanding of the most frequent pattern of their episodes of violent behavior (as described in Chapter 12), as well as the range in the variability among episodes. It rapidly became clear that there were many similarities, and some differences, among the violent acts of the clients I was working with. As time went on, however I began to get a sense of the profile of the typical violent act of our clients.

I have since used these continua to help me compare our violent clients with clients described in the literature. This comparison helped me to identify a gap. Most severely-violent clients described in the literature are housed in custodial institutions (prisons and hospitals), while the less severely-violent are not institutionalized; the typical client referred to us is not institutionalized, but is more severely violent than the non-institutionalized clients described in the literature. Our clients are also from lower socioeconomic levels than the violent outpatients typically described in the literature. In effect, therefore, the literature to date has rarely described clients like ours living in circumstances like ours. Hence, a selective review of the literature on this subject is warranted.

Table 11.1

Continua on Which Episodes of Violent Behavior can be Characterized

1.	Sudden	Slow
2.	Unprovoked	Provoked
3.	Undirected	Directed
4.	Unpredictable	Predictable
5.	Unstoppable	Stoppable
6.	Patient will stop short of causing injury to the target	Patient will not stop short of causing severe injury to the target
7.	Patient will stop when others verbally intervene	Patient will not stop unless totally physically restrained
8.	Unplanned	Planned
9.	No memory	Memory
10.	Remorse	No Remorse
11.	Not righteous	Righteous
12.	No reason(s)/stimulus(i) cited	Reason(s)/stimulus(i) cited
13.	No values cited	Societal, religious or personal values cited
14.	Stressors/triggers not identifiable	Stressors/triggers identifiable
15.	Control issues not involved	Control issues involved
16.	No audience necessary	Audience usually present
17.	Short duration (lasts seconds)	Long duration (lasts hours)
18.	Subject expresses displeasure	Subject expresses pleasures (before, during, after)
19.	Not verbal	Verbal
20.	Physical	Not physical
21.	Life-threatening	Not life-threatening
22.	Not directed at (an) object(s)	Directed at (an) object(s)
23.	Not directed at a person or animal	Directed at a person or animal
24.	Constant pattern	Variable pattern
25.	Overcontrolled	Undercontrolled (also subcultural)
26.	Drive mediated	Instrumental
27.	Respect-disrespect involved	Not involved
28.	Revengeful	Not revengeful
29.	Substance use/abuse involved	No substance use/abuse involved
30.	Seeming scripted or ritualistic	Not seeming scripted or ritualistic

Neurological Correlates

The extreme, dangerous, and sudden explosions of violent behavior that generally lead to institutionalization have often been equated with a condition known as intermittent explosive disorder or episodic dyscontrol. At the behavioral level, these terms are usually reserved for individuals with a history of violent outbursts upon little or no provocation. Although the terms imply a neurological substrate, some confusion surrounds the neurological correlates of the condition.

Among the neurological studies conducted on people meeting the behavioral definition, neurological results conflict even when one looks at studies with similar methodology (Riley and Niedermeyer, 1977; Hughes and Hermann, 1984). Elliott (1982) studied a sample of 245 subjects with histories of uncontrollable rage upon little or no provocation and found that about 40 percent of these individuals showed no EEG abnormalities. Such findings may be related to technical problems, such as relying on recordings from scalp electrodes rather than on recordings from subcortical structures (Smith, 1980), or relying on recordings taken only during quiescent periods. On the other hand, the findings may indicate that no fundamental brain abnormalities are related to the violent outbursts of some people. As far as I see at present, we must consider the relationship between episodic violent behavior and specific pathology of the central nervous system to be an open question.

Another neurological process does appear reliably correlated, and may even become a reliable predictor of violent outbursts. This, as discussed in Chapter 3, is the sudden activation of the SNS, or the sympathetic branch of the autonomic nervous system. In fact, the literature on central nervous system abnormalities that are correlated with violent outbursts contains frequent mention of pronounced signs of sympathetic hyperactivity (Stone et al., 1986). Our own data (described in Chapter 3) provide solid support for this observation. Specifically, we have seen that in violent clients, SNS arousal, as indexed by upward shifts in skin conductance, correlates with the client recounting situations that provoked anger or violent behavior. Numerous other investigators have observed such correlations between autonomic function and violent behavior (e.g., Malta et al., 2001). Van der Kolk and Greenberg (1987) summarized much of the literature on this relationship and offered a number of observations and suggestions that are compatible with my own experiences and ideas. In the following paragraphs, I will relate their observations and those of other investigators to some of the more important aspects of assessing and treating violent clients.

Early Environment

I will not review the possibility that a separate genetic bias toward violent behavior might occur in some people; support exists for this possibility, and has been reviewed (e.g., see Holden, 1987; Gilligan, 1996). We will focus instead on the environmental factors that were considered in the preceding chapters. It is important to note that are many good arguments for focusing on environmental factors. For example, although it has been clearly shown that tendencies toward aggression are significantly heritable in rodents, it has also been shown that these tendencies toward aggression can be dramatically modified by environmental factors (e.g., see Reiss and Roth, 1993).

One environmental cause for the neurological impairment that can lead to violent behavior can be quickly identified. Violent adults are likely to have been physically abused as children (Heath et al., 1986; Eron, 1987). Physical abuse is likely to have long-term effects that result from organic damage (and also, as discussed below, from factors such as modeling and post-traumatic stress disorder). The medial temporal structures, which are more susceptible to injury than those in other brain locations (MacLean, 1986), are the structures that have a high probability of showing abnormalities in violent individuals.

Other identified environmental determinants of adult violent behavior are nonphysical. Table 11.1 includes two labels for aggressive behavior, subcultural and instrumental, that imply emulation of parents and others who have been observed using aggressive or violent behaviors to obtain desired outcomes or objects. In recent years it has been found that the relationship between the experience with violent models and the later appearance of violent behavior is quite complex. For example, Hannon and colleagues (2001) used a violent attitudes scale and found that social variables, including subcultural forces, peer pressure and opportunities to possibly gain from a violent act, have their greatest impact on violent delinquency among those who start out with violent attitudes. On the other hand, those within the same subculture who had a higher level of attitudinal or moral opposition to violence were far less likely to become involved in any sort of violent behavior. Eron (1987) and others have made a very strong case for the contribution of emulation or modeling to the development of adult violent behavior. Presumably, those youngsters in the study by Hannon who had the higher attitudinal or moral opposition to violence are more likely to have at least some experience with models and mentors who showed nonviolent attitudes.

In Chapter 14 we will consider another possible learned pathway to development of adult violent behavior-one based on negative reinforcement, on learning to be violent in order to terminate aversive stimuli. When we consider the case histories of four clients in Chapter 13, we will see that in some clients, all of these environmental causes appear to converge.

Hyperarousal and the Binary Switch

Van der Kolk and Greenberg (1987) cited evidence that an abusive early environment can contribute to the development of hyperarousal states that will have long-term detrimental effects on the child's ability (and later the adult's ability) to modulate both anxiety and aggression. This chronic hyperarousal state in traumatized persons "often causes them to go immediately from stimulus to response" (Van der Kolk and Greenberg, 1987, page 66). The sudden overreaction to even minor stimuli as if they were emergency situations has been characterized as an "all-or-nothing" response pattern. The all-or-nothing response, the sudden transition from stimulus to major response without apparent internal dialogue, characterizes most of the violent clients whom I have seen.

In reconstructing some episodes of violent explosion with most clients, one does see some evidence of internal dialogue. Most of this dialogue appears to involve pre- or post-violence rehearsal of the expectancies and dispositions that lead to the "binary switch" or the all-or-nothing explosive response. Eron (1987) supported this observation in his summary of a longitudinal study of the development of aggression: "Over the 22 years of this study, it was what the subjects were saying to themselves about what they wanted, what their environment would permit or expect, what might be an effective or appropriate response, and what were the likely consequences of such action that helped determine how aggressive they are today"(page 441). The repetition of such well-practiced internal dialogue facilitates the observed automaticity and rapidity of transition from stimulus to response. On this point, Goldfried said, "Because of the habitual nature of one's expectations or beliefs it is likely that the thinking processes and images become automatic and seemingly involuntary like most overlearned acts (in Staub, 1980, page 324)."

Many reports of successful therapy with violent individuals have focused on developing new forms of internal dialogue. On the other hand (as already mentioned several times), most of the clients I have worked with appear unable to pause between stimulus and response for internal dialogue until considerable work is done in training them to monitor and to modulate the emotional fire in their boiler.

Level-Setting Functions of the ANS

As mentioned in Chapter 3, the autonomic nervous system (ANS) appears to perform a level-setting and modulating function. This function leads to changes in the probabilities and likely speed of certain kinds of responses. Van der Kolk and Greenberg (1987) gave an excellent example of level setting and modulating mediated by the ANS: "An illustration of the association between autonomic arousal and flashbacks is provided by the case of a former parachutist who had a three-month period of post-traumatic symptoms after his second parachute failed to open during a jump until he was a few hundred feet above the ground. Five years later the only remaining symptom is a flashback of this event after autonomic arousal, such as occurs in a near accident on the road" (page 70). In this case, autonomic arousal appeared to reach a level at which the probability of retrieving a particular memory was dramatically increased.

Such shifts in response probability may be related to either a high chronic resting level of autonomic arousal or to a sudden and high-amplitude autonomic reaction. In most of our violent clients, we have seen both high resting levels and high reactivity. In all of them, we have seen high reactivity, as indexed by skin conductance level. Most reactions, at the outset of treatment, are followed by a long period of high arousal (i.e., slow recovery). My observation of long-duration episodes of hyperarousal suggests that levels and episodes of activity in the ANS may interact in the violent client. This interaction is depicted in Figures 11.1 and 11.2. Figure 11.1 is hypothetical, an example of a priming effect when successive stimuli are too close together for the system to recover. Figure 11.2 depicts actual data obtained during the assessment of one of our violent clients (Mr. D, who is described in several other chapters). The point is this: in a system that might initially be at a low resting level, the inability to recover rapidly from episodes of subpathological autonomic arousal may have the end result of priming the system so that an apparently minor stimulus can produce the all-or-nothing response.

PRE TREATMENT Violent client shows:

1) High resting level.
2) Low input reaction threshold – <u>expectation</u> – more stimuli are processed as threatening.

3) Low output reaction threshold – <u>disposition</u> – more stimuli are overtly reacted to.
4) Fast arousal rise after stimulus.
5) Very slow recovery (slow drop in arousal) after stimulus.

6) Typical starting posture (obvious expectation/disposition) and typical response (threat/attack) rapidly alters environment to alter (↑ or ↓) provocative power of stimuli.

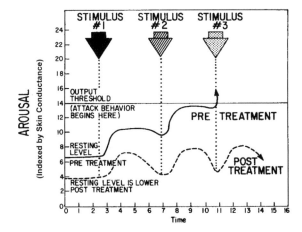

Figure 11.1. *Hypothetical example of the priming effect that occurs when successive stimuli are too close together for the system to recover.*

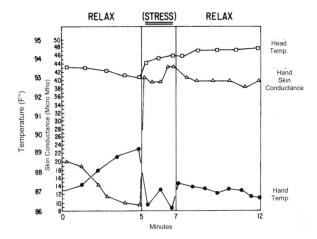

Figure 11.2. *Assessment of an assaultive client.*

In reality, I think I have seen at least three variations on the relationship between arousal levels and episodes of surge in arousal:

(1)   The arousal level is chronically high, and minor stimuli always produce sudden violent outbursts.
(2)   The moderately high level interacts with episodes of arousal to prime the system as depicted in the accompanying figures.
(3)   The level is, relatively, chronically low, but may show a rapid increase to a high level when confronted with certain apparently minor stimuli.

With numerous clients, I have seen what appears to be a progression during treatment through these three stages, and in the order listed. In the third stage, clients are much more selective, in terms of which stimuli they respond to. Even though I may feel that the stimuli are minor, the client will still perceive them as major. In the third stage, the violent outbursts are often as severe as they are in the first stage; however, the speed of onset of the outbursts seems somewhat less and the duration of the outbursts, and any sub-outburst surges of autonomic arousal, are generally much shorter in duration than those typical of the first stage (when an episode of arousal occurs from a high baseline), or those typical of the second stage (when the episode occurs from a relatively lower baseline). To be helpful to most of the clients I have seen, success must be attained in lowering resting levels of autonomic arousal, in decreasing the duration of episodes of autonomic arousal, and in developing some discrimination among the stimuli that might cause autonomic arousal. Somewhere between the second and third stage, the speed of onset of episodes also seems to decrease and we are able to begin doing effective work with internal dialogue.

Self-Concept

Looking for Trouble

One of the most dramatic differences among the members of our sample has involved the tendency to repeatedly expose themselves (either in imagery or reality) to stressful or dangerous stimuli that seem somehow related to the traumatizing event. Many of the clients referred to us for violent outbursts have been Vietnam combat veterans. Van der Kolk and Greenberg (1987) have noted that approximately 20% of Vietnam veterans who sought treatment for Posttraumatic Stress Disorder (PTSD) reported that they often exposed themselves to dangerous situations or went to movies that reminded them of their experiences in Vietnam. In some of our clients, the tendency to seek out dangerous situations (such as in taverns or pool halls) has been quite troublesome early in treatment. Several clients have recognized a pattern in the occurrences of their desire to expose themselves to such situations. One Vietnam combat veteran told me, "When I began treatment I needed to do it about once every one or two weeks. Now I only do it about once every month, and it's different now. I seem to sit and watch, while before it was like a command performance. Everybody knew I was there and everybody knew something was going to happen. The last two times I went nothing happened." Another veteran told me, "I can go into a strange town and find a place like that within 15 minutes. I can smell it—it's where the action is. I'm like an animal, and when I want to get violent I can always find somebody else who is willing to oblige me.[1] I used to need to do that sometimes."

Both of these individuals were terribly abused as children. One was locked in a closet for at least three days, and the other was locked in a trunk. Both experienced numerous beatings, broken bones, lacerations, and so forth. One was raped by an older male relative, and the other was raped when in a juvenile detention home. Both of these men have verbal IQs above 130. They both have rich fantasy lives and can vividly describe images of combat experiences, of being terrorized and of terrorizing.

These observations are in accord with those of Brett and Ostroff (1985). In considering the relationship between imagery and PTSD, they hypothesize a two-dimensional framework for understanding PTSD based on repetitions and defensive functioning. Indeed, the imagery and behavior of both clients I have just

---

[1] One important aspect of this behavior—discussed further in Chapters 1, 7 and 14—is the fact that many violent individuals can communicate their readiness for violent behavior to a total stranger in a few seconds without any physical or verbal contact. The violent client assumes a facial expression, a posture, and a gait that communicates to others that he is ready to be violent. This feed forward influence can be observed when some of our clients enter a room full of strangers. In other words, these sometimes subtle behavioral cues regarding a response disposition—a readiness to be violent—are quickly communicated to other people and bias their first response to our clients.

described suggest the presence of a compulsion to repeat trauma-related images and actions and to repeat a definitive form of defensive behavior namely, violent outbursts. Some of these violent individuals spend much of their time thinking and behaving as if there are only two possible states—being terrorized or being the terrorist.

The above quotes from clients illustrate the fact that some of these individuals actually look for trouble. The idea that one might feel a need to be violent, to fight, or to be in a dangerous situation has been considered by many authors, and many possible contributing factors have been cited. Terms like "adrenaline junkie" (implying someone who thrives on a high level of adrenaline and ANS arousal), "risk-taker," and "thrill-seeker," have been applied to this behavior. Alternatively, it may be that these situations provide opportunities to gain clear signs of respect from others (or perhaps from the self). Finally, these situations may serve to distract the client from their own limitations and problems and may briefly focus their attention away from the ordinariness or dreariness of their own lives, and somehow allows them the feeling of being special, or (using a phrase from one of my clients) "being back in action."

Secondary Gains

The issues regarding clients looking for trouble were well considered by Horowitz (1981). His theoretical orientation and terminology are very different from those used in this book, but are easily translatable. He pointed out that violent individuals may persist in this behavior because it is enlivening and provides a type of secondary gain. Horowitz described one patient:

> *The liveliness of the rage extricated him from the states of apathetic dullness so common in narcissistically vulnerable persons. That is, he experienced the rage states as 'fuel' or 'energy'. The rages were idealized and, like an old friend, were embraced to avoid further loss. Only gradually did he learn to enliven himself by healthy, sublimated forms of exhibitionism rather than by reactive rage at being deprived of such pleasures. (page 1237)*

I am reminded here of Adler's statement that can be roughly paraphrased, "Ask what the symptom or problem does for the client." Sometimes this question pays off well. The prototypical example is where one can identify clear secondary gains for a client, as with the phobic person who maintains control of his or her spouse by the phobic behavior. At other times, this question does not pay off in a simple way, since it seems the symptom/problem is a total loss to the client. And sometimes the symptom or problem both pays off and hurts the client. This is the case with most violent clients. The symptom or problem seems an effective short-term way of coping with challenges to self-esteem. To some clients, it even seems an effective short-term way of dealing with any sort of dysphoria. Here we are again reminded that the client is abolishing or somehow brushing away an unpleasant experience by indulging in the problem behavior. Again we see the power of the principle of negative reinforcement.

For most of our clients, the losses are also very clear—loss of trust from other people, alienation from family and former friends, problems with police, inability to hold a job. To realize these losses are occurring entails recognition of facts that many violent clients are unable or unwilling to acknowledge. Much of the work of treatment focuses on getting these violent individuals to acknowledge the losses. We must train them in the endeavor of becoming personal scientists and theorists, and help them to identify relationships between the essential audience and critic function as these impinge upon their fragile self-esteem.

Critics, Heroes, and Monsters

In accord with our own observations, Horowitz (1981) observed that many episodes of self-righteous rage are triggered by injuries to the self-concept or drops in self-esteem. He observed that the states mind displayed by parents are often emulated by their children, and that certain forms of violent behavior appear to be passed on as styles of emotional expression in a subculture. He attends to the role of parental attention in development of the "critic function" (a similar concept to our "essential audience"). It is in this latter area that I find his ideas most helpful. Horowitz described a specific three-party model or role structure that "contains a hero, a monster, and a critical audience. The critic admires the hero and loathes the monster" (page 1235). This three-party role structure is useful "in understanding why a usually restrained person, when confronted with triggers that instigate this model, may freely express fierce, brutal, but pleasurably exciting hostility. The pleasure is an assumption of dominance over a dehumanized other, a pleasure heightened by feelings of merger with a powerful critic (or group) and exhibition of the self to that critic (or group) to gain attention, admiration, and praise" (page 1235). The locus of the critic function is ambiguous and changing. "Sometimes a given appraisal of blame may be seen as instigated from within and sometimes as instigated from outside of the self. Even when the critical function is located externally, inconsistency is expected as blame is assigned and withdrawn in shifting judgments" (page 1235).

In considering the development of the critic's role, Horowitz said:

> *Precursors to the critic's role probably occur during the earliest phases of mother and infant interaction ... [Later in development] the child watches for responses to its behavior—an admiring smile or nod, a gleam in the eye, a scornful look, a pursed mouth, or simply the absence of any response. Parents with changeable mental states and inconsistent styles of response will affect the child differently from those who provide relatively stable reactions to the child's behavior. Eventually, the child watches its own behavior in the manner that had been experienced as parental reflection and criticism ... (In a triad of family interactions) each pair may bond, with some critical empathy or contempt for the person who is "left out." The patterning of such episodes is internalized, leading the child to learn and revise the critic's role ... If the critic's role patterns are etched more deeply without development of stable autonomous value structures and blame–attribution processes, the person arrives at adulthood with a special vulnerability to labile state changes. This would occur because it is sometimes itself and sometimes the conceptualized other who assigns the self-concept to positions as worthy or unworthy, whole or fragmented, competent or incompetent, to blame or blameless for unleashing evil into the family or group. (page 1236)*

An extension of these ideas appears valid for my violent clients. Specifically, it appears that the strategies of "get them before they get you" and "always be ready" (which I often hear repeated by these clients) could involve a combination of terror, on the one hand, at possibly being blamed by the critic and joyful anticipation, on the other, of any opportunity to take on the role of hero. And thus ensues their search for despicable monsters and vigilant avoidance, or violent rejection, of any criticism.

Therapeutic Possibilities

With regard to therapeutic procedures, Horowitz said:

> *Change that is more than the institution of compensatory controls requires a deeper level of analysis. [Most therapists] encourage patients to recognize the self-images and self and other schemata by which they organize a situation and the unconscious interpersonal fantasies by which they provoke situations. The addition of the critic's role and the three-party role structure is a subtle but useful supplement to the clear examination of conflicted interpersonal relationship patterns (page 1237).*

I suspect that Horowitz would approve of the formats that I have depicted in Figure 1.1 and Table 1.1 in Chapter 1 and Figure 9.1 in Chapter 9. Indeed, he says, "Reconstruction of episodes in the treatment situation usually is necessary also during such examinations of the critic's role" (page 1237). Our specific strategies for this will be spelled out in more detail later. For now, it is worth noting that both Horowitz and I have spent much of our energy considering the assessment and treatment of people who are quite intelligent. The particular strategies he described, and most of those that I will describe in subsequent chapters are most appropriate for people with at least normal intelligence and verbal skills.

Wong et al. (1987) described many procedures for use with less intelligent and more regressed individuals. The assessment procedure they use at the outset is similar to that depicted in Table 1.1 of Chapter 1. Because of the limitations of their clients they would be unable to make use of the collaborative and multilevel strategies we have described here. In Chapter 13, I will describe our attempts to make use of these procedures—and some alternatives—with less able individuals.

A New Self-Concept

With some clients, we eventually reach a point where the highly stressful, anger-provoking stimulus must be faced without the easy short-term solution of exploding. Here we must be creative and energetic in developing, with the client, viable alternative responses for dealing with the stimulus and the feelings of upset. We are aided in this endeavor by the realization on the part of the client that he or she now has the ability to detect a high level of the fire in the boiler and to detect some increases, as well as the ability to lower the level and slow or abort the increases.

The interdigitation of the fundamentally biological maneuvers of controlling the fire in the boiler and the fundamentally psychosocial maneuvers of considering and employing other cognitive and overt behaviors in response to this stimulus represent both a new life-style and a new self. As we proceed in therapy with a violent client (as well as with any other client), we must keep constant focus on the evolving transactions between the shifting self-concept and the effect of various stressors. In some cases, we now walk a tightrope. Here I am reminded of some of the stutterers I have treated. In several of them I could see the reluctance to give up the symptom. One stutterer told me that his stuttering behavior represented a comforting aspect of himself (or a safety signal). Giving up stuttering was to him akin to cutting his ties with "cute little Bobby" and forever casting his lot with "adult Bob." This was, at times, a terrifying prospect.

As I began to work with some clients referred for violent behavior, I have discussed with them the necessity that they become willing to lose the power over people that accrues from their reputation as a violent and dangerous person. With some clients, I have discussed the need for them to learn to tolerate humiliation. Needless to say, most are initially reluctant to accept such conditions, and I generally have better luck with these issues later in treatment. Eventually, many clients begin to tell me that they have "let an insult pass" or "didn't let it get to me" or "stayed calm"; at this point, I realize that we are on the way to some level of success. Sometimes clients will later describe feeling less powerful, less entitled, less special, less righteous, less ready for anything. When we reach this stage, a fundamental change in self-concept is underway. These changes take many forms and much time. Some aspects of the new self-concept that clients can accept two years after therapy begins would have been very hard for them to even consider at the outset.

Seizures

In this review, I have not yet addressed the treatment possibilities for violent behavior that is related to seizures. For some individuals with seizure-based intermittent explosive disorder (this has also been called episodic dyscontrol), a high resting level of activity in the sympathetic nervous system (the fire in the boiler), or a high reactivity, or both, might prime for a seizure or trigger a seizure. The reciprocally-determined relationship between the fire in the boiler and the psychosocial variables, however, suggests that even a client with seizure-based explosive disorder might respond to treatment based solely on psychosocial interventions. Accordingly, Feldman and Paul (1976) videotaped some of their clients' seizures, along with the usual psychosocial antecedents, and observed the therapeutic benefits of playing these videotapes for their clients. One could easily imagine that this experience would help to destigmatize and demystify the seizure event, and clarify the relationship between the seizure and some psychosocial antecedents. The whole process is probably akin to a form of desensitization, which might lead to a lower level of general anxiety, and thus to a lower level of fire in the boiler. The net effect would be to decrease the priming and triggering contributions of the fire in the boiler to the onset of seizure activity. This form of treatment may also help some clients to develop the personal scientist and theorist attitude that aids in developing and using adaptive strategies in all three domains (bio, psycho, and social).

We have used the format shown in Figure 1.1 of Chapter 1 to essentially replicate the procedure of Feldman and Paul with one client who had a seizure disorder (without violent behavior or episodic dyscontrol) that had been caused by a bullet wound to the brain. Our results were consistent with those obtained by Feldman and Paul, and support the above suggestions regarding the contributions of psychosocial variables and a priming effect of the fire in the boiler. Specifically we observed a reduction in the frequency of seizures and a dramatic reduction in the resting level and lability of the SNS. (These issues are addressed again in Chapter 12.)

Recommended Reading

I will conclude this selective review by calling your attention to some literature that may be helpful in the further consideration of these issues.

There are reviews that cover many of the issues raised here and provide excellent background on the specific problem of violence and the general problem of therapy/rehabilitation. One very useful review is a long multiauthor section on violence in the annual review of the American Psychiatric Association (Tardiff, 1987). This review is multifaceted, thoughtful and broad. One of its most interesting features is the section on "attacks." Attacks (or assaults) that are not motivated by sexual or financial desires, and that do not result in death, are the most frequent forms of violent behavior that psychiatrists deal with. The review points out that they are also the least studied of the violent crimes. Again, it is important to note that attacks of this sort are one of the most frequent problem behaviors of the clients I describe in this book.

A valuable paper by Gendreau and Ross (1987) reviewed the rehabilitation literature from 1981 to 1987. It included a section on violence and pulled together some promising information on attempts to match rehabilitation strategy to individual differences.

There are now several journals devoted to this area. One is *Violence and Victims* (published by Springer, beginning in 1986), a valuable reference.

There are many useful books. One of the most useful is by LeDoux (1996). It presents the best available description of the biological underpinnings of emotion. Several earlier books are also worth reading. One, by Hays et al., (1981) summarized a symposium on *Violence and the Violent Individual* that was held in 1979. This volume provides ideas, theories, methods, data, and legal and ethical considerations regarding violence. A second book, edited by Roth (1987), covered much of the same ground, but is more recent. These two books should be consulted by a reader who wants to obtain a broader view than my narrow and personal account. A third book is a thought-provoking effort from Samenow (1987). He addresses the topic of "the criminal mind" with an anecdotal discussion from his work and that of his mentor (Yochelson). Even though the book is uneven, and presents only rare glimpses of an empirical base, it is of value. My impression is that Samenow's criminals bear only a slight resemblance to a few of my violent clients.

Two other more recent books purport to take a look at "the criminal mind." Gilligan (1996) has published an outstanding discussion of violence that I find much more comprehensive and well reasoned than the book by Samenow. The experiences described in the book come from the same setting, namely long years of work in penal institutions. Although the Gilligan book describes individuals who are generally quite different from my clients, he comes to very similar conclusions regarding the most frequent origins of violence. Anyone who reads Gilligan's book after reading mine will be able to see very clearly that "negative reinforcement" is pervasive in the lives of violent individuals.

The second recent book focusing on "the violent mind" area is *Why They Kill* by Richard Rhodes (1999). This is an unusual book, written by a professional writer that is based in large part on the work of the criminologist L. H. Athens. Rhodes became intrigued with the issue of violence, at least partly, because of his personal experience of beatings, starvation and torment between the ages of 10 and 12. Athens's thinking is similar to my own and to that of Gilligan. Athens concluded, as described by Rhodes, that "individuals who decide to use violence need the fearful respect of their intimates." Another way to say this is that the violence leading to fearful respect is armor and it is born of the experience of being tormented in some way. I have argued that this pattern is a playing out of the learning principle "negative reinforcement."

I will mention one more book. Gaylin (1984) has given us a very personal account of the issues in his widely publicized book, *The Rage Within*. Gaylin's book is a particularly valuable contribution of a sort quite unlike the present volume and unlike anything else I know of in the literature. Gaylin described many of his own experiences with anger, rage, and violence. In doing so, he validates many of Horowitz's ideas, such as the critic's role and, I feel, he provided support for my general strategy of carefully attending to the specific interactions between stressful situations and working self-concept. Gaylin ended his book with a consideration and elaboration of a position that Freud developed in his later years. The basic idea is that we are locked in a struggle to manage anger. In this regard, Freud "embraced the concept of love as man's hope" (page 196). Gaylin concluded that Freud thought we should enlarge the population with which we identify. In this way, the population of others (despicable monsters, hostile critics, potential enemies) becomes smaller, while our own population expands. "In doing so we magnify ourselves, and reduce our sense of vulnerability" (page 196).

12: Population, Treatment Method, and Results

In this chapter, I will review the characteristics of our population of violent adults treated prior to 1984. You will then read about assessment and treatment methods that my colleagues and I have used with these clients. Finally, I will describe results, with an emphasis on physiological and behavioral findings with a smaller sample of violent clients on whom we obtained very long-term follow-up data.

The total population studied by 1984, and followed since whenever possible, consists of 113 men and two women referred for outbursts of violent behavior (physical assault on a person or object). These people were referred to the Psychology Section at the White River Junction (VT) Veterans Administration Hospital between 1974 and 1984. Of the 115, I had enough personal contact with 62 of the men to gather details about their histories and to follow most aspects of their assessment and treatment.

The 115 clients were all military veterans, mostly from the lower to middle socioeconomic classes. They had an average of ten years of education. More than half of them had been in trouble with the law for assault. Of these 115 clients, 41 reported having made some sort of physical assault on another person during the week before beginning treatment, and 35 of them were reported to have beaten someone to unconsciousness. Public fistfights were very frequent in this group of clients. Many had spent considerable time in jail on charges that included assault, armed robbery, and murder.

Description of the Sample

Table 11.1 in Chapter 11 shows the 30 continua that I use to characterize violent clients; reference to these continua will assist us in this general description of behavior of the 62 people I am most familiar with. (Others have worked on describing the behavior of, and developing a typology of violent individuals (e.g., Waltz, Babcock, Jacobson, & Gottman, 2000). These workers have used different, and much more complex strategies in this endeavor. It is worth noting that the complete repertoire of violent episodes of any one of my clients can be characterized using only 5 to 10 of these thirty continua.)

On continua 1 through 3, our subjects typically show *sudden, provoked,* and *directed* episodes.

On continuum 4—*unpredictable/predictable*—their behavior is usually predictable in categories of triggering stimuli and in profile, both by themselves as well as by an observer who has some experience with the client's prior behavior.

On continua 5 through 7—*stoppable/unstoppable*—and the continua that define the conditions for stopping, our clients vary. Some of them (like Mr. A, described in Chapter 13) initially showed the pattern of not stopping until either he or the other person is unconscious, or unless he is completely restrained. However, many of our clients, in at least some episodes, have shown the ability to stop as soon as the opponent submits or "gives up." (During the first few sessions Mr. A developed the ability to stop, and later he developed the ability to resist violent urges altogether.)

On continuum 8—*unplanned/planned*—the episodes vary. Most episodes show some signs of being briefly planned; they also show signs of being well-practiced and even rehearsed, perhaps both overtly and in imagination.

On continuum 9—*no memory/memory*—almost all of the episodes of all clients are clearly remembered. No client in this sample has remembered fewer than half of his violent outbursts.

On continuum 10—*remorse/no remorse*—most initially show no clear signs of remorse. This corresponds with findings for continua 11 through 13—*not righteous/righteous, no reason(s)/reasons, no values/values.* Most episodes are accompanied and/or followed by righteous justification, with reasons cited and some form of value cited, usually societal or personal.

On continua 14 and 15—*stressors, triggers not identifiable/ identifiable—and control issues not involved/involved*—stressors or triggers are always identifiable, and control issues are often involved.

On continuum 16—no audience necessary/audience usually *present*—I believe an "essential audience" with its "critic function" is always present, even when the client destroys an object with no one else around. In fact, most of the violent episodes that caused these clients to be referred to me occurred in public, with one or more observers present.

On continuum 17—*short duration/long duration*—even when the violent behavior lasts for a very short time, the feelings of anger and violent urges may last for hours, or even days.

On continuum 18—*subject expresses displeasure/subject expresses pleasure*—clients often expressed displeasure immediately before and during the violent episode; the displeasure would be expressed as if it were about the behavior of some despicable monster. But when the episode has ended my clients typically express pleasure with their own heroic behavior and righteous attitudes. Some would go even further and actually express feeling joy while being violent. One of the subjects described in Chapter 13 (Mr. B) recalled an episode of his violent behavior as a "spiritual orgasm"; while I'm not sure exactly what he means by that, I can assume there was some joy involved.

On continua 19 and 20—*not verbal/verbal* and *physical/not physical*—these clients are much more likely to get into trouble for showing physical than verbal violence, but most of them are also well practiced in delivering verbal abuse.

On continuum 21—*life threatening/not life threatening*—at least some episodes of more than half of these 62 clients have apparently been life threatening, and indeed at least two of these people have been responsible for the deaths of others outside of military combat situations. However, even in those individuals who show the most severely life-threatening forms of violent outbursts, the vast majority of their outbursts do not result in loss of life.

On continua 22 and 23—*not directed at object/directed at object*—and *not directed at a person or animal/directed at a person or animal*—many of the violent behaviors are aimed at another person, but a very high percentage also involve objects. For example, several of my clients have attacked their own houses with chain saws, and their own cars with sledge hammers. On the other hand, very few violent episodes (except in the case of one client) have been directed at animals.

On continuum 24—*constant/variable*—most clients show several sorts of violent behavior, with at least some of them being quite reliable in pattern, and others showing high degrees of variability.

Continuum 25—*overcontrolled/undercontrolled*—(Megargee, 1966) is clearly related to issues of modeling and subculture. Undercontrolled violence is typical of individuals whose parents, relatives, neighbors and peers expressed positive attitudes about violent behavior. Masters, Burish, Hollon, and Rimm (1987) point out that these under-controlled clients are the most difficult to work with. On the other hand, over-controlled violence is the sort one would see in a person who was brought up in an entirely different cultural setting, who struggles to control violent urges, and who explodes only rarely. Most of my clients (with no more than five exceptions) show undercontrolled violence.

Continuum 26—*drive mediated/instrumental*—(Feshbach, 1970) is also related to cultural issues, but not as clearly as the previous continuum. The prototypical example of instrumental violence occurs in the service of obtaining some desired object. On the other hand, the prototypical example of drive-mediated violence occurs in the service of intense emotion. Most clients show predominantly drive-mediated violence. A few had histories of some episodes of instrumental violence (e.g., armed robbery), but such episodes are vastly outnumbered by episodes of drive-mediated violence.

These last two continua mix in a complex way with many of my clients. Their acts of violence are instrumental in developing and keeping their "dangerous" reputations. These reputations are protective and important to their self-concepts and involve issues such as pride and masculinity. Thus it is that instrumental, under-controlled and drive-mediated may all describe the same act. This mixture of drive-mediated and instrumental violence is supported by a description I recently heard of an interview with a man who had repeatedly been convicted of armed robbery, and who had no history of violent outbursts. Interestingly, he said something along the lines of "I never got so much respect as when I put a gun in someone's face during a robbery." This anecdote further supports the frequent observations of the power of issues such as pride, masculinity, the development of protective reputations or armor, and the pervasiveness of issues involving respect and disrespect.

Accordingly, continuum 27—*respect-disrespect involved/not involved*—is quite clear in its application. Issues of respect and disrespect seemed to be present in almost every episode of violence shown by my sample of clients.

Continuum 28—*revengeful/not revengeful*—is similar. When an issue of respect or disrespect is involved some element of revenge is usually present, although it is often somehow obscured.

Continuum 29, regarding—*substance use/abuse*—seems to be less important in my clients than it is in the literature reviewed by Gilligan (1996). Gilligan says "Alcohol use has repeatedly been found to be correlated with violent behavior; for example more than 50 percent of the perpetrators or victims of murder and other serious violence...have alcohol in their blood streams at the time...." Alcohol and other substances appear to play some role in less than one quarter of the violent acts perpetrated by my clients.

Continuum 30—*seeming scripted or ritualistic/not seeming scripted or ritualistic*—came to my attention very recently. Gilligan and a young reporter who had written a book about a double murder that recently occurred near Dartmouth College spoke at a Dartmouth Ethics Institute dinner in the spring of 2002. They agreed that many acts of violence seemed to have characteristics of being somehow scripted or ritualized. I have thought back over the violent acts of my clients, and realize that this element is present in many of these acts. The element of scripting or ritualization may be reflected by the fact that many of the violent episodes of many of these individuals show a rather consistent pattern. Scripting or ritualization may also be reflected by the fact that the presence of an audience seems to increase the likelihood of a violent episode among my sample of clients.

The above descriptions should give you an idea about who these clients are. But a final note with regard to intermittent explosive disorder/episodic dyscontrol is in order. Of the 62 clients I know best, 25 have had at least one neurological evaluation with an EEG, and only nine of these show any neurological abnormality. Only one of the four clients described in Chapter 13 has a documented neurological abnormality that shows up in the EEG, although all four were subjected to numerous neurological exams with EEG. On the other hand, a history of head injuries with loss of consciousness is the rule among these clients.

Assessment and Treatment Methods

By 1984 I had designed and evaluated a multimodal assessment and treatment program for use with individual violent clients. The program includes various techniques—relaxation training, biofeedback, and elements of systematic desensitization and various strategies of cognitive behavior therapy, including "stress inoculation" (Meichenbaum, 1977). Other investigators have reported some success with one or several of these techniques (e.g., Goodwin and Mahoney, 1975), but none has used biofeedback of autonomic activity in the way that we have, and none has attempted to influence all three realms (bio, psycho, and social) of the clients' lives in the way that we have. Furthermore, as mentioned earlier, our sample of clients is unlike any sample of outpatients with whom comparable procedures have been evaluated. We used variations on this program with all 115 of our population of violent clients; the sequence had been essentially standardized by 1983. (Individual treatment variations will be spelled out in Chapter 13.)

The program has three phases. Most of the program and its elements are applicable to clients with problems other than violent behavior. Where I have included a special technique for the violent client, I will so indicate in the discussion.

Phase I

Phase I consists of a behavioral interview and a psychophysiological assessment (stress profile). The interview identifies the stimuli that trigger the individual's violent episodes (or other stress reactions) and his or her characteristic biological, emotional, behavioral, and cognitive responses.

I obtain informed consent prior to the psychophysiological assessment. This assessment entails monitoring autonomic activity (as indexed by at least two variables—electrodermal activity and finger temperature) during the 12-minute relaxation-stress-relaxation sequence that was described in Chapter 10. The variable, which shows the greater change, is then picked as the more suitable physiological variable for the subsequent biofeedback (in all cases described here electrodermal activity was selected). The psychophysiological assessment also establishes one of the baselines for eventual evaluation of the impact of treatment.

At the first session and each subsequent session, detailed reports are obtained from the client regarding some specific behavioral and subjective variables. For this purpose, I use the general format shown in Figures 12. la and 12. lb. When I am assessing a violent client, I also obtain detailed reports regarding anger felt and expressed during the prior 24 hours. (Specifically, the report format determines if clients felt or expressed anger; threatened, grabbed, pushed, or hit anyone; or hit anyone until they or the other person became unconscious. The general strategy depicted in Table 1.1 of Chapter 1 is used for this purpose, along with a general questioning strategy that is tailored for the client and for the situation being described.)

At the end of the first and each subsequent session, the clients who are being treated individually are asked to keep a daily record, to be filled in between suppertime and bedtime, of one of the following:

(1)   The most powerful stress- or anger-producing experience of the day;
(2)   The worst experience of the day;
(3)   The best experience of the day;
(4)   The most powerfully emotional experience of the day.

Corson
Dartmouth College
1988

Scale 0=None, 3=Moderate, 5=Highest

Additional Comments	Dependent Variables	0	1	2	3	4	5	Date
	Quality of sleep – when you got up this morning, were your rested?							
	Severity of ____ _____ (highest, greatest since this time yesterday)							
	General anxiety (worst since this time yesterday)							
	Frequency of _____ (since this time yesterday)							

Figure 12.1a. *Data gathering format for use at outset of each session (side a)*

Corson
Dartmouth College
1988

Scale 0=None, 3=Moderate, 5=Highest

Additional
Comments

negative mood				positive mood			Dependent Variables	0	1	2	3	4	5	Date
-3	-2	-1	0	+1	+2	+3								
							Mood right now							
							Energy level right now							
							Feeling of mastery of control over (highest since this time yesterday)							
							General feelings of depression (greatest since this time yesterday)							
		Feelings of self-satisfaction 1. Highest since this time yesterday 2. What was happening? 3. Lowest since this time yesterday 4. What was happening?												

Figure 12.1b. *Data gathering format for use at outset of each session (side b)*

Name:_____ Date: _____

Therapist Name:_____ SS #: _____

Best Experience
Fill out each day after supper and before bedtime

Date	Time Period	Situation	Rating: See Below
1.			
2.			
3.			
4.			
5.			
6.			
7.			
8.			
9.			
10.			
11.			
12.			

Scale:

+5 (as good an experience as I can ever imagine); +4; +3; +2; +1 (just noticeably good); 0 (neutral);

-1 (just noticeably bad); -2; -3; -4; -5 (as bad an experience as I can ever imagine).

Figure 12.2. *Record-keeping format for daily use.*

I decide which of these to request on the basis of an assortment of hunches. I usually select the third or fourth item. A sample format for this assignment is shown in Figure 12.2. The scales shown in this figure require some comment. When I first began using this assignment, I found that some clients were avoiding record keeping with the excuse "I didn't have any good experiences, so I didn't have anything to keep a record of." Because I want each client to keep a record of something each day, I changed the scale. Now I say, "If you don't have any good experiences, just fill in your least lousy experience of the day. That way you will have something to record each day." These records and the behavioral interview are used to select stressful and anger-producing stimuli for use in the third phase of treatment.

Phase II

Phase II entails at least three one-hour sessions for practicing relaxation and biofeedback. The client first learns a simple relaxation technique based on the procedure of Benson et al. (1974). The technique takes about 20 minutes, and the client is asked to practice it once a day for the duration of treatment. The client then learns to lower sympathetic tone using relaxation and biofeedback (with a continuous analog tone). At the end of the second phase, the client is taught a rapid relaxation strategy (similar to that of Stroebel, 1982) using the following instructions:

> *Focus on your breathing—take a deeper than normal breath and breathe out through your nose—on the out breath think the word "calm" and smile to yourself. Let a warm comfortable sensation develop in your hands and stomach. Do it again. Each breath takes about 10 seconds; the whole exercise takes about 20 seconds. At the end of this quick calming response notice how much better you feel. Try to do this at least 12 times per day. (Some people have reminded themselves to practice this response by doing it each time they look at a watch or a clock, each time they enter a bathroom, and each time they hear a phone ring.)*

The first two phases are usually completed within four to five sessions.

Phase III

Phase III includes an average of 13 one-hour treatment sessions as well as daily homework (record-keeping assignments and relaxation practice, aided for many clients by a portable biofeedback unit). During the treatment sessions, two-minute, semi-structured "stress interviews" (Almy, 1978) alternate with five-minute relaxation periods. As mentioned above, the stressful material for the two-minute interview is based on previously gathered (and continuously updated) information about stress- or anger-producing situations appropriate for the particular client. During the first few stress interview periods the client is instructed, "Let yourself feel and express anger (or upset), without becoming physically violent." During the first few sessions the client receives continuous visual analog biofeedback during several cycles of two-minute stress and five-minute relaxation periods. The array of equipment shown in Figure 1.1 of Chapter 1 is often used at this stage. In early sessions, and at the outset of other sessions, the stress interview often includes simulation (via role playing) of the stressful or anger-producing situation. At the end of each two-minute stress interview, the client is instructed, "Put those things out of your mind and relax deeply and quickly."

After the first several sessions of this phase, clients are also taught to alter their cognitive processes (covert verbalizations and imagery) in response to simulations and descriptions of situations that would previously have provoked stress or anger. For example, the violent client is asked to consider anger as a secondary emotion that rapidly follows a drop in self-esteem, which is accompanied by an emotion such as humiliation, frustration, or fear. The client is asked to identify and describe aloud the original emotion (much individual tailoring is necessary here).

In the later sessions of this phase, the feedback system is occasionally turned off (i.e., feedback tones and video feedback are not presented to the client during a cycle of relaxation-stress interview-relaxation). Following this, we discuss feelings and events that occurred during the cycle. Particular attention is paid to the client's estimation of his or her own stimulus value (i.e., how others might perceive him or her) at various points during the stress interview. We also attend to a violent client's feelings of, perception of, and control over the fire in the boiler, without the aid of simultaneous biofeedback. Following this discussion, the videotape of the cycle is replayed, and the actual relationships of the behavioral and biological variables are observed as they occurred together in real time. At the end of each session, the client is shown a simple graph of the results of at least one cycle of relaxation-stress-relaxation, which is compared with graphs from prior sessions; changes in duration and level of arousal are highlighted.

With most clients, models, mini-models, and a personality theory are developed and discussed during some sessions. Often small experiments (for the client to try in "real-life") are planned (along with development of a format for gathering data on the outcome of the experiment). The feedback on outcome of these experiments is obtained at the subsequent session, or over the telephone. After approximately 17 sessions, treatment is terminated and follow-up visits are scheduled; for most violent clients, follow-up continues for at least 2 years, with visits scheduled every one to three months. It is worth noting that in 2006 I am still occasionally following up with some clients from this sample whom I have worked with for more than 20 years. Some of these clients are seen occasionally in-group settings, and a few others are seen in individual sessions on an approximately once every three months schedule.

Results

With the sample of 62 violent clients, we have monitored treatment effects on numerous dependent variables (behavioral, physiological, and subjective). The remainder of the chapter will examine the impact of the treatment program in the context of several crucial dependent variables. But first, I will briefly review an important result that directly relates to the client as coinvestigator and personal theorist.

Record Keeping

By the end of formal treatment the data on compliance with record-keeping instructions are very clear. Of the 62 clients I followed most closely, 37 complied with the record-keeping assignments. Of these 37, 30 showed at least an 80% reduction in frequency of physically violent episodes, with marked reduction in severity and duration. Improvement was such that police were not involved in subsequent episodes, while police had been involved with many of their episodes prior to the start of treatment. Of the 25 clients who did not comply with record-keeping assignments, only two showed an 80% reduction in frequency of physically violent behavior.[1]

Follow-up Fourteen Years Later

By late 1988 we had been able to obtain a detailed follow-up on 25 of the 62 clients. The results are shown in Table 12.1. These data show that reductions in the severity and frequency of most clients' angry feelings and violent behavior (henceforth collectively referred to as "hostility") were maintained from six months to ten years after the end of formal treatment. In many of the cases shown in Table 12.1, we were able to obtain the cooperation of people who know the client well (probation officers, spouses, friends, children) in order to get independent corroboration on such data as the types and frequencies of violent outbursts.

The comparison of the follow-up data (shown in the last column of Table 12.1) with behavioral status at the end of treatment (not shown) indicates a surprising degree of stability. Only one of these 25 clients (#11) was clearly worse since the end of treatment. Coincidentally another client (#12) had improved, to the same extent, since the end of treatment. Among these 25 clients there is a statistically significant point —biserial correlation of record keeping with hostility change (degrees of freedom = 23; t value is 1.18; p<0.05 one-tail) indicating that greater hostility change was shown among those clients who kept records. This comparison provides support for the observation made with the 62 clients described above.

Table 12.1 and its footnotes explain the methods of converting hostility levels and frequencies into numbers. Table 12.2 presents a comparison of the ten clients showing the greatest hostility change

---

[1] The correlation between compliance with record keeping and treatment success is now used as the basis of the following printed policy, which is handed out to each client at the start of treatment: "All clients must keep records during each week of treatment. The second failure to comply with this requirement will result in immediate discharge; at the time of this discharge the client will be given two weeks' worth of blank record-keeping sheets and an envelope addressed to us. If the client decides that he/she would like to get back into treatment, he/she should complete two weeks' worth of record keeping and return the complete data sheets to us. When we receive these two weeks of complete records, we will put the client at the bottom of our waiting list."

Table 12.1
Individual Data Pre- and Post-Treatment for Clients in Follow-Up Sample

| | | | SKIN CONDUCTANCE LEVELS (scaled to range from 0 to 1) | | | |
| | | | Minimums | | Maximums | |
Client	Sessions	Record Keeping?	Pre	Post	Pre	Post
1	15	Y	.18	.10	.30	.10
2	11	Y	.30	.10	.73	1.00
3 (Mr. B)	40+	Y	.60	.20	1.00	.50
4	09	Y	-	-	-	-
5	20	Y	-	-	-	-
6	33	Y	.04	.02	.07	.03
7 (Mr. A)	40+	Y	.65	.40	1.00	.98
8	40+	N	.65	.10	.70	.15
9	10	Y	.16	.46	.25	.58
10 (Mr. D)	40+	Y	.55	.15	.90	.20
11	18	Y	.85	.40	.89	.61
12	21	N	.61	.30	.90	.80
13	19	Y	.71	.80	.90	.86
14	10	N	.87	.62	.92	.01
15	09	N	.30	.58	.59	.70
16	28	Y	.20	.08	.25	.10
17	10	Y	.46	.48	.80	.78
18	15	Y	.23	.09	.26	.15
19	11	Y	.45	.20	.70	.52
20	07	N	-	.10	-	.41
21 (Mr. C)	40+	Y	.55	.25	.71	.36
22	11	N	.06	.04	1.00	.06
23	36	Y	.65	.18	.69	.22
24	10	Y	-	-	-	-
25	18	N	.85	.80	.90	.82
MEANS	20.8		.498	.293	.689	.488
SD	12.2		.246	.241	.291	.324

NOTE: Y=Yes, record keeping was done; N=Not done. (-) = No data for that variable.
  a)   ½ "life" refers to how long it takes, in minutes, to return ½ way to the pre-stress level of skin conductance.
  b)   Feel no anger = 0, Feel anger = F, Express anger = E, Threaten = T, Grab or push = G, Hit = H. These items are scored using the following numbers:
         O = 1, F = 2, E = 3, T = 4, G = 5, H = 6
Mean and SD of frequencies are expressed in decimals and presented in parentheses.

Table 12.1 (continued)

Skin Conductance Arousal Duration (1/2 Life in minutes)[a]				Highest Level of Anger or Violent Behavior in prior week [b] (frequency in prior week)	
Stress Profile		Stress Interview			
Pre	Post	Pre	Post	Pre	Post [c]
1.0	1.0	2.0	0.5	H (1)	E (5)
-.-	-.-	-.-	-.-	T (1)	F (2)
4.0	0.5	5.0+	0.5	H (1)	F (1)
-.-	-.-	-.-	-.-	E (7)	0
-.-	-.-	-.-	-.-	H (1)	E (1)
5.0+	2.0	5.0+	3.0	T (1)	E (1)
3.5	1.0	5.0+	0.5	H (2)	F (2)
1.0	0.5	4.0	2.75	H (1)	G (1)
2.0	0.2	5.0+	0.75	H (1)	T (1)
2.5	0.6	5.0+	0.75	H (4)	E (1)
3.25	-.-	3.0	1.25	H (1)	H (1)
5.0+	5.0+	5.0+	2.0	H (1)	E (1)
0.5	0.5	2.25	1.0	E (4)	E (1)
1.5	-.-	0.5	1.5	E (7)	E (1)
3.75	1.5	2.75	0.75	T (1)	0
-.-	1.25	1.25	0.75	E (1)	F (7)
1.25	1.25	5.0+	2.0	T (1)	0
-.-	-.-	0.5	1.5	H (1)	E (3)
5.0+	-.-	0.5	1.0	T (1)	E (1)
-.-	-.-	-.-	5.0+	G (7)	G (4)
5.0+	0.5	5.0+	0.5	H (1)	T (1)
5.0+	-.-	5.0+	-.-	E (3)	E (4)
-.-	-.-	-.-	5.0+	H (4)	E (2)
-.-	-.-	-.-	-.-	E (1)	0
1.0	0.5	2.0	1.0	T (4)	T (1)
4.25	2.24	4.83	2.70	4.76 (.232)	2.72 (.168)
2.10	1.46	2.28	1.64	1.30 (.210)	1.59 (.170)

NOTE: c) This measure was taken in a follow-up questionnaire and/or phone conversation (follow-up durations ranged from 6 months to 10 years after the end of formal treatment); all other Post measures were taken at the client's last formal treatment session, or during a follow-up visit.

Table 12.2
Data for Top vs. Bottom Ten Clients in Terms of Hostility Change from Pre-Treatment to Follow-Up (Some Clients Have Incomplete Data)

VARIABLES	ALL CLIENTS WITH DATA			TOP TEN CLIENTS		
	MEAN	SD	N	MEAN	SD	N
Sessions	21.75	12.22	20	24.0	13.6	10
Record Keeping	.650	.489	20	.800	.422	10
Skin Conductance Pre Minimum	.55	.24	.17	.51	.16	8
Skin Conductance Post Minimum	.31	.26	18	.30	.17	8
Skin Conductance Pre Maximum	.73	.29	17	.77	.25	8
Skin Conductance Post Maximum	.48	.32	18	.54	.32	8
Stress Profile S C Arousal Duration Pre	3.30	2.08	14	3.50	1.59	6
Stress Profile S C Arousal Duration Post	1.42	1.60	11	1.81	2.09	6

Table 12.2 (continued)

BOTTOM TEN CLIENTS			STATISTICAL OBSERVATIONS
MEAN	SD	N	
19.5	10.9	10	There is no significant correlation between number of sessions and hostility change when all 25 subjects are included.
.500	.527	10	There is a significant point biserial correlation ($p<.05$, 1 tail) showing that complying with record keeping assignments is related to greater hostility change.
.58	.30	9	The most important feature here is that more successful clients have a
.32	.32	10	higher range of Skin Conductance Level pre treatment; among all 25
.70	.33	9	men the correlation of hostility change with Skin Conductance range is .43 ($p=0.027$).
.44	.33	10	
3.16	2.49	8	These numbers are not significantly different.
0.95	.57	5	

Table 12.2 (continued)

VARIABLES	ALL CLIENTS WITH DATA			TOP TEN CLIENTS		
	MEAN	SD	N	MEAN	SD	N
Stress Interview S C Arousal Duration Pre	3.67	2.31	16	4.75	2.23	7
Stress Interview S C Arousal Duration Post	1.90	1.71	17	1.75	1.83	8
Hostility Level (With Frequency Added as a Decimal Value) Pre	4.97	1.24	20	5.53	1.09	10
Hostility Level (With Frequency Added as a Decimal Value) Post	3.12	1.35	20	2.31	0.99	10

NOTE: Statistical observations are based on correlational analyses, analyses of variance and analyses of covariance for all variables except the record keeping. Record keeping was evaluated using point biserial correlational analyses. All p values were 2-tail unless otherwise noted.

Table 12.2 (continued)

BOTTOM TEN CLIENTS			STATISTICAL OBSERVATIONS
MEAN	SD	N	
2.83	2.12	9	In all 25 clients, there is a significant correlation (r=.61, p=0.003) between interview duration decreases and hostility change. ANOVA shows the top 10 men have greatest interview
2.03	1.69	9	decrease (p<.02), but ANCOVA shows that when the difference in pretreatment duration is covaried out, there is no remaining difference in duration change.
4.40	1.16	10	These numbers represent a significant difference between pre treatment levels and a persisting significant difference in change scores when the pre treatment differences are covaried out (p<.001).
3.92	1.19	10	

Table 12.3
Data for Top vs. Bottom Six Clients in Terms of Hostility Change from Pre-Treatment to Follow-Up (All Clients Have Complete Data)

VARIABLES	ALL TWELVE CLIENTS		TOP SIX CLIENTS	
	MEAN	SD	MEAN	SD
Sessions	26.67	13.26	26.67	15.20
Record Keeping	Four of the top six and four of the bottom 6 clients kept records; however, in all 25 clients, record keeping was found to be related to hostility change. (See Figure 12.2)			
Skin Conductance Pre Minimum	.51	.23	.53	.13
Skin Conductance Post Minimum	.38	.26	.35	.17
Skin Conductance Pre Maximum	.73	.29	.87	.15
Skin Conductance Post Maximum	.56	.31	.66	.27
Stress Profile S C Arousal Duration Pre	3.13	2.07	3.50	1.59
Stress Profile S C Arousal Duration Post	1.25	1.58	1.81	2.09

NOTE: Statistical observations are based on correlational analyses, analyses of variance and analyses of covariance for all variables except the record keeping. Record keeping was evaluated using point biserial correlational analyses. All p values were 2-tail unless otherwise noted.

Table 12.3 (continued)

BOTTOM SIX CLIENTS		STATISTICAL OBSERVATIONS
MEAN	SD	
26.67	12.71	These numbers are not significantly different.
.49	.32	
.41	.34	
.59	.35	
.47	.35	
2.75	2.56	The pre treatment duration is related to change in duration (F is significant at .02), but significant differences do not show up in change scores when the pre treatment differences are statistically controlled.
0.70	.65	

Table 12.3 (continued)

| VARIABLES | ALL TWELVE CLIENTS | | TOP SIX CLIENTS | |
	MEAN	SD	MEAN	SD
Stress Interview S C Arousal Duration Pre	4.92	1.67	5.46	1.33
Stress Interview S C Arousal Duration Post	1.29	.90	1.08	.71
Hostility Level (With Frequency Added as a Decimal Value) Pre	5.27	1.13	5.50	1.09
Hostility Level (With Frequency Added as a Decimal Value) Post	3.01	1.26	2.08	0.94

Table 12.3   (continued)

BOTTOM SIX CLIENTS		STATISTICAL OBSERVATIONS
MEAN	SD	
4.38	1.91	The pre score is related to change score (F is significant beyond .001) but significant differences do not show up in change scores when the pretreatment differences are statistically controlled.
1.50	1.08	There is also a significant correlation (r=.59, p=.02) between change in duration of arousal during stress interview and change in hostility.
5.03	1.21	These numbers represent a significant difference between pre treatment levels and a persisting significant difference in change scores when the pre treatment differences are covaried out (p<.001).
3.93	.75	

with the 10 clients showing the least hostility change. We have complete data for only 13 of these clients, and the top and bottom six (in terms of hostility change) are separately presented in Table 12.3. The statistical analysis strategies are specified in the footnote of Table 12.2.

The hostility differences between the top and bottom groups show up clearly in analyses of covariance. These differences are evident in both the evaluation of groups of ten (Table 12.2) and groups of six (Table 12.3). The results indicate that those clients who showed the most change in hostility also showed greater hostility levels prior to treatment, and when this difference is covaried out they continued to show highly significant differences in hostility change. In other words, although the level and frequency of hostility at the outset of treatment is related to change in hostility over the course of treatment, the statistical analyses indicate that improvements occurred which were not merely due to the pre-treatment hostility level. Therefore the changes observed cannot be explained merely by "regression to the mean."

Examination of the relationship between number of sessions and amount of hostility change shows no significant relationship when the 25 clients are taken together. Furthermore there is no significant difference when the top ten and bottom ten clients are compared. However, it is worth noting that in some parts of our sample we can see a correlation between sessions and degree of hostility change. (For example among the top six men of the 13 for whom we have complete data, a higher number of sessions correlates with a greater degree of hostility change, $p=.02$.) A higher number of sessions also correlates with some other variables; the most statistically significant of these correlations shows that the higher number of sessions correlates with higher levels of pretreatment hostility ($p=.006$).

Physiological Data

Five different generations of skin-conductance detection systems were used between 1974 and the present (different apparatus, electrode type and size, and gel). While these changes do not appear to influence the recorded duration of the arousal response, they do alter the absolute values. To deal with these differences in detection systems, I have related each minimum and maximum value obtained for a violent client by a particular detection system to the total range obtained with that system for all clients (violent and nonviolent), using a transformation method described by Cohen et al., (1978) and by Berman and Johnson (1985) for obtaining range-corrected standardized scores. The range extends from 0 to 1. For example, with a client whose minimum value is halfway up the range obtained with that particular detection system, the transformation would result in a .5 being given as the minimum value for this client. Use of these transformations permits us to examine a variety of relationships for the group as a whole.

Perusal of the tables indicates that there is a reduction in skin-conductance values (both maximum and minimum), and a reduction in durations of skin conductance arousal in both the stress profile and the stress interview. Among the skin conductance minimum and maximum measures there is one difference that stands out as being particularly robust, indicating that a higher range of skin conductance pretreatment is characteristic of those clients who will show greater hostility change. Note that these same clients also show a higher range of skin-conductance after treatment, but that the maximum and minimum values are lower at the end of treatment (the change scores are also significant in some of the comparisons).

Turning to the duration measures, we see that the durations of skin conductance arousal in the stress-profile evaluation do not show a clear relationship with overall hostility change, even though some subsets of the data show statistically significant relationships. One of the largest is a relationship between change (pre- to post-treatment) in duration of arousal in the stress profile and change in duration of arousal in the stress interview ($r=.566$; $p=.02$).

Initially I was surprised to see that the stress profile did not show greater relationship to other variables. However, later reflection reminded me of my own observations, as well as published observations, which indicate that stressors selected for each individual client are more likely to show diagnostic effects than are standardized stressors (e.g., Flor, Turk, and Birbaumer, 1985). Accordingly, the individualized stress interviews do show much greater relationship between the duration variables and hostility change than is shown between the standardized stress profile and hostility change. (I dropped the standardized stress profile from our individual subject protocol on the basis of this observation.)

The one variable which shows the most clear relationship with hostility change (as revealed in the analysis of variance and all correlations) is the arousal duration during the pretreatment[2] stress interview (all p values are beyond the .02 level with 2-tailed tests). In the statistical observations section of Table 12.2, the analysis of covariance shows that the change in duration of arousal during the pre-treatment interview is not significantly different between the top and bottom ten men when the large differences in duration of arousal during the pretreatment stress interview are covaried out. However, in other comparisons (with all 25 men and with the 13 men for whom we have complete data) we find a strong relationship between duration of arousal in the stress interview and hostility change. The clients who show the greatest hostility change also show lower durations of arousal following the stress interview at the end of treatment, as well as the expected difference in degree of change in duration of stress interview arousal between pre-and post-treatment.

These relationships suggest that it may be possible to predict which clients will do well (in terms of decrease in hostility as a result of treatment) by attending to a combination of variables that can be measured at the outset of treatment.[3] In fact, in the sample of only 13 clients for whom we have complete data, a multiple regression analysis shows that the combination of range of skin conductance prior to treatment and level of hostility prior to treatment predicts change in hostility, accounting for over 60% of the variance ($r=.78$; $r^2=.61$).

Possible Explanations

An attempt to explain these behavioral and biological observations brings to mind the issues of habituation, placebo effects, and skill acquisition. From another study we have some data that pertain to the habituation and skill-acquisition issues: we found no signs of habituation to the stress profile when ten normal subjects were tested twice (using alternative forms of the quiz), with at least 34 hours separating the two experimental sessions. On the placebo issue, we have subjective reports from some individuals who failed

---

[2] This is a liberal use of the word "pretreatment": the first stress interview is conducted in the fifth or sixth session, when some treatment has actually started.

[3] As mentioned earlier, the compliance with record-keeping instructions is an excellent predictor; after a few sessions it becomes obvious which clients are going to comply with these instructions.

to show reductions in the recovery time for autonomic function, and nevertheless report that they have developed some mastery over their emotional arousal as a result of the treatment sequence. The data on the ten normal subjects argue for a skill-acquisition explanation of these results, while the data on those who showed no reduction in duration of autonomic arousal argue for the possibility of a placebo effect.

Between these two extremes are many points at which habituation has probably played a large role. For example, it seems likely that some habituation may have occurred as a result of repeated exposure to stress interviews between the first and second exposures to the standardized stressors. Even the least successful clients, in terms of reduction of violent behavior, showed shorter duration of autonomic arousal in response to both the stress interview and the stress profile at the end of treatment. Note again that the stress material is constantly updated and that the amplitude of response to a stress-interview stimulus item that produced a large response at the end of treatment was almost the same as that observed at the beginning of treatment. By the end of treatment, the number of stimuli capable of producing an episode of clear autonomic arousal was typically reduced; however, we were usually able to identify at least one arousal-provoking stimulus for each session.

As I look back on all of my experience with this general strategy, I conclude that habituation, skill acquisition, and placebo effects probably all play important roles in the success of treatment. The simple exercise of considering troublesome stimuli—as well as alternative responses to these stimuli—in a relatively safe situation, with no behavioral outbursts occurring, seems likely to have had a variety of effects. Further work will be necessary if we are to clarify the approximate contributions of placebo effects and such factors as habituation, skill acquisition, response prevention, and changes in expectancy and disposition, as well as changes in the working self-concept. However, it is my guess that very little generalization will be possible from client to client concerning the contribution of these various factors because of the wide individual differences.

To illustrate and perhaps to help resolve the role of these individual differences, the next chapter presents the details of treatment features, results, and very long-term follow-up for four individuals.

13: Case Histories, Treatment Details, and Long-Term Follow-up[1]

This chapter demonstrates how all the concepts and strategies discussed up to this point can be put together to help some of the most stressed and stressful people I have ever known. The chapter is divided into five sections. In each of the first four sections I will present an individual member of our sample of violent clients. In the course of these presentations, I will describe how we used the assessment and treatment methods outlined in Chapter 12, and the results, as well as very long-term follow-up, for each individual. In the fifth and final section, you will read about some adaptations in procedure for three clients who could not profit from the strategies described in Chapter 12.

Mr. A

Mr. A was 47 years old when he began treatment with me in 1980. When I first met him his violent behavior was more severe and frequent than most of our clients. (His status at the time of our initial assessment is shown in Figure 13.1.) He had an eighth-grade education and normal intelligence. He was five feet, ten inches tall, and at the beginning of treatment he weighed 210 pounds. His parents were not married and he had spent some of his early years in

---

[1] Informed consent was obtained from all clients and demographic details have been altered to protect anonymity.

foster homes. In Mr. A's early years he was repeatedly abused by foster parents and older neighbors. He became suspicious and uncooperative. This probably accounts for his obtaining a low score on a childhood IQ test and eventually being placed in an institution for retarded children for several months. He also spent some time in reform school, and when I first met him, in 1980, he had been in prison (for robbery or assault) or in mental hospitals at least once each year since he was 15 years old, with the exception of years in the military.

He recalled an episode when he was 11 years old during which he was being tormented by two older, larger boys. He broke free and was able to seriously injure one of the boys; the other boy left Mr. A alone (this episode is depicted in Figure 13.2). From this episode Mr. A got the reputation of being a very hostile and dangerous person who would hurt others if he got a chance. Even when he was overpowered, he would not give in or cease trying to hurt other people. Mr. A perceives this as a very important time in the development of his reputation—a reputation that he said "saved me from a lot of hassles—because the other guys knew I didn't fool around." This appears to have been the pivotal episode of negative reinforcement in Mr. A's early life. In each new situation involving a move to a new neighborhood or a new institution, Mr. A had to reestablish his reputation—and thus experienced further episodes of negative reinforcement that further strengthened his tendency to quickly become violent when he was upset.

At 16-and-a-half years of age, Mr. A took an assumed name and lied about his age to enlist in the military. He was in combat in Korea and Vietnam (taking a second assumed name to get into the service during the Vietnam era). His military record was spotty, with excellent ratings in some activities, but with evidence of great difficulty in dealing with authority figures; this resulted in his spending much time in the brig. After his discharge, he continued to have trouble with the law, and, in fact, other than his time in the military, his longest single period out of jail or a mental institution from age 15 to age 47 was about three months. During his brief periods of freedom he worked in construction and other forms of manual labor.

He was once convicted of manslaughter, and at one point he spent 12 consecutive years in prison. He reported that he spent most of his prison time in solitary confinement because of his violent behavior. Prior to working with us, Mr. A had been extensively treated with electroconvulsive shock therapy, and with medication (including 16 months of lithium) and some forms of psychotherapy, for a variety of problems, including bipolar disorder, paranoia, impulsive behavior problems, and outbursts of rage. A neurological exam, including EEG, however, was within normal limits. Prior to treatment, Mr. A's violent behavior patterns included threats and shoving on the average of more than twice a week. If his antagonist showed any resistance, Mr. A immediately escalated to hitting until he or his antagonist lost consciousness, or until Mr. A was firmly restrained. Attempts to restrain Mr. A generally required more than one individual, and usually resulted in injury to several people because of Mr. A's considerable strength and general physical fitness (he had been doing calisthenics, lifting weights, and running for years).

At the time of my initial assessment of him he was very agitated and emotionally labile, and he talked loudly. He did not seem to listen to or respond to anything except for direct commands and questions. These problems became much less severe during the first few relaxation and biofeedback sessions. During the first six sessions of treatment, Mr. A's violent behavior also decreased rapidly, and at no time since the beginning of treatment has he spent a night in jail—in marked contrast to his pretreatment jail record. Since starting treatment, he has been directly involved with the police only one time, and this was between the third and fourth sessions.

The duration of his autonomic arousal after the standardized stress profiles and the stress interviews has decreased (see Figures 13.3 and 13.4). While there was only a slight decrease in the amplitude of arousal during the stress interviews, Mr. A explained that he could now detect in himself the early signs of increasing arousal without the use of biofeedback. Duration of arousal outside the therapy sessions was also dramatically reduced. Prior to treatment, Mr. A became angry frequently, and stayed angry long enough, so that he reported being angry "most of the time." Prior to treatment his expressions of anger or violent eruptions occurred about twice each week. The angry feelings stayed with him for about two days. After the sixth treatment session, these episodes of expression of anger were much more mild—involving very few violent eruptions, and less explicit threats. By this time his angry feelings were lasting for only hours (rather than days), and the frequency of his expressions of anger was reduced to about once per week.

Mr. A lived far from the hospital and obtained a full-time job shortly after we began working with him. Because of this, we were not able to schedule sessions as close together as we would have preferred. In the ninth month of treatment (after 12 sessions), Mr. A described a wave of calm that came over him while he held the shirt of a man whose dog had bitten him. Mr. A released the man and dealt with the situation in a reasonably calm manner. (He attributed this wave of calm to the biofeedback training and claimed that he had visualized the therapy room and biofeedback apparatus. One of my colleagues has said: "John Corson is now Mr. A's essential audience.") Shortly after this episode, we gradually decreased the frequency of Mr. A's visits from once monthly to once every three months to maintain his coping skills and to allow follow-up. The follow-up program with Mr. A (and many other clients) included occasional record-keeping assignments and reminders about continuing practice of strategies he had learned. The following paragraph is the text of a letter I sent to Mr. A in late 1982.

September 20, 1982

Dear Mr. A:

We recently received your record keeping—we only saw three dates entered on it. The idea is to use this thing every day.

Please use the enclosed form every day. Fill it out between suppertime and bedtime each day. Describe the most successful use of the quick calming response during that day.

You should be using the quick calming response at least twelve times each day—as directed on the back of the record-keeping sheet. Use it every time you hear a phone ring, use it every time you go to the bathroom, use it every time you look at your watch. This should add up to about twelve times per day.

When you have completed a week of this record keeping, please mail it back to us in the envelope we have provided.

Sincerely,

John A. Corson, Ph.D.
Psychology, Veterans Administration Hospital

enclosures

Over the past 17 years, Mr. A has been physically violent twice, but he has stopped himself short of inflicting any serious physical injury; one episode of violence occurred in a restaurant in response to an insult from an old antagonist, and the other occurred during an episode when Mr. A's automobile was vandalized. Mr. A reported that his feelings of persecution (which were a constant preoccupation prior to treatment) have decreased "a little," and that his ability to predict and control feelings of anger has increased "a lot."

Mr. A, like several other clients, has noticed changes in his energy and eating behaviors since treatment. Mr. A's childhood experiences apparently gave rise to self-doubt, profound insecurity, anger, and the general strategies of "always be on guard" and "get them before they get you." These strategies suggest that chronically high resting levels of sympathetic activity were accompanied by a high degree of sympathetic reactivity. This pattern was confirmed in our initial psychophysiological assessments. This chronically high arousal seemed to affect both eating behaviors and energy levels. Mr. A described bouts of overeating and periods of intense fatigue prior to the onset of treatment. He now weighs 180 pounds (down from 210) and reports that he is able to eat normally and that he very rarely feels fatigued. He also reports that his sleep patterns and his ability to concentrate have improved since treatment, and he describes a dramatic reduction in his subjective feelings of muscle tension and general agitation. He was fully employed until he reached retirement age, and now continues to work part-time. For some years he returned for individual follow-up sessions once every three months. He now occasionally attends a weekly solution-oriented group that I run. He continues to report persisting paranoid feelings, but he states, "I just don't let it get to me... I mind my own business." He appears to be very physically fit and he still "works out." He still has a steady relationship with a woman, but does not describe having many other friendships. He describes enjoying litigation, and he does considerable reading on case law. He has been very helpful to several of my other clients in suggesting lawyers and particular legal strategies to deal with financial and legal difficulties. He does not smoke, drink alcohol, or use any other substances.

His status in 1987 is depicted in Figure 13.5. I am pleased to report that his status today, with the exception of those changes mentioned above, is identical to that of January 1987.

Figure 13.1. *Pre-treatment flow diagram for Mr. A.*

State Hospital; Jails and prisons.	Feared Possible Selves: Victim	Social Behavior: Talks loudly, Doesn't listen; Emotional lability (laughed loudly 2x and cried 3x during initial interview); Litigious, takes offense easily.	Was in state hospital and had ECT before age 20; At various times was on Lithium, Haldol, Librium and other medications. Had 2 ½ years "off" and on"	Wechsler Memory = 82; Halstead-Reitan index = .7 (suggests possible diffuse bilateral impairment). Zung = 56 (significant depression).
Combat Experience Korea and Vietnam	Chronic high arousal and high reactivity.	Hypertension	Psychotherapy – ended 1 year ago.	Notes: Had psych testing before age 16–IQ=67, was placed in an institute for retarded people for several months, failed 3rd grade in school, longest period out of jail (other than in Military) about 3 months since age 15; longest jail term was 12 years.
Memory of getting a "reputation" by fighting			Hopes, Interests, Hobbies: A better job, more pay. Interested in dogs, cares for dogs, lifts weights, "works out."	Neurology work up and EEG normal.

Name   Mr. A (pretreatment)   Education   8th Grade (GED?)   Marital Status Divorce x2   Referred by   Dr. P.

Date   12/20/80   Age   45   Occupation   Laborer   Presenting Problems   Violent Behavior, etc.

STIMULI	PRESUMED INTERNAL PROCESSES	TARGET PROBLEMS	TREATMENT METHODS	EVALUATION METHODS
<u>Authority Figures</u> "Police" "Local Politicians" "Injustices"	Fear? Humiliation? "Anger"	<u>Violent Behavior</u> Many fist fights; Shoves, threats; Many arrest; One manslaughter conviction.	Relaxation, Biofeedback, Anger management training (stress interview/role playing interpolated between periods of relaxation and biofeedback throughout), Social skills training, assertion training.	Record keeping best and worst experiences. Psychophysiological monitoring; SCL=.65 to 1.0, BP = 147/97. # Arrests, # Days in jail, # Fights (at outset hit twice last week). Paranoid scale –
<u>Life History</u> of abuse, isolation and violence. Foster homes; Reform School; Institution for retarded people;	<u>SELF-CONCEPT:</u> "Hair trigger"; "I get even"; "Outsider"; "Paranoid about some things"; "I'm always ready"; "I get them before they get me"; "I'm a hard worker"; "Hostile"; "I've got a reputation". Hoped for Possible Selves: Respected, Dominant	<u>Substance Abuse</u> History of ETOH, Heroin and other drugs (not for the last 5 years). <u>Depression</u>. Made a suicide attempt at age 14.	Is now on BP meds – has been for 2 years. Prior treatments:	Hi; Anger/violence scale = Hi; WAIS V = 94, P = 99, FS = 96.

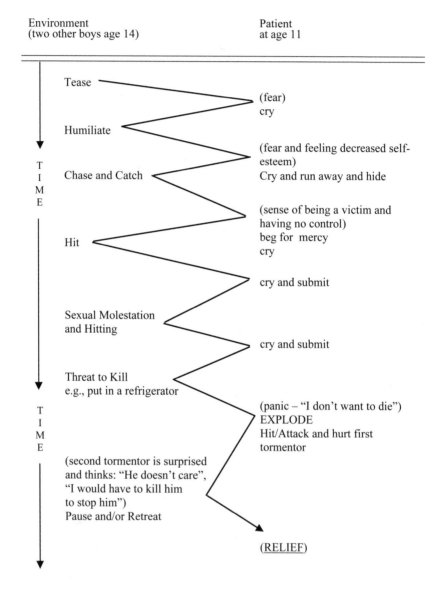

Figure 13.2. *Mr. A's violent episode at age 11.*

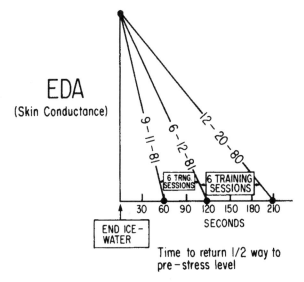

Figure 13.3. *Mr. A's recovery from stress profile is more rapid as training progresses.*

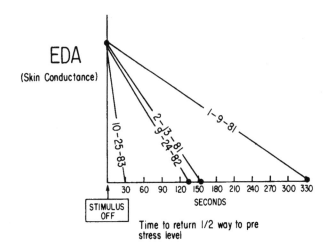

Figure 13.4. *Mr. A's recovery from stress interview is more rapid as training progresses.*

Figure 13.5. *Post-treatment flow diagram for Mr. A.*

obvious emotional liability.

Hypertension ⟶

Is on same BP meds – same dose as in 1980.

Hopes, Interests, Hobbies: Is dating "A nice woman"; still lifts weights and "works out."

Paranoia Scale = medium to high;

Anger/Violence Scale = low.
Client's ratings:
(on a scale from 0 to 5)

Sleep-rested? 1980 – 2-3, now – 5.

Anger 1980 – 5, now – 0-1.

Anxiety 1980 – 3-4, now – 0.

Depression 1980 – 5, now – 0.

Self Satisfaction 1980 – 2-3, now – 5.

Name Mr. A (post-treatment)   Education 8th Grade (GED?)   Marital Status Divorce x2   Referred by Dr. P.
Date 1/12/87   Age 52   Occupation Laborer   Presenting Problems Violent Behavior, etc.

STIMULI	PRESUMED INTERNAL PROCESSES	TARGET PROBLEMS	TREATMENT METHODS	EVALUATION METHODS
Same as in 1980 Now the "ordinary hassles" of daily life shift from session to session, e.g., over the last 2 sessions 1) lazy co-worker, 2) woman friend having financial problems.	Self-Concept: "I'm still paranoid, I just don't let it get to me"; "I mind my own business"; "I'm a hard worker"; "I've got a pretty good life now". Hoped for Possible Selves: Respected Feared Possible Selves: Victim Lower resting arousal level and lower reactivity.	Violent Behavior Reports persisting paranoid feelings and occasional feelings of anger. Substance Abuse "None since 1975" Depression "Not now" Social Behaviors? Listens better, talks more quietly, less	Follow-up once every 3 months; anger management booster sessions.	Assign occasional record keeping (results are uniformally good, compliance is excellent). Pyschphysioliogical monitoring: SCL = .25 - .5 BP = 140/85. #Arrests = 0 in 6 years #Fights = 2 in 5 years (both brief and relatively mild compared to pretreatment).

Mr. B

Mr. B was 59 years old when he began treatment with me in 1981. He had some post-high school education and a verbal IQ of over 130, initially established on the Ammons Quick Test and later on the Wechsler Adult Intelligence Test. He had been taken to police stations more than 50 times by his own count. He had also spent a total of six years in psychiatric hospitals for problems related to assault and episodes of violent behavior. His status at the time of assessment is shown in Figure 13.6. Mr. B was five feet, six inches tall, and weighed 241 pounds at the start of treatment. The results of Mr. B's neurological exam, with EEG, were within normal limits.

Mr. B is the illegitimate child of a very young woman, and his grandparents brought him up as her brother. He was disciplined very harshly as a child, and he cites family tradition as the reason for his harsh treatment. For example, Mr. B was repeatedly locked in a dark closet for long periods of time (at one time for more than 24 hours), and he had all of his fingers broken by a female relative as a punishment for lying. Many pejorative labels were applied to Mr. B during his childhood. Those that had the greatest impact were "bastard," "coward," and "liar." Mr. B was raped by a male neighbor and severely beaten by relatives and other neighbors.

When Mr. B was approximately nine years old, he won a fight against three brothers who lived near him (two of these boys were older than Mr. B, and one was bigger and heavier). This victory came after three battles, the last two of which were watched by Mr. B's father and the father of the brothers. In a situation similar to that described by Mr. A, Mr. B then developed a reputation as one who was not only dangerous and "always ready," but as one who would persist in fighting—he would not give up. Early in Mr. B's teenage years he began to lift weights and started to experience increasing success in fistfights. By his middle and late teenage years he had acquired a reputation of being a very dangerous person whom no one should "mess with" (he said, "they called me 'lethal'"). Mr. B felt that this reputation helped keep him out of many situations in which he might have been tormented by others; however, he also acknowledges that this reputation probably also got him into many altercations. Again, this early memory represents an episode of very powerful negative reinforcement, with the violent behavior becoming a reliable way of terminating unpleasant experiences.

Mr. B graduated from high school and enlisted in the Army during World War II. He was in combat in Europe and had an excellent record until the war ended, when he quickly got into trouble. He finished his military career in a "neuropsychiatric" hospital.

He is a very articulate man with considerable talent for writing. In an attempt to help us understand the relationship between his early experiences and his violent adult behavior, he has dictated over a dozen tapes and written hundreds of pages over the years since he was first referred to us. From these sources we have been able to construct a detailed history and have developed an understanding of how his working self-concept has evolved through various experiences, and of how he is now able to interact with other people without becoming violent.

Some aspects of Mr. B's medical and behavioral history indicate that several of his episodes of violent behavior when he was between 17 and 50 were driven primarily by a neurologically-undetected seizure disorder. Evidence in support of this includes Mr. B's description of a strange aura or a sense of impending doom that would occur up to 20 minutes before some of his violent episodes. He also reported having no memory of those violent episodes preceded by an aura. His first recollection after each of these episodes was waking up, totally restrained, either in jail or in a psychiatric setting. His information about what had happened during these violent episodes was gathered from accounts provided by other people. A summary of two such episodes follows.

Episode 1: During an 18-month stay on a locked ward in a psychiatric hospital, Mr. B was walking in a ward hallway near his room when he felt an aura. He recalls reaching out to the wall for a "panic button" that the attendants pushed when they needed help— and this is his last memory prior to awakening in his room totally restrained. He was later told that he began making strange noises and attacking people and eventually had to be restrained by four large men and two women. During the altercation, he inflicted the following injuries on staff members trying to restrain him: two dislocated shoulders, a broken arm, three broken ribs, a broken nose, and a broken jaw.

Episode 2: When Mr. B was in his early 30s, he recalls riding in a car with his wife and another couple while he was on leave from another mental hospital. It was the Fourth of July and a very warm day. His car was stopped in a line of traffic in a small rural town when the public fireworks display suddenly began. He recalls only a loud noise and a blinding flash (he describes no aura prior to this episode); he later learned that he had left the automobile and begun attacking people. Among the injured were police officers, women and children. His first recollection following this episode is of being totally restrained in the town jail.

When we began treating Mr. B, we noted that his skin conductance rested at a very high level and was also very reactive. From his reports it was clear that his life at that time could be characterized by constant scanning of his social environment for any sign of disrespect or provocation. I assumed that the high autonomic resting level and reactivity reflected this general disposition. This disposition and his history suggested that he had shown three types of violent behavior. The first type involved only a few episodes, such as those recounted above. These were apparently ictal, or seizure-related in nature; they seemed to involve his high resting level of autonomic activity, which had the effect of priming or setting levels in damaged central nervous system structures (although, as mentioned above, this damage was not detectable by neurological examinations). For some unknown reason, the various factors combined to cause his system to cross a threshold and go into a seizure. The second type had a rhythmic temporal quality, and involved going to taverns and slum areas to seek out violent encounters (looking for trouble) at times when he felt the urge to do so.[2] The third type of violent outburst occurred when Mr. B felt that he had been shown any sign of disrespect, or that he was "called upon to right some unforgivable wrong"; in other words, the third type involved "righteous rage." My best guess now is that this third category encompasses most of Mr. B's violent episodes. These episodes were triggered by identifiable psychosocial stimuli and were consciously guided throughout and remembered afterwards.

The first of these types of violent episodes did not occur during our period of working with Mr. B. The second type of episode dropped out by the third month of treatment. Prior to that time, such incidents had been occurring at intervals of once every two to six weeks. The third type did not occur after the 15th session, even though a strong urge to indulge in such behavior can still be triggered by certain experiences (such as observing a man being mean to a woman or child).

---

[2] In a letter he wrote to me in the early 1990s, Mr. B added a postscript saying "I might add: self-induction of mania, together with willful intent, was part of my dysfunction for many, many years."

When I began working with Mr. B (and for several years before and after), he was undergoing supportive psychotherapy, which appeared to be of considerable help. Prior to that time he had been extensively treated with insulin shock, ECT, and medication (including lithium for two years) for problems including bipolar disorder, paranoia, and impulsive behavior. None of these earlier treatments appeared to have had much beneficial effect. At the time of beginning treatment with us, he had reduced his drinking to occasional bouts—once or twice per month. About once a year a violent episode would occur at the time of alcohol use. One such episode occurred during the early months of treatment, and another occurred during a very stressful period in 1984, when Mr. B was on a follow-up schedule of one visit every three months. Between 1984 and 1988 he was rarely intoxicated. Since 1988 he has not been intoxicated at all, and it is my understanding that he now has no more than two drinks in any month.

After initial assessment, we conducted 18 weeks of treatment using the format described in Chapter 12 (one session per week). After the sixth session, Mr. B's episodes of violent behavior decreased rapidly from three or more per month to none (unless alcohol was involved). His feeling of persecution decreased, and his ability to predict and control feelings of anger increased, while the duration of his angry emotions decreased. The duration of his skin-conductance response to the stress profile decreased over the first six training sessions (see Figure 13.7). The duration of his skin conductance responses to the stress interviews also decreased during this period, from over five minutes at the outset to under four minutes. By the 18th treatment session, the duration was usually under two-and-a-half minutes. By the end of treatment, Mr. B's autonomic level (indexed by skin conductance level) was within the normal range in three out of four sessions I; it had been above the normal range for the first eight sessions. After the initial 18 treatment sessions the frequency of Mr. B's visits was reduced to one per month, for assistance in maintaining his coping skills and to allow for follow-up. After 14 months on this schedule, he was seen once every three months, except for during two highly stressful periods that are described below. Since the initial 18 sessions, he has not grabbed or struck another person. On one occasion in 1982, after drinking a large amount of rum, however, he damaged some property.

As was the case with Mr. A, Mr. B noted that he no longer had the uncontrollable urge to overeat. His weight had dropped from 241 to 189 by the end of the 18 weeks of initial treatment and has fluctuated between 180 and 210 since then. In 2006 he weighs 170. Mr. B reports that his sleep pattern and his ability to concentrate have improved since the initial period of treatment, and he describes a dramatic reduction in the subjective feelings of muscle tension and agitation. He even goes so far as to say he now feels serene. He also says that the biofeedback helped him "learn more about the forces within me" and "tune myself to the right level when things get tough."

The first of the two highly stressful situations that occurred after the beginning of Mr. B's treatment concerned pain, immobility, and "hassles" with the medical profession regarding his degenerative arthritis. It had been recommended that he have bilateral knee replacements, and he had been judged to be totally disabled by the Veterans Administration. While he has some trouble walking, he is able to block out pain and do heavy physical labor for short periods of time, even though his physicians have urged him to refrain from this. Over the past 17 years, he has generally abided by his physicians' suggestions regarding physical activity (although in May of 2002 he saw fit to reject help from others and shovel two yards of topsoil into low places on his lawn.) All things considered, however, he is now doing quite well, and is still postponing the knee replacements. The most intense upset over his arthritic condition occurred during a period of approximately 18 months, starting in late 1982, when he experienced steadily increasing pain and difficulty in walking. The initial diagnosis was couched in psychiatric terms, and the primary medical aspects of his condition were not acknowledged until he had become seriously incapacitated. His anger and paranoia (some of which may have been justified) regarding these issues led to many urges to do violence; however, he never acted upon these urges.

The second highly stressful episode occurred in the 1980s when his fifth wife became attached to another man and began spending a great deal of time with him. Again, urges to do violence were frequent, but Mr. B had no behavioral outbursts. It is important to note that while Mr. B's arthritic condition is indeed severe, it only has slight effects on the mobility and strength of his upper body. His 1987 post treatment status is shown in Figure 13.8.

In several written summaries of his thoughts regarding his status and history, Mr. B expressed the idea that he had no sense of being a self or a person, was chronically afraid and felt ugly and deficient and that he always "had something to prove." His account strongly suggested that the cognitive behavior therapy, combined with the supportive psychotherapy, helped him develop a general working self-concept, with accompanying attitudes and expectations toward himself and others, that made his life much more pleasant.

While his accounts of earlier episodes of violent behavior—of the second and third types listed above—include internal dialogue, these episodes of dialogue were clearly in service of very simple expectations and dispositions. However, his internal dialogue became much richer during our work with him and now allows him to consider of a variety of behavioral alternatives. Mr. B indicated that before beginning the biofeedback he often felt controlled or driven by bodily forces that he could not understand. After the first 18 sessions of biofeedback, he reported the he could "now pause and question my initial urge—I can talk it over with myself before taking rash action." In fact it seems that many of the gains made by Mr. B have been directly relatable to his ability to take on the "personal theorist" frame of mind. He has repeatedly told me that the scientist/theorist attitude and the modeling activities gave him a feeling of control and understanding, both of which were very important to him.

Mr. B is now over 80 years old at present. Since 1987 he has completed a paralegal course, and I was told by one of his instructors that he was the best student they had ever seen. He is retired. Like Mr. A, he has been very helpful to several of my other clients, occasionally with suggestions about legal matters, and frequently with very sensible supportive comments. At one point he joined Mensa (an organization for particularly bright people), but apparently became bored with the meetings and stopped attending. He has had no fights since 1987, and has actually become a very peaceful individual. He has practiced Tai Chi since 1994, and describes doing "isometrics—framed in a Zen-like system." Several years ago he was divorced from his sixth wife. He has subsequently stopped smoking several times, but I think he is smoking again. He has occasionally attended the relapse prevention, support, and crisis management group described elsewhere in this book. However he has not done so for several years, and I now see him individually every two to three months. The sessions involve conversation about his current life, and a short period of psychophysiological assessment, during which he proves to himself that he can still remain very calm, even when discussing difficult experiences.

Figure 13.6. *Pre-treatment flow diagram for Mr. B.*

| Memories of being called "bastard"; "coward"; "liar"; of being locked in a closet for many hours (once for more than 24 hours); of fingers being broken for lying; of being raped; of getting torment to end by fighting. | Feared Possible Selves: Victim, Humiliated, Incompetent, Controlled. Chronic high arousal and high reactivity. | Bipolar (now refuses Lithium) | Prior Treatments: Psychiatric hospitalizations (in for a total of six years; 18 months on a locked ward). ECT, various meds including Lithium for two years. Psychotherapy – sporadic with therapists other than Dr. F. Hopes, Hobbies, Interests: A better job, interested in dogs, gunsmithing, drawing, carpentry. | #grab, shove = 4 per month, #hit = 1 time in last week, #hit to unconscious = last time was two years ago. Paranoia scale = high; Anger/violence scale = high. IQ (Ammons Quick Test) = 130+. Notes: Is very articulate writer and draws very well. Neurological work-up/ EEG normal. |

Name __Mr. B (pre-treatment)__   Education __High School, some College__   Marital Status __M 5th Wife__   Referred by __Dr. F.__

Date __2/13/81__   Age __59__   Occupation __Skilled Laborer/Technician__   Presenting Problems __Violent Behavior, (5' 6", 241 lbs.)__

STIMULI	PRESUMED INTERNAL PROCESSES	TARGET PROBLEMS	TREATMENT METHODS	EVALUATION METHODS
Social Situations; Social slights	Fear? Humiliation?	Violent Behavior: Many brawls, fights, threats; many arrests (some violent outbursts between periods of relaxation may have been seizure related).	Relaxation, Biofeedback, anger management training (stress interview/role-playing interpolated between periods of relaxation with biofeedback throughout).	Record keeping – best and worst experiences each day. Psychophysiological monitoring: skin conductance level = .6 to 1.0.
Hot weather, sudden noises, explosions	Self-Esteem drops; "Anger"			Weight = 241.
	Self-Concept: "Lethal"; "Always ready"; "I love a good fight"; "I hit until someone drops"; "You might say I overdo everything".	Substance Abuse: History of alcohol "Now only about once every two weeks".	Psychotherapy with Dr. F (Has been going for 2+ years)	#Arrests = none in the last year, #days in jail = none in 1 ½ years, #expressions of anger = 5 per week, #threats = 3 per week,
Life history of abuse and violence. Multiple admissions to psychiatric hospitals; multiple (over 50) arrests.	Hoped for Possible Selves: Dominant, Respected, In control.	Overweight		

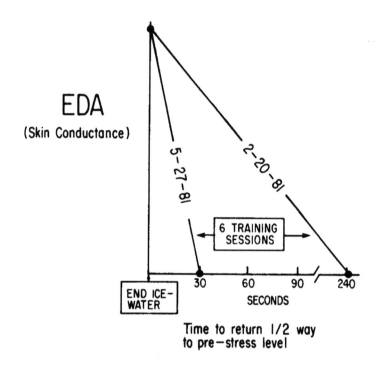

Figure 13.7. *Mr. B's recovery from stress profile is more rapid as training progresses.*

Figure 13.8. *Post-treatment flow diagram for Mr. B.*

Name __Mr. B (post-treatment)__ Education __High School, some College__ Marital Status __Divorced__ Referred by __Dr. F.__

Date __2/20/87__ Age __65__ Occupation __Part-time clerk__ Presenting Problems __Violent Behavior, (5' 6", 180 lbs.)__

STIMULI	PRESUMED INTERNAL PROCESSES	TARGET PROBLEMS	TREATMENT METHODS	EVALUATION METHODS
Life history and memories – see Pre-treatment flow diagram	Self-Concept: "In control," "serene," "lonely". Hoped for Possible Selves: competent, respected, loved, in control.	Violent Behavior? no violent behavior in several years.	Follow-up occasional visits and monthly contact by mail.	Record keeping – best and worst experiences each day.
Financial Problems (paying alimony)		Substance Abuse? None for over a year.	Hopes, Interests, Hobbies: Started working again, hopes to make new friends, would like to have a woman friend, no longer raises dogs, no longer does gunsmithing or carpentry.	Psychophysiological monitoring: skin conductance level = .2 to .5.
	Feared Possible Selves: old, lonely, crippled, incompetent, controlled, victim.	Overweight? not currently a problem.		Weight = 180.
	Lower resting arousal level and lower reactivity	Bipolar still notes some tendency to highs and lows, but is able to control them.		No arrests, violence or threats; occasional feelings of anger.

Paranoia scale = low; Anger/violence scale = low. Notes: Is lonely and often sad.			
		Degenerative Arthritis pain, difficulty moving (takes no medication).	

Mr. C

I first saw Mr. C in 1981 when he was 34 years old. He had completed most of his college education and had a verbal IQ of over 130 (Ammons Quick Test). He had been convicted of manslaughter and had spent several years in prison and many months in psychiatric hospitals for problems related to assault and episodes of violent behavior, as well as for other problems related to depression, substance abuse, and posttraumatic stress disorder. He was five feet, nine inches tall, and at the beginning of treatment he weighed 145 pounds. Neurological examination, with EEG, showed results within normal limits (His status at the time of assessment is shown in Figure 13.9.) Mr. C was the younger of two children born to a career military officer. Both parents were alcoholics. In his early years, his family moved frequently, and Mr. C promptly developed a reputation in each new neighborhood and school for being very quick with his fists, short tempered, and dangerous. Mr. C's brother often engineered situations so that Mr. C would feel compelled to get into a fight with someone. Mr. C studied a variety of martial arts and was very careful to keep himself physically fit (except for times when he was abusing drugs or alcohol—at these times he generally avoided situations in which he might feel compelled to fight). With Mr. C, fights took many forms—some being fistfights, others involving knives, and some involving guns. Mr. C reports that he first killed a person, in self-defense, at the age of 15. The incident involved three other people and was a fundamentally racial matter. Mr. C had never seen his victim before, and he was not completely sure that it was as a result of the wounds he inflicted that the victim died. Mr. C was not prosecuted for this assault.

Portions of Mr. C's childhood experience are described in earlier chapters. He was abused physically and psychologically by his father and psychologically by his mother. At one point, one of his fingers was almost totally amputated during a beating by his father, and at another time, while Mr. C. was a helpless observer, his older brother had several teeth broken by his father during a period of abuse. When Mr. C was 11 years old, his father was beating his mother and Mr. C made him stop by threatening him with a pistol. While pointing the pistol at his father and watching his father beg for mercy, Mr. C decided that "from now on I will be the terrorist." This episode appears to have been the pivotal episode of negative reinforcement in Mr. C's developmental period.

Mr. C enlisted in the military and had a tour of combat duty in Vietnam. Mr. C was briefly a prisoner of war (he escaped) and was brought up on charges twice (once for killing a civilian and once for assaulting an officer). Both charges were dropped. During his time as a prisoner of war, Mr. C reported being tortured and raped by his captors. He was also severely wounded in his arms and legs in combat in Vietnam. Mr. C was diagnosed with posttraumatic stress disorder and, when I met him, was considered totally disabled.

At the time of Mr. C's referral to us, he was indulging in a wide range of violent acts. These acts included threats to the lives of others (for example, he would talk about explicit details regarding the type of high-powered rifle, explosive, or poison he intended to use) and the occasional severe beatings he administered to other people. Mr. C carried a knife, and frequently a gun. The most severe physical assault we know of since we first assessed him was a pistol-whipping (hitting with the butt of a handgun) that he administered to his former wife. During this period, he was making threats of physical violence on an average of twice each week and was involved in public fistfights once every one to three weeks. In the previous 12 months, he had rendered at least two people unconscious.

After 20 sessions with very little progress, Mr. C left treatment when we asked him to reduce his use of marijuana (he was smoking from one to three times each day). Mr. C resumed treatment twice, and only during the last series of sessions, during 1987, did he make significant and durable progress. He reduced his use of marijuana to less than once a week, he developed skill in controlling autonomic arousal, and at our last follow-up session he showed a lower resting level and more rapid recovery from episodes of high autonomic arousal (see Figure 13.10). He also showed a dramatic reduction in both threatened and actual violence. My colleagues and I saw Mr. C for over 40 sessions. I conducted the last 20 sessions. The first 12 of these 20 sessions were conducted weekly or biweekly, and when progress was noted, the frequency was reduced to once every two to four weeks. (Figure 13.11 shows Mr. C's status in August of 1987.)

Further understanding of Mr. C's status during treatment, his coping strategies, and some of his problems can be gathered from looking at Figures 13.12, 13.13, and 13.14. These figures depict three points of view on the same episode. Mr. C was having financial problems, his wife was sick, and his daughter was in jail; in short, he was in deep trouble. His first impulses at that time are shown on these various diagrams. While he was in a session with me, I drew these with his input. At the end of the session, I photocopied these figures and gave them to him to take along and think about. When he came back the next week, we discussed the figures again. He told me he had come to a peaceful solution of the problems that were bothering him during the previous week. He asked me to write "solved" across these diagrams. Close examination of these figures, particularly Figure 13.13, shows the relationships among the fire in the boiler, the working self-concept and the feared possible selves. Making this explicit in a session with a client, such as I did with Mr. C, often seems to be of great help. The impact may be, in part, akin to a sort of desensitization to the worst possible outcome; this desensitization may allow the client to indulge in a fruitful internal dialogue, which in turn allows more effective problem solving than had been previously possible.

Another way of examining the relationship between the feared possible self and the working self-concept is to pay careful attention to the client's responses to the last two questions in Figure 1 of Chapter 12—specifically, What is the lowest level of self-satisfaction in the last 24 hours, and what was the situation in which this lowest level occurred? The client's responses to these questions (asked at the start of each treatment session) can serve as a guide to a discussion or the development of a model that will help put his worst fears into perspective, and may help facilitate problem solving and improve outcomes.

The primary gains that Mr. C experienced from our work together appeared in three areas: (1) a sharp reduction in both the expression of threats and physically violent behavior; (2) a better relationship with his immediate family and reconciliation with his oldest child; and (3) a realization that he had learned to choose whether or not to abort his feelings of agitation before they turned to anger and violence.

I am very sorry to report that he committed suicide several years ago. He had made remarkable progress since he stopped active treatment in 1987. He had completely stopped using marijuana, and all other substances except alcohol, which he used occasionally. He had stopped threatening other people, and was applying to colleges and universities in the hope of completing his bachelor's degree, so that he could go on to law school. As I understand it, he went to the house of a friend and consumed most of a bottle of wine. His friend, also one of my clients, told me that they discussed many things that night. Apparently some of the discussion reflected the fact that Mr. C was struggling with the possibility of again taking on the role of a student, and with facing the losses involved in the attempt to completely turn his back on his well-practiced role of warrior or terrorist (his old, primary, available self). In any event the alcohol apparently disinhibited him and he shot himself with his friend's shotgun.

Figure 13.9. *Pre-treatment flow diagram for Mr. C.*

Name   Mr. C (pre-treatment)   Education _____ College Graduate _____ Marital Status _____ M 2nd Wife _____ Referred by ____ Dr. S.

Date ____ 8/26/81 ____ Age ____ 34 ____ Occupation ____ Disabled (30% Service connected) ____ Presenting Problems ____ Violent Behavior, Pain

(5' 9", 145 lbs.)

STIMULI	PRESUMED INTERNAL PROCESSES	TARGET PROBLEMS	TREATMENT METHODS	EVALUATION METHODS
Memories of combat in Vietnam, of being a POW, being raped, a victim.	Frustration, Humiliation	Violent Behavior Many fights with fists, knives, and guns. Has been convicted of manslaughter. Carries a knife at all times. Keeps a gun in his car. Frequently threatens.	Relaxation, Bio-feedback, anger management and pain management training.	Record keeping – best and worst experiences each day.
Veterans Administration Denied increased in disability payment.	Self-Esteem Decreases Anger		Alcohol Rehabilitation Program (Client refuses to attend)	Psychophysio-logical monitoring: SCL = .55 - .71. Monitor pain levels, sleep, etc.
Financial Problems Crowds	Anxiety Self-Concept: "I can't relax"; "I can't get close to people"; "I was terrorized"; "I have no conscience"; "I am a loner"; "I don't lie but I've been lied to all my life".	Substance Abuse Current marijuana, and alcohol, occasional cocaine. Previously Heroin, cocaine and alcohol.	Vietnam Vets Group (sporadic attendance) Elavil "has helped with some of these problems" (Wants Demerol)	#Arrests = 1 (2 mo. ago), #Days in Jail = 1, (2 mo. ago), #Threats = 7+ last week,

Wife ("hassles me"),	Hoped for Possible Selves: Respected, In Control, Rich	Post-Traumatic Stress Disorder Nightmares, sleep disorder, startle response, flashbacks.	Prior Treatments: Transcutaneous nerve stimulation, surgery, medication, psychotherapy.	#Grab, shove = 7+,
Daughters ("one is always sick, the other is always in trouble").	Feared Possible Selves: Terrorized, Victim, Poor	Chronic Pain Left leg and both arms (still has some shrapnel).	Hopes, Interests, Hobbies: 100% Service connection. Interested in guns, explosives and motorcycles.	#Hit = 1 time in last week.
Childhood abused by father (and mother).	Chronic high arousal and high reactivity.	Disability Issues "I want 100% disability – I'm unemployable."		Paranoia Scale = Hi;
Memory of terminating abuse by threatening father with a gun. Developed a reputation as a terrorist and "ready to kill."				Anger/Violence scale = Hi.
Wounded – shrapnel is still in left arm and leg.				High IQ (Ammons Quick Test) = 130+.
				Notes: Is articulate, Neurological Work-up/EEG Normal.

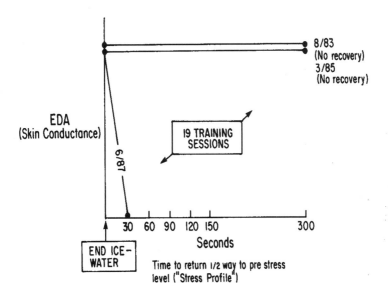

Figure 13.10. *Mr. C's recovery from stress profile is more rapid as training progresses.*

Figure 13.11. *Post-treatment flow diagram for Mr. C.*

Name   Mr. C (post-treatment)   Education   College Graduate   Marital Status   M 3rd Wife   Referred by   Dr. S.

Date   8/27/87   Age   40   Occupation   Disabled 100% Service connected)   Presenting Problems   Violent Behavior, Pain

(5' 9", 140 lbs.)

STIMULI	PRESUMED INTERNAL PROCESSES	TARGET PROBLEMS	TREATMENT METHODS	EVALUATION METHODS
Same as in 1981, except he now has 100% Service-Connected Disability and is married to a different woman – "who doesn't hassle me – at least not in the same ways".	Frustration, → Anger Self-Esteem decreases	Violent Behavior? No fights for 4 months, occasional threats.	Follow-up and continuing work on remaining problems, 1 session every 2 weeks.	Assign occasional record keeping (compliance is excellent).
Financial Problems	Self-Concept: "I have a better family life now", "I'm being screwed financially"; "I've let go of some old problems and solved some tough problems".	Substance Abuse? No alcohol for 2 years, no cocaine for 2+ years, marijuana less than once per week.	Antabuse	Psychophysio-logical monitoring: SCL = .25 - .36.
	Hoped for Possible Selves: Respected, In Control, Rich Feared Possible Selves: Victim, Trapped, Poor	PTSD? Symptoms persist but somewhat more bearable and less frequent.		Blood flow in arms and legs is asymmetrical-left side lower than right. Monitor pain levels, (still Hi).

Lower resting arousal and lower reactivity	Chronic Pain? Persists (methadone helps)	Methadone (and other medications) Hopes, Interests, Hobbies: "I need more money".	Monitor sleep (only slight improvement). Paranoia Scale = Mod-Hi; Anger/Violence scale = variable (Mod-Hi). #Threats = 1 in last week (no hits). #Arrests = None in 12 months.

PERSONAL SCIENCE – FORMAT FOR DEVELOPING A MULTILEVEL **ABC** DIAGRAM

Use this format to describe the most recent (or most memorable) occurrence of your problem and fill in as many of the spaces you can.

ANTECENDENTS: <u>As</u>k yourself what was going on in yourself and your environment just before the problem occurred;

BEHAVIORS: <u>As</u>k yourself what behavior did you show and what was going on in yourself and environment during the behavioral episode;

CONSEQUENCES: <u>As</u>k yourself what happened after the behavioral episode ended.

		ANTECEDENTS	BEHAVIORS	CONSEQUENCES
THINGS OTHER PEOPLE	DO	Debt, bank agent telephone	Listen	Bank sends foreclosure
	SAY	"You know you owe us 2000 and what will happen if you don't pay."	"We'll see about that."	
OTHER ENVIRONMENTAL EVENTS		Wife sick, baby sick and crying, daughter in jail.		Police "watching me."
MY OVERT BEHAVIOR		Sit and listen	Swear at him; threat – "You hassle me again & you've had it." Hang up.	"Nothing I can do."
MY COVERT BEHAVIOR		"Got to get them before they get me."	"Get him." "Gather ammo."	"I told him I could kill him." "They'll know who did it."
THOUGHTS		Angry Depressed Anxious	ANGRY	Joy Trapped, angry, depressed, anxious
MOODS, EMOTIONS & FEELINGS		Stressed, shafted, trapped, warrior	Warrior	victim, poor trapped
LABELS I USE FOR MYSELF				
THE LEVEL OF MY SELF-ESTEEM	HIGH			high
	MEDIUM		medium	
	LOW	low		low
THE LEVEL OF MY EXCITEMENT	HIGH	high	high	high
	MEDIUM			
	LOW			

Figure 13.12. *Mr. C – ABC depiction of an episode.*

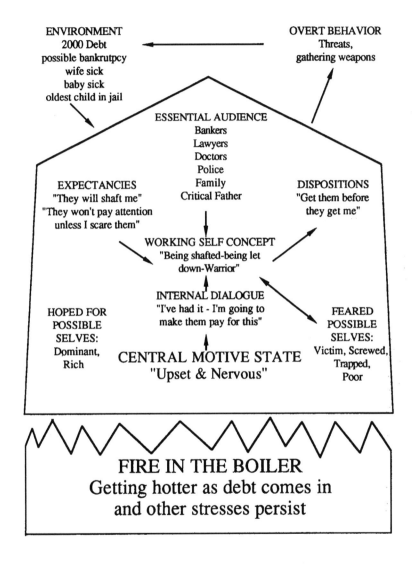

Figure 13.13 *Depiction of Mr. C dealing with same episode as in Figures 13.12 and 13.14.*

Figure 13.14. *Flow diagram of Mr. C dealing with same episode as in Figures 13.12 and 13.13*

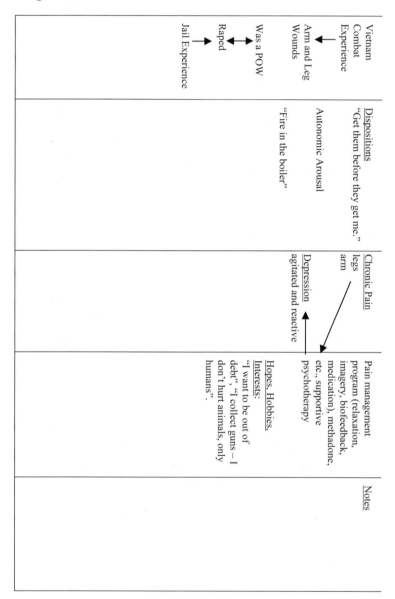

Name Mr. C   Date 2/7/87   Age 40   Occupation Disabled (100% Service-connected)   Education College Graduate   Marital Status M 3rd Wife   Referred by Dr. S.   Presenting Problems Violent Behavior, Pain

STIMULI	PRESUMED INTERNAL PROCESSES	TARGET PROBLEMS	TREATMENT METHODS	EVALUATION METHODS
ST	Self-Concept (working): "Terrorist; I've been shafted; I'm fed up; I'm wired".	Violent Behavior Threats ("I've killed before and I'll kill again – in a second").	Anger management program (biofeedback, relaxation, cognitive behavior therapy, stress management)	Count # threats. Self-report on: anger, violence, anxiety, depression, pain, etc.
LT History Triggers	Hoped for Possible Selves: Hero, Feared, Respected, Rich	Impulse Control Problems		
Abused as a child	Feared Possible Selves: Victim, Raped, Scorned, Poor			
Negatively reinforced as a terrorist	Expectancies "They will shaft me"; "They won't pay attention unless I scare or hurt them."	Substance Abuse Alcohol (not for 24 months) Marijuana (3x last week Cocaine (?), etc.	On Antabuse (won't go to AA) (won't go to NA)	
Financial problems $2,000 Debt				
Family Problems Wife sick Baby sick Daughter in jail				

Mr. D

I first met Mr. D in 1975, when he was 27 years old. He had a high school education and a verbal IQ of over 125 (Wechsler Adult Intelligence Scale), and was known to the police in his small southern Vermont town as someone who occasionally made threats with weapons. He had spent a few months in psychiatric hospitals for problems related to anxiety and impulse control. (His status at the time of assessment is shown in Figure 13.15.) Mr. D was five feet, 10 inches tall, and he weighed 150 pounds at the start of treatment.

Part of Mr. D's case history was presented in Chapter 6 (in connection with his treatment for anxiety and abuse of his preverbal stepdaughter). Further details of his background follow. Mr. D is the oldest of five children. Both of his parents were still alive at the start of treatment, and his father was an alcoholic showing clear signs of an Alzheimer's type disorder. Prior to entering the service, Mr. D's social behavior was within normal limits and he did well in school. While Mr. D was serving in Vietnam with the Army, he was rendered unconscious by coming into contact with a high-voltage wire. This appears to have been a turning point in his life. Since that time, much of his behavior can be characterized as disorganized and impulsive. He has lapses of memory and judgment and he is frequently unkempt. Mr. D's neurological exam with EEG was indicative of diffuse neurological impairment. Neuropsychological evaluations using the Halstead Reitan Battery also indicated diffuse neurological impairment. When Mr. D was about to be discharged from the service, he met and married a 16-year-old girl who was pregnant with another man's child.

At the time of referral to us for neuropsychological assessment and treatment for anxiety-related problems, Mr. D was not a member of an organized religion. He later joined a fundamentalist church and often gives credit to the church for "cleaning up my act." At the time of referral, Mr. D held occasional odd jobs and earned about $2,000 a year, which was supplemented by a service-connected disability payment of several hundred dollars a month. This income was insufficient to meet the family's expenses, and they were having trouble with both the water supply and the heating system in their small house. They were not able to afford an automobile, and Mr. D had no driver's license. Mr. D spent much of his time hunting and fishing.

Shortly after the end of the treatment described in Chapter 6, Mr. D came to us saying that he was considering killing one of his neighbors and had publicly threatened to shoot this man with a rifle. The apparent stimulus for this threat was the neighbor's statement that he would "keep your wife warm while you are in the hospital." Mr. D inferred from this that his neighbor was going to try to seduce Mr. D's wife while Mr. D was in the hospital for elective surgery (for a hernia). Shortly after Mr. D's confession of this threat to us, we learned that he had frequently threatened his wife and many other people (see Figure 13.16). While he had rarely carried out his threats, many in his neighborhood were afraid of him. His immediate family suffered the brunt of his anger and threats. When Mr. D was angry with someone outside the family, he would talk of nothing else but the details of his plans for revenge. Following an altercation, Mr. D would stay angry for at least two days, and he would get little sleep during this period. Because of the fact that most people took Mr. D very seriously, they would stay away from him, or they would somehow let him know that they were intimidated by his threats. One individual told Mr. D something like "I know you're crazier than I am, and you might just do it."

Much of the treatment of Mr. D has been described in parts of other chapters and is summarized below. Mr. D was unable to follow, or uninterested in following, the sort of complex mini model shown in Figures 13.16, 13.17 and 13.18. The first two of these depict his general stance in response to many social situations. The last depicts a specific episode when his wife had a miscarriage. He only occasionally participated in development of such models and responded best to the simplest—such as shown in Figure 13.16. The treatment procedure that appeared to have the greatest impact on Mr. D was the training in autonomic control during stress interviews and the extension of this training into real-life settings by way of a simple recipe (described in detail in Chapter 3). Mr. D learned to detect high levels, and shifts in the level, of his emotional fire in the boiler. He was able to use this learning to almost always respond effectively to the following command: "When you notice the fire in the boiler say, 'I'm upset,' and then quickly start using your relaxation response to lower the fire in the boiler." His frequent rehearsal of this simple formula led to changes in his behavior outside the treatment setting and laid the foundation for the development of a new working self-concept, with attendant changes in expectancies and dispositions, and with occasional adaptive internal dialogue.

An important feature of Mr. D's treatment was a review and discussion, following each session, of the graph of autonomic function during the session. He became very accurate at perceiving shifts in his autonomic arousal and became justifiably proud of his ability. He would often take several copies of the graphs home with him to show other people.

The status of Mr. D as of late 1987 was dramatically changed since the end of the first two years of our work with him; his status in 1987 is shown in Figure 13.19. His wife had left him and he had a new live-in girlfriend whom he later married and divorced after having two children with her. He was no longer in touch with his stepdaughter or his two sons, and although he missed them, he said, "Maybe it's for the best that they get a new start." Mr. D was employed part-time as a laborer, but was noting persistent memory problems. His family was concerned with a continuing weight loss (he weighed 135 pounds) and apparent sadness (which he denied to us). They also noted that he had not expressed any anger in the previous nine months and had made no threats since April 30, 1986 (a year-and-a-half prior to the moment at which I wrote the account in the 1989 book).

For Mr. D we can identify no specific instance of the operation of negative reinforcement prior to the onset of his violent behavior. Therefore we must assume that the head injury in Vietnam had much to do with his present status. Of the first four clients presented in this chapter, Mr. D was least likely to profit from considering mini models and theories regarding his own personality. However, his relatively high level of intellectual function in some areas, and his development of skill at controlling autonomic responses to previously anger-provoking situations, permitted us to use many of the same treatment procedures that we employed with the other three men.

I am sorry to report that since 1987 Mr. D has shown considerable psychometric decline. The decline may be secondary to his electrocution in Vietnam in 1968, or to early onset of an Alzheimer's-like disorder (there is a family history of Alzheimer's and a CAT scan in the early 1990s indicated the presence of remarkable signs of premature aging). Although he has been in occasional legal trouble, it is my understanding that he has not resumed the violent behavior patterns that he showed during the early months of his work with me. He has had two brief admissions to our inpatient unit between 1987 and 1996. Both admissions seemed to have been triggered by psychosocial stressors. He spoke of feeling very depressed and said he was considering suicide. I have not been able to follow him up for the past 9 years.

Case Histories, Treatment Details, and Long-Term Follow-up   215

Figure 13.15. *Pre-treatment flow diagram for Mr. D.*

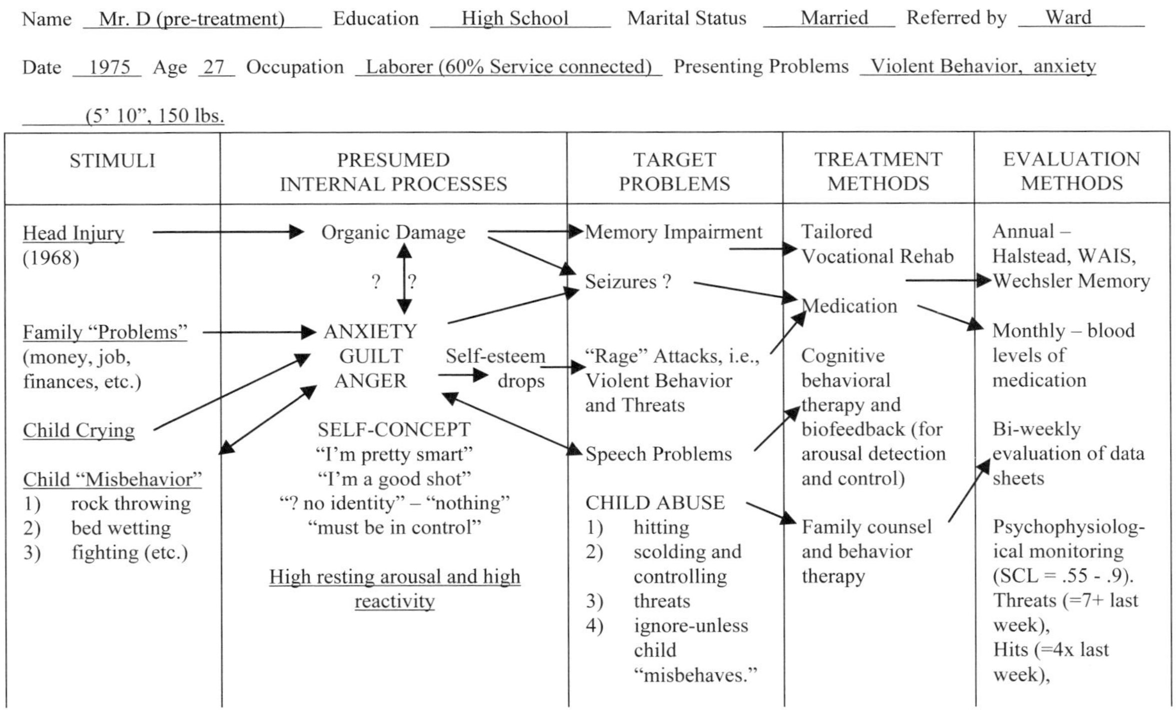

Name Mr. D (pre-treatment)   Education High School   Marital Status Married   Referred by Ward

Date 1975   Age 27   Occupation Laborer (60% Service connected)   Presenting Problems Violent Behavior, anxiety

(5' 10", 150 lbs.)

STIMULI	PRESUMED INTERNAL PROCESSES	TARGET PROBLEMS	TREATMENT METHODS	EVALUATION METHODS
Head Injury (1968)	Organic Damage	Memory Impairment	Tailored Vocational Rehab	Annual – Halstead, WAIS, Wechsler Memory
	? ↔ ?	Seizures ?	Medication	Monthly – blood levels of medication
Family "Problems" (money, job, finances, etc.)	ANXIETY GUILT ANGER Self-esteem drops	"Rage" Attacks, i.e., Violent Behavior and Threats	Cognitive behavioral therapy and biofeedback (for arousal detection and control)	Bi-weekly evaluation of data sheets
Child Crying	SELF-CONCEPT "I'm pretty smart" "I'm a good shot" "? no identity" – "nothing" "must be in control"	Speech Problems	Family counsel and behavior therapy	Psychophysiological monitoring (SCL = .55 - .9). Threats (=7+ last week), Hits (=4x last week),
Child "Misbehavior" 1) rock throwing 2) bed wetting 3) fighting (etc.)	High resting arousal and high reactivity	CHILD ABUSE 1) hitting 2) scolding and controlling threats 3) threats 4) ignore-unless child "misbehaves."		

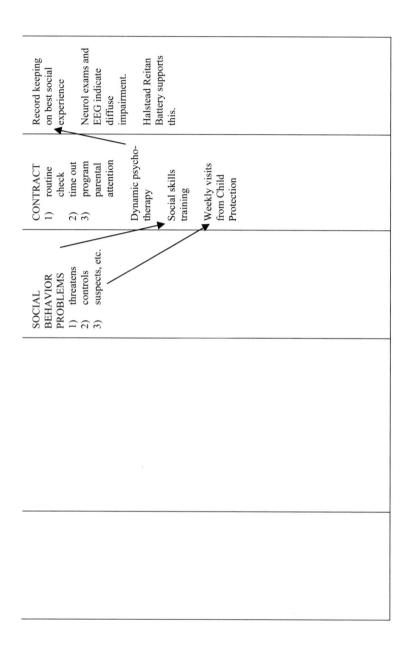

SOCIAL
BEHAVIOR
PROBLEMS
1) threatens
2) controls
3) suspects, etc.

CONTRACT
1) routine
   check
2) time out
   program
3) parental
   attention

Dynamic psycho-therapy

Social skills training

Weekly visits from Child Protection

Record keeping on best social experience

Neurol exams and EEG indicate diffuse impairment.

Halstead Reitan Battery supports this.

Figure 13.16. *Prototypical ABC sequence when Mr. D yells, threatens and/or hits.*

Antecedents	Behaviors	Consequences (short term)	
Someone behaves so as to cause client to have the (expected) perception that he is being ignored or otherwise belittled.	Yell, Threaten and/or Hit	Opponent Attends, Responds Retreats or Otherwise Submits.	Society and/or Opponent actively avoids or otherwise isolates client.
Mr. D.			

Figure 13.17. *Mr. D's general stance in social situations and our plans for treatment and assessment (including the sequence shown in Figures 13.16 and 13.18).*

Name ___Mr. D___ Education ___High School___ Marital Status ___Married___ Referred by ___Ward___

Date ___1975___ Age ___27___ Occupation ___Laborer (60% Service connected)___ Presenting Problems ___Violent Behavior, anxiety___

(5' 10", 150 lbs.)

STIMULI	PRESUMED INTERNAL PROCESSES	TARGET PROBLEMS	TREATMENT METHODS	EVALUATION METHODS
Someone acts so as to give client the perception of being ignored or otherwise belittled.	Expects people to be rude, (i.e., low self-esteem and low trust). Perceptual Processing Lowered Self-Esteem Self-Concept Memories and Fears of 1. being a victim; 2. being humiliated; 3. loss of control; Fears "Anger"	THREATEN, YELL AND/OR HIT	1. Relaxation Training 2. Biofeedback 3. Cognitive behavior therapy 4. Role playing and biofeedback 5. Homework assignments (e.g., Q Calm, say "I'm upset"; practice	Record keeping – most severe anger episode each day -best experience of the day Stress Profiles a) general/ standardized b) individualized Self-esteem measures Locus of Control measures

apologizing; help someone without "pay"; tell them it's because it makes you feel good.)

Memories of relief (via "identification with the aggressor") i.e., via behavioral outburst

DISPOSED TO DO IT AGAIN, i.e., "ALWAYS READY"

HIGH FIRE IN THE BOILER

Figure 13.18. *Multilevel ABC diagram of Mr. D's "problem in the hospital" when his wife had a miscarriage (a specific example of the generalizations shown in Figures 13.16 and 13.17).*

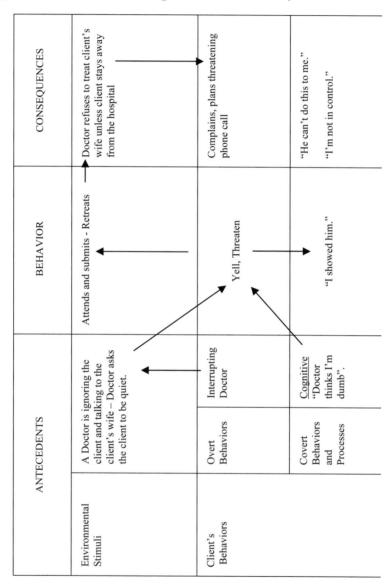

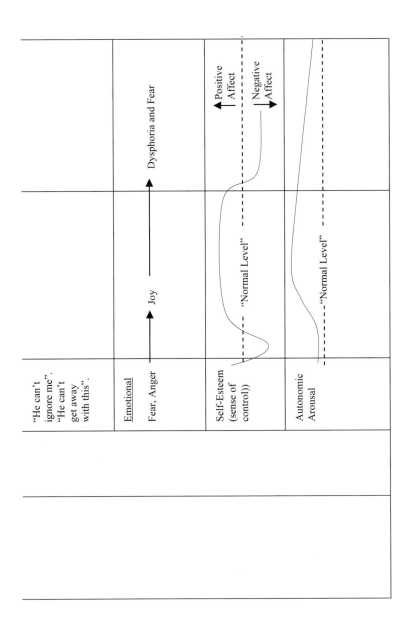

Figure 13.19. *Post-treatment flow diagram for Mr. D.*

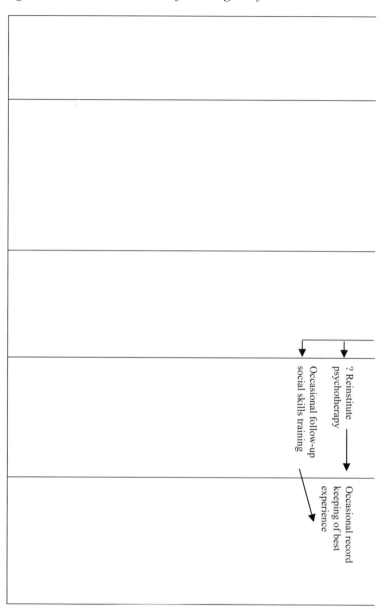

Name Mr. D (post-treatment)   Education High School   Marital Status Divorce: living with a woman   Referred by Ward
Date 1987 Age 39 Occupation Laborer (Disabled) (60% Service-connected) Presenting Problems Violent behavior, anxiety
(5' 10"; 135 lbs.)

STIMULI	PRESUMED INTERNAL PROCESSES	TARGET PROBLEMS	TREATMENT METHODS	EVALUATION METHODS
Head Injury (1968)	Organic Damage	Memory Impairment	Ongoing tailored vocational rehab	Job performance
Family "Problems" (money, job, finances, etc.)	? ? ANXIETY GUILT ANGER	Seizures (under control)	Medication	Occasional blood levels of medication
	SELF-CONCEPT "I'm getting by" "I believe in Jesus" "I've got a good woman" "I miss the kids"	? Thoughts of doing violence	Follow-up sessions biofeedback (for arousal detection and control)	Occasional Wechsler Memory Test
		Speech Problems		
		Depression? Weight loss?	Occasional follow-up family counsel and behavior therapy and cognitive behavior therapy	
		Social Behavior Problems 1) withdraws 2) controls 3) suspects, etc.		

Treatment Adaptations

We have worked with a number of clients who have been unable to profit from full application of the general method for treatment. For these clients, we adapt our overall method, or we may employ only one technique out of the array. For example, the one-sentence rationale used with Mr. D has been a helpful core intervention with some very difficult organically impaired individuals. I will now present excerpts of the treatment records of two violent clients for whom we have substantially adapted the general method, and then review the case of Ms. E, for whom I applied directly the personality theory I outlined earlier in the book.

Mr. G

Mr. G began treatment with me in 1983, when he was 33 years old. I worked with him for 20 sessions spread over three years. He had experienced a severe head injury while he was in the service. He had been a very involved abuser of many substances, and he had a family history of severe alcoholism (father), schizophrenia and Alzheimer's disorder (mother). It was clear that he was severely impaired, and that his greatest impairment was shown in noisy or confusing situations. In fact, my work with him gave remarkably vivid examples of the general concept of "noise" in a system, and the subtleties of individual differences in strengths and weaknesses resulting from organic impairment.

As far as I could determine, the injuries sustained by Mr. G, from being hit with an iron pipe in the forehead and sustaining a fractured skull, were very similar to those of Mr. K, the next patient to be described. Their neuropsychological testing results, neurological exams and EEG findings were quite similar. However, Mr. G showed remarkable differences in performance that varied with "noise," while Mr. K showed similarly amazing differences in performance that varied with time of day.

Evidence of Mr. G's susceptibility to "noise" was obtained in several ways. I tested him with the Wisconsin Card Sort test when he was in a quiet and familiar room with me, after he had come to know and trust me. He performed at the normal level (error rate of 23 percent) in that situation. On a subsequent day, in the same room, with me alone, I tested him with the Wisconsin again. This time I added white noise (radio static at a mildly noxious level) his error rate rose to the profoundly impaired level (error rate of 50 percent).

On the digit span test from the Wechsler Memory Scale he performed within the normal range when it was quiet. Subsequent testing was done with alternate forms of the digit span test. I was somewhat surprised to find that he also performed within the normal level in the presence of the same white noise that had impaired his performance on the Wisconsin. However, his digit span performance dropped far below the normal level when I added a different sort of "noise" by bringing into our familiar and quiet room two of my co-workers, who were relative strangers to Mr. G.

These observations led me to carefully interview his outpatient caretakers and the personnel on our psychiatry ward, where he had been occasionally housed. From these interviews it became clear that he did not show any violent behavior when he was in a quiet, familiar, and structured environment. Accordingly I made a specific set of behavioral management proposals (shown below). These proposals have been followed fairly closely by his caregivers, and I understand that he has not shown any violent behavior since I last saw him. Also, it has not been necessary to hospitalize him since our last session.

The following is a slightly abridged copy of the final report for Mr. G.

Psychology Section (116B) Patient Report: Mr. G

Date: 1/86 Therapist: John A. Corson, Ph.D.

ASSESSMENT

Extensive assessment (described elsewhere) indicates diffuse organic impairment—somewhat more impairment in frontal lobes than elsewhere—considerable memory impairment—and near—or above—normal performance in some areas (e.g., Verbal IQ as indexed by Ammons Quick Test of Intelligence). His performance on some standard neuropsychological tests indicates impairment unless he is in a quiet and familiar environment—and then he can perform within the normal range. For example, on the Wisconsin Card Sort Test—which is a standard tool for assessing frontal lobe impairment, addition of a white noise (radio static—at a mildly noxious level) raises his error rate from 23% (normal) to 50% (profoundly impaired). On the Digit Span Test of the

Wechsler Memory Scale he was not influenced by white noise, but when two relative strangers came into the room during testing his score dropped (from 9 to 6). On another test—the Category Test from the Halstead Reitan Battery—he performed in the severely impaired range unless he was asked to reconsider the rules, and heard the instructions reiterated when he expressed confusion or began to respond randomly (his Categories performance and its implications are discussed in detail elsewhere). The basic point here is that he is impaired—and his greatest impairment is shown in distracting, confusing, unfamiliar or "noisy" situations. If he can remain calm, work in a quiet, familiar, and structured environment, with occasional prompts regarding rules and objectives, he should do quite well.

Conclusions from Psychometric and Behavioral Observations since 9/19/83:

Mr. G shows psychometric and behavioral signs of impairment that are made much worse whenever some form of social stimulation (e.g., strange people, demands, humiliation) is combined with a high noise level in the environment and/or confusion regarding what is expected of Mr. G ("cognitive noise"). These conditions rapidly lead to a high arousal state which Mr. G is often unable to manage in an adaptive manner.

(Note on arousal state: During white noise and psychological testing Mr. G's skin conductance level went from 7 micro mho—normal level—to 50 micro mho—a level we rarely have seen in anyone. At the end of the session, his hands were soaking wet.)

BEHAVIORAL MANAGEMENT PROPOSAL

As indicated above, Mr. G should be placed in a quiet, structured, and supportive environment—where staff personnel are trained to provide prompts regarding rules and objectives. (Specific vocational training suggestions are provided elsewhere—e.g., see report of 11/85.) Specific behavioral management procedures are as follows:

I. The Quick Calming Response

Mr. G has been asked to practice the quick calming response: "Practice calming down for two breaths—breathe a little deeper than usual; on the outbreath think the word 'calm' and smile to yourself, breathe in again—a little more deeply than usual—on the outbreath say the word 'calm' to yourself and smile to yourself."

He has been asked to practice this whenever he hears his watch "beep" (every 1/2 hour), whenever he hears a telephone ring, whenever he looks at a watch or a clock, and whenever he goes to the bathroom. This will result in more than a dozen practice episodes per day, and will keep the calming response ready for use if he gets upset. **He should be reminded of this daily.**

II. The Anger/Frustration/Confusion Management Strategy

In response to feelings of anger or frustration or confusion, Mr. G has been trained to use the general strategy of (1) saying (quietly) "I'm upset" and then (2) doing the quick calming response. Following the announcement of his being upset and the quick calming response (taking about 20 seconds) he is to (3) quietly problem solve with the most appropriate person(s). **He should he reminded of this daily.**

III. The Role-Playing Strategy

Whenever Mr. G shows signs of being upset, a role-playing session should be conducted—along with a reminder that he must be responsible for his self-control. In the role-playing session (2-5 minutes), a staff person should reenact the problematic situation with Mr. G and remind him of the quick calming/anger management strategies, and then show him one or two calmer and more adaptive ways of coping with the same situation. (While Mr. G was at the VA Hospital in 1984, we found that it was necessary to repeat such role playing and advice [involving quick calming and anger management strategy] at least three times after each episode of upset;

when he was here in 1985, he did not become upset to the extent of being disruptive.)

Mr. K

Mr. K was not physically violent, but was verbally belligerent. For him, we used a variation of the above procedure.

The following is a brief description of Mr. K: He began treatment with me in the early '80s when he was 30 years old. At the time of referral he already had been subjected to a complete neurological examination and clear evidence of head injury had been established. Psychological testing in a quiet environment showed that Mr. K, like Mr. G, retained high average verbal intelligence as tested by the Ammons Quick Test, while showing a variety of other difficulties (motor coordination, concentration, and memory). His intellectual performance, as far as we could tell, was not influenced by the sorts of "noise" that had degraded the performance of Mr. G. After several sessions, and several conversations with his supervisors and his significant other, we began testing Mr. K's eye-hand coordination at various times of the day. His deterioration over the course of a day is described below. It is important to note that he also became more irritable and less rational during the late afternoon and evening.

Mr. K was extremely belligerent verbally, but did not have a significant history of physically violent behavior. He is a small man with a very large vocabulary and a loud voice. In fact, the problem that led to the head injuries was that a bit of alcohol consumption produced a dramatic escalation in his verbal belligerence. He went out drinking when he was a 20-year-old soldier. After being arrested for drunkenness and disorderly conduct he was put into a jail cell with other men. Apparently, his verbal belligerence led to a severe beating by one of the other men in the cell. Our problem was to work with him and his employer on a rehabilitation and behavior management program that would help him make use of his "wise mind" (at one point during this work he said "I need to use my wise mind instead of my wise mouth"). Follow-up indicates that he has done quite well, and holds down a relatively low stress part-time job that requires his presence early in the day, avoiding the late afternoon and evening hours. I understand that he is now married and has lived at the same residence for several years.

The following is a combination of several reports we have completed on Mr. K.

Psychology Section (116B) Patient Report: Mr. K

Date: 8/86 Therapist: John A. Corson, Ph.D.

ASSESSMENT

Extensive assessment (described elsewhere) indicates organic impairment that apparently resulted from injuries received in 1972.

Organic Impairment—Performance Changes With Time of Day:

Mr. K retains considerable ability in some areas (e.g., vocabulary) but has considerable difficulty in other areas (e.g., motor coordination, concentration, and memory). Over the last few months, we have determined that his problems get worse in the late afternoon and evening. We used a test of eye-hand coordination that showed that Mr. K performs at approximately 80% of the normal level before 2 P.M. and performs at between 20 and 40% of the normal level after 5 P.M.

TREATMENT PLAN

Behavior That Interferes With Performance in the Workplace—An Extinction Plan:

I have had extensive discussions with Mr. K's employer and supervisor. They have informed me that he has managed to be a good employee "as long as he keeps his mouth under control." We developed a plan with Mr. H of vocational rehabilitation and presented it to Mr. K's employer. The plan is spelled out in the following paragraph:

Mr. K's employer and co-workers have noted that Mr. K has a tendency to argue and talk too much and/or talk about the wrong things. We have developed an "extinction" procedure which involves explaining to Mr. K the difficulty regarding arguing too much/talking too much/talking about the wrong things/"beating a dead horse," etc., and we made an agreement with Mr. K. This agreement—presented by Mr. K's supervisor (with the knowledge and consent of Mr. K)—was phrased as follows: "In the past we have had trouble with your arguing or talking too much, or harping on things. So that we can work together effectively we need to make a new arrangement. I propose whenever I feel that you are talking too much, arguing too much, harping, or otherwise being unproductive in conversation I will raise my hand and you must stop. The other side of this coin is that you can do the same to me. If you feel that I am talking too much, or harping on something that you already understand you can raise your hand and I will stop. If either of us fails to stop at the sign of the raised hand the other one should simply walk away. If we can understand this as a constructive agreement, entered into by two adults we should be able to make this work. This is a way of me teaching you about what irritates other people. You have had trouble with this in the past, and I am going to do my best to help you improve so that I, and other people, will be able to get along with you more easily.

Results of the Extinction Procedure—A New Two-Part Plan:

The above procedure worked for a while, but eventually the employer complained that "the stop signal only stops him temporarily—and he always seems to have an excuse to start up again right away." On the basis of this information we developed a new two-part procedure that combined the stop signal with a quick relaxation exercise (which Mr. K had learned earlier). The instructions to Mr. K were as follows:

To Mr. K from Dr. Corson:

When you and I met this morning we discussed some problems and put together a new program. This letter summarizes our discussion and plan—please use it as a reminder.

First, you and I agreed that it is important for you to maintain the attitude that you and your employer are working together on a rehabilitation program.

This program is designed to help you cope with your organic and behavioral problems to the extent that you will be able to stay in the workforce. You and I have worked for a long time on a relaxation strategy (the quick calming response) that you must now remember to use whenever you see the "stop signal." You have a well-practiced relaxation response that will help you keep from quickly starting up again. We also expect that the quick calming response will keep you from becoming overly upset about minor hassles at work.

Remember that whenever you receive the "stop signal" (the raised hand) you must use the quick calming response—focus on your breathing—take a deeper than normal breath and breathe out through your nose—smile calmly to yourself. Let a warm comfortable sensation develop in your hands and stomach. Do it again. Each breath takes about ten seconds; the whole exercise takes about 20 seconds. At the end of this quick calming response notice how much better you feel.

Remember that you must practice the quick calming response at times other than when you see the "stop signal." You should be doing it at least 12 times a day. To help yourself to get enough practice you should do the quick calming response each time you look at a watch or a clock, each time you enter a bathroom, and each time you hear a telephone ring.

As you consistently practice the quick calming response (at least 12 times a day) you will notice that the calmness you feel during the response will last longer and longer. You will notice that you are able to calm down more quickly after you see the "stop signal." You will also notice that you will be able to use the quick calming response to quiet yourself down quickly after feeling tension and stress. Remember—practice makes perfect; practice 12 times a day on your own; use the quick calming response whenever you see the stop signal; use the quick calming response whenever you feel tension or stress coming on.

Mr. G, Mr. K and Mr. D had all experienced head injuries that were documentable by neuropsychological testing and neurological examination, as well as by EEG. Mr. G and Mr. K did not seem to profit as much from the biofeedback training as had Mr. D, but they did make some gains, at least in terms of developing a sense of control over themselves in response to this training.

Ms. E

Another seemingly intractable case involved a severely troubled and extremely violent young woman. Ms. E had been able to get through two years at a university even though she had begun to show episodic periods of psychosis in her early teenage years.

These episodes of psychotic behavior included inflicting severe injuries on herself and on others. At the time of my involvement in this case, Ms. E was incarcerated in the secure psychiatric unit of a maximum-security facility. I did not visit with the woman, but discussed her history and status with two senior psychiatrists who knew her case well. I made the following set of suggestions, which I understand led to improvement in her behavior. Ms. E was able to return to an open ward in a state hospital, and seven months after this program was implemented she was able to spend the weekend with her family. An abridged version of my consultation report follows:

Date: 2/87

To. Dr. W

From: John A. Corson, Ph.D.

Re: Consultation regarding Ms. E, currently housed at Secure Psychiatric Unit

From conversations with Drs. X and Y, I have learned some details of Ms. E's history, medical and psychiatric status, current behavior, and prospects.

I spoke with Dr. X on 2/5/87, and offered the following observations and suggestions:

1. Return of Ms. E to the State Hospital seems advisable even though future violent behavior seems quite likely;

2. An assessment/compilation of activities and specific Staff people she has previously shown signs of enjoying (e.g., those she has chosen to spend time with) should be put together;

3. On the basis of this assessment, a long-term management program might be put together along the following lines:

> A. Ms. E should be given reliable clock-contingent attention from someone (preferably someone she seems to enjoy) on each shift (this could be a 10-minute conversation at every hour—a timer should be set so this is not omitted at any time during the day and evening shifts);
>
> B. Whenever possible she should be given opportunity to engage in some enjoyable activity—and she should be given positive attention for doing these activities (in other words, give her opportunities to do good things, and show her some enthusiasm when she is observed doing good things);
>
> C. Whenever she misbehaves, she should be given only the level of perfunctory attention necessary to protect her and others, while clearly informing her of the category of unacceptable behavior that has occurred, and why it is unacceptable, and what a specific appropriate alternative behavior might be. These should not be occasions for extra attention and/or emotionally loaded interactions—her needs for interaction and attention should be satisfied by aspects A and B.

The most important key to this program is aspect 3A. If this is reliably provided, the other aspects should be relatively easy to implement. From my understanding of Ms. E's history and prior treatment, the idea that any additional program features should be aimed at punishing Ms. E, or at teaching her by way of punishment (physical or verbal) not to hurt herself or others, should be abandoned.

This total program should be continued systematically for the duration of her stay at the State Hospital. Any additional rehabilitative or therapeutic features should be seen as add-on features.

Please let me know if you have any questions or observations regarding these suggestions.

From reading the report on Ms. E, you may have recognized some of the principles spelled out in earlier chapters. In particular, I made use of the following ideas:

(1) Individuals are addicted to attention;

(2) Attention must be dissociated from episodes of negative behavior, and, preferably, must also become independent of specific episodes of positive behavior. That is, attention must become automatic and reliable, and some caution must be taken to make sure that the attention does not come so close in time to a particular episode of negative behavior that it appears to be contingent on that behavior;

(3) Episodes of misbehavior must be dealt with so as to insure safety, but only with application of the minimum necessary perfunctory attention;

(4) The attention given for misbehavior must be informationally strong—it must clearly specify the category of unacceptable behavior that has occurred;

(5) The environment must be structured so as to allow the client maximum opportunity to indulge in enjoyable activities that are appropriate to normal adults of their age.

Ms. E could not be adequately followed up for several reasons. I served only as a consultant to two of my colleagues who were senior psychiatrists at the institution where she was housed. Both psychiatrists retired in the early 1990s, and have had no further interaction with her. However, it appears that the program worked fairly well, even though she had been hospitalized several times between the initiation of our program and the early 1990s. After initiation of the program, she was able to re-enter the State Hospital population, and, up to the point that my friends retired, she had not been in restraints, nor had she been physically violent. Also, we have been able to determine that she eventually completed her college education.

Some Thoughts on Long-Term Follow-up

As I read through what I have just written I am reminded of one of my favorite books, *Lives in Progress* by R. W. White (1952). This book describes many years in the lives of three people, a housewife/social worker, a male physician, and a businessman. White led the reader to know each of these three individuals, and to appreciate their complexity and depth, and the vast differences between them. White's book had a lot to do with my decision to attend carefully to individual differences. However, when I compare these three rather normal, somewhat privileged people to my clients, I realize more clearly than ever that most of the clients I deal with have had severely limited opportunities, and many of them have lived lives of chaos and trauma.

14: Theoretical Perspectives and Practical Advice

Now I invite you to reflect on all of the foregoing material and to consider a developmental theory of violent behavior. Then I offer answers to two perennial questions.

Self-Concept and Violent Behavior

During the initial interview, or in early treatment sessions, almost all 62 of the clients I described in 1989, and the vast majority of the violent clients I have interviewed since then, reported some form of traumatic experience early in life. This usually involved chronic physical abuse at the hands of parents, foster parents, or other caretakers. This abuse was usually accompanied by negative labels (such as coward or liar) and led to humiliation, low self-esteem, and assorted negative expectancies regarding both self and others. A very frequent feature of the history, usually between the ages of 9 and 15, was an episode in which the client struck back at the tormentor(s) with such vigor that the torment was ended (at least temporarily).

On the basis of these observations I developed a variation on the developmental sequence[1] presented in Chapter 4; this variation

---

[1] Many other theories have been offered to explain developmental influences, which might lead to violent adult behavior; a good summary is provided by Hays et al. (1981). As far as I know, no one since then has proposed a fundamentally new explanation.

is shown in Figures 14.1 and 14.2. It seems likely that the first few weeks of most infants' lives have a similar course to that shown in Chapter 4.

Parental attention (PA) becomes a powerful conditioned incentive stimulus, and the process of addicting (again I am using this word intentionally) the child to parental attention begins. However, at the stage depicted by Figure 4.5 in Chapter 4, clear difficulties may begin to occur. Specifically, the child may learn that he or she is "not OK." As shown in Figure 4.7 of Chapter 4, this self-labeling eventually becomes independent of behavior. The figures here characterize some important aspects of the development of our typical violent client. In such a client, parental attention is typically negative, with positive attention having more to do with the parents' moods than with the child's behavior. Very early severe beatings often occur, accompanied by negative labeling of the child. In addition to the beatings, prolonged periods of torment, which may involve restriction, or even incarceration of the child in dark closets or trunks can occur. The parent is responding to the child's crying and other behaviors as if they were personal insults to which the parent must respond.

In reviewing the case histories, I am reminded of Alice Miller's book *For Your Own Good* (1984), in which the causes of violence are traced to an unequal power struggle between the parent and child. The parent justifies abuse by saying it is "for the good of the child," "an essential part of child-rearing." An important idea in Miller's book is the idea that the tendency to be abusive is passed from one generation to the next generation: "For parents' motives are the same today as they were then; in beating their children they are struggling to regain the power they once lost to their own parents" (page 16). It is worth noting that I have repeatedly seen clients who justify their own severe physical punishment of their children with such statements as "it was good enough for me" or "spare the rod, spoil the child."

Eventually, as shown in Figure 14.1, the child grows larger and can retaliate effectively in response to an episode of torment. When retaliation is effective in terminating the torment, the mechanism of negative reinforcement (the termination of an aversive stimulus by a behavior leads to an increase in the future probability of that behavior) is mobilized. Subsequently, the child may tend to become violent in response to a slight hint of humiliation, a loss of self-esteem, or the like. In fact, this pivotal episode of negative reinforcement seems to galvanize a whole new working self-concept.

As discussed in Chapter 2, a possible self puts a particular working self into action. In this case, the possible self is the highly-salient, feared possible self of the tormented and cowering victim. The relationship between the feared self and the new working self is established by the sudden realization (which may not be conscious in the usual sense of the term) that there is a response in their repertoire (violent behavior) that has the guaranteed positive outcome of ending suffering.

Now, as Figure 14.2 shows, a transformation has occurred here from terrorized to terrorist, with appropriately-transformed expectancies and dispositions. The biopsychosocial patterns that are established by this transformation result in a self-perpetuating positive feedback loop. Now, any sign of a feared self, or in some clients even a feeling of upset or dysphoria, will put the working self-concept of the violent warrior into action. This suddenly shifts the dynamics in the system (see the system depicted in Figure 3.1 of Chapter 3) to select which expectancies are to be present and which dispositions are to be played out, and is the basis of the binary switch mode of behavior. The case histories help illustrate this.

From the above, one might conclude that these clients are all very large and strong, but this is not the case. Even very small people can develop in this manner. The control they exercise over many other people is based on their communicating that they will fight to the point of dying—or kill their opponent at the slightest provocation.

A few months ago one of my clients asked if he could borrow a copy of my 1989 book. I gave it to him on a Friday morning, and on the following Sunday evening he telephoned to tell me of his experiences in reading the book. He said everything was going along fine until he came to a part of the book that is very similar to what you have just been reading. He said he suddenly saw himself and experienced a new understanding of his predicament.

When my client told me about this experience I decided to put together a small document that summarizes the central point made here. That point is that a tormented child may eventually come to a moment when he decides to fight back. This is generally after he has grown larger and has a chance to retaliate effectively. When that retaliation is effective in terminating the torment, this mobilizes a powerful learning mechanism known as "negative reinforcement" (the termination of an aversive stimulus by a behavior leads to an increase in the future probability of that behavior). Subsequently this child, now grown larger, may tend to become violent in response to a

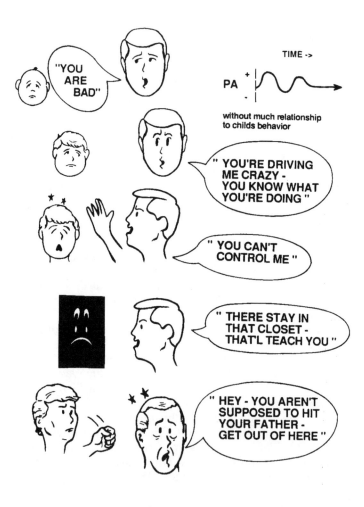

Figure 14.1. *Variation on the developmental sequence – 1.*

" I'M ALWAYS READY"

(Expectancy)

"I'M A WARRIOR"

(Disposition)

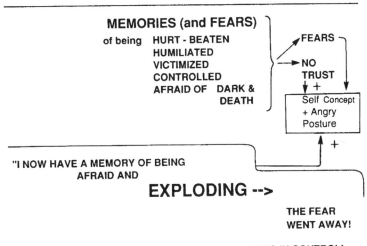

MEMORIES (and FEARS)

of being   HURT - BEATEN
HUMILIATED
VICTIMIZED
CONTROLLED
AFRAID OF   DARK &
DEATH

FEARS

NO
TRUST
+

Self Concept
+ Angry
Posture

+

"I NOW HAVE A MEMORY OF BEING
AFRAID AND

EXPLODING -->

THE FEAR
WENT AWAY!

I WAS IN CONTROL!

I WAS A HERO!   THE CRITICS APPLAUDED!

NOW I'M READY - NO ONE MESSES WITH ME . . . ."

(ie - "I'M BAD - A JUNK YARD DOG")

Figure 14.2. *Variation on the developmental sequence – 2.*

hint of disrespect, humiliation, a loss of self-esteem, or the like. In this small document I pointed out that some of my clients did not experience abuse from their parents, but something else has gone on, perhaps on the playground, or the street, or in boot camp, or in combat, that brought them to the point where they also have developed the readily available self of the violent warrior.

Interestingly, when I gave this little document to my solution-oriented group (which is also, depending on which day you look at it, a relapse prevention, crisis management, stress and anger management, or support group) two-thirds of the people present (6 of the 9 attending on that day; all of those attending were Vietnam combat veterans) said they had beaten up their father or stepfather shortly after returning from Vietnam. It is worth noting that several of my total sample of clients had hit their father or stepfather before entering the military, but many more did so after returning from the military. It is also worth noting that many of these violent adults are very intelligent, and some have very high levels of education. It does not seem to matter how intelligent or how well-educated they are, the legacy of the experience of successfully standing up to a tormentor is that a readily available self is very likely to be a violent warrior.

Response to the Violent Person

In these final paragraphs, I will consider two questions that people invariably ask when I make presentations on the subject of violent behavior:

(1)   How do you deal with individuals who are threatening to do violence to others?
(2)   How do you deal with individuals who are threatening to do violence to you?

When Someone Threatens Others

Much has been written on this topic. What I can add will primarily reinforce what I have found to be valuable in the published literature and folklore. When I am faced with a client threatening to do violence to someone else, my stance is to attempt to validate their feelings of upset, and to attend to the disruptions in self-concept so as to make them feel less alone, and perhaps to feel somewhat more "understood." With many clients part of this task involves determining details of the stressful stimulus or—as some of my combat veteran clients have called it—the incoming fire. We can imagine the sequence from the incoming fire to the outgoing fire to be a linear temporal sequence. I work to draw a curtain, or barrier between the temporal point of sensing a feeling of upset and disruption in self-concept, on the one hand, and, on the other, the point of feeling anger, and/or the planning of retaliatory violent behavior. The following depicts this temporal sequence:

(1) Stimulus

⇓

(2) Upset and Drop in Self-Esteem

⇓

(3) Anger

⇓

(4) Violent Behavior

I have frequently shared such a diagram with clients who are threatening to do violence.

About 25 years ago I heard an address by a psychiatrist who was experienced in dealing with violent individuals. One of his admonitions was along the lines of "get on the same side of the fence as the patient with regard to the stimulus issues, but avoid validating the response plans."

Of course, if the client continues with the plan to do violence, I discuss and, if necessary, initiate appropriate and legally mandated protective steps.

When Someone Threatens You

I have been directly threatened a few dozen times. Thus far I have not been attacked. My strategy is to face directly toward the threatening individual without changing posture dramatically. I particularly refrain from standing up while the client is seated. If he stands, I may stay seated. I am careful to think about managing the vertical and horizontal space between us. I make it clear to the client that I am going to listen patiently to what he or she has to say. I control my facial expression and eye contact to help the client perceive me as being neither threatened nor threatening. (I confess that I have several times taken off my glasses, in case the client suddenly kicks or punches me.)

Simply put, I work to present myself as an interested person trying to help an individual who is expressing a threatening working self-concept under highly stressful circumstances. I may be able to understand more clearly the forces involved in that working self-concept if I am careful to ask the right questions and make the right responses. I have continued to find that episodes of being threatened often provide me with an outstanding opportunity to move ahead in work of therapy.

15: Conclusions Regarding Work with Individual Violent Clients

We have covered much ground in this consideration of work with individual violent clients. You have been introduced to people, ideas, methods, and data, as well as to anecdotes and hunches. My objective here is to pull it all together, and to identify some remaining problems and possibilities.

Assessment and Treatment

Early in this book, I described a general strategy for developing a new personality theory for each client (Chapter 2). I said that the client and I must work consistently to update the theory so that we are aware of the particular working self-concept that is operating when the client is interacting with a particular stressor. I also said that I would attempt to redefine stressors for each new situation, and that the stress—or impact on the individual—would also need to be reconsidered in each new stressful situation. In other words, the three aspects of the biopsychosocial model (bio, psycho and social) must be considered carefully in each new situation; a change in one domain (say, a change in the bio domain, which is part and parcel of the stress response, or fire in the boiler) would be expected to influence variables in the other two domains (the psycho and the social domains).

Throughout the book, I have attempted to elaborate on methods of tracking shifts in self-concept and of monitoring variables in each of the three domains. The following is a review of the strategies I have described for keeping track of the assorted variables. As illustrated in Chapters 12 and 13, I put these strategies together in a format that enables me and the particular client to understand what is going on.

We assess the present working self-concept in several ways—primarily by the daily tracking of self-satisfaction and the situations that coincide with the highest and lowest levels of self-satisfaction (see Chapters 7 and 12). A second-order assessment strategy is the frequent review, in the context of the general flow diagram (Chapter 9), of the presumed internal processes and the assorted self-statements that apparently constitute the present working self-concept. I frequently review these self-statements with the client, and we use various strategies to help determine what the current list membership and rank order or weighting should be. (See, for example, Figure 13.18 in Chapter 13.)

When there is a particular identifiable stressor, I may draw a new flow diagram, with new self-referent terms, ordered and weighted to depict the working self-concept interacting with this particular stressor (as in Figure 13.14 of Chapter 13). As mentioned earlier, the stress response (fire in the boiler and central motive state), and the expectancies and dispositions attendant to the working self-concept, can often be elaborated in a telling manner when we are dealing with a particularly compelling stressful situation (as in Figure 13.14 of Chapter 13).

Sometimes I do this work in the context of a conversation, and I draw a flow diagram during the conversation in collaboration with the client (as in Figure 13.15 of Chapter 13). At other times, the multilevel ABC format, depicted in Table 1.1 of Chapter 1, is used to examine and display these various factors and their relationships (see also Figure 13.16 and 13.19 in Chapter 13). As I have so often mentioned, the client and I must collaborate closely if we are going to do our job well. Many times, the particular discussion of situation, psychological, biological, and self-concept variables is not interesting or helpful to a client. I will then create a special, or simplified, chart (as in Figure 13.16 of Chapter 13). In some sessions with almost all clients, the lights seem to come on and the client assumes the stance of the personal theorist. At these times, the client clearly sees a particular working self-concept as the superordinate variable in controlling the fire in the boiler, expectancies, and dispositions. For most clients, at some point in therapy such a realization leads to a quantum leap toward considering, and often toward trying out new ways of behaving. Sometimes this leads to new ways of being and new life-styles. When these leaps occur, all of the technical nuts and bolts that I have been describing seem to have been worthwhile.

Biofeedback

Since I have no control groups, I cannot prove that our clients are better off as a result of the particular set of strategies I've used—and I've not really proved that the addition of biofeedback had a helpful impact (see Chapter 12). I am forced to cite a set of less-than-optimal supports for my argument that the biofeedback has in fact been helpful:

(1)   No client improved while on the waiting list, for periods ranging from one week to three months.

(2)   Most clients had previously received many other therapies without achieving a reduction in their violent behavior.

(3)   Some clients (e.g., Mr. A) were difficult to communicate with prior to the introduction of biofeedback.

(4)   Some clients showed clear correlations of reduction in autonomic levels and reactivities, and durations of episodes of high arousal, with reductions in the level and frequency of their angry feelings and violent behavior.

(5)   Among the clients for whom we have data on the effects of biofeedback, we have some evidence (described in Chapter 12) that those who showed the most progress in reducing their autonomic levels and reactivities, and durations of episodes of high arousal also showed the greatest reductions in their violent behavior.

(6)   Most of our successful clients have offered testimony about how the biofeedback helped them.

Nevertheless, the relationship has not been proven in the way that it would have been if control groups had been used.[1]

---

[1] In this type of work, control groups (other than waiting list controls—and documented periods on other treatment) would be very difficult to organize in such a way that they meet the criteria set by most researchers. Also, there are important ethical considerations of not treating individuals who are at high risk of causing harm to self or others.

Violent Behavior

A more general remaining problem is the disturbing fact that a number of these clients may be still terrified and terrifying. Even in my most optimistic moments, I realize that at least some of these individuals will still suffer and will also cause much suffering for others. Their problems have not been completely solved.

There are many clients with whom I have not dared to sever ties completely, even though I have worked with them for many years, and even though most of them have not had even a minor episode of violent behavior over the last decade. The longest time I have gone without seeing most of these clients is three months, and in most cases our follow-up schedule is rigidly established, with appointments once every three months. Why do I continue to work with these men who have taken on new lifestyles and have hurt no one for years? Because I believe the available self of the warrior is still close at hand, and that the follow-up sessions are necessary to keep them practicing their new way of being. One of these clients, Mr. A, recently told me of things that at the very least illustrate the need for ongoing follow-up:

> *I am just as paranoid as I used to be. ...I used to get a lot of pleasure out of kicking ass. ...I just realize it's not worth it, and I keep my mouth shut whenever somebody tries to bother me. ...I've learned to mind my own business. ...It's a lot of work for me to stay like this. ...It's like my old self is just under the surface looking for an excuse to break out -even though life is much better now—I'm still just as paranoid as I used to be—but I'm less agitated.*

Another client told me in the late 1980s that he had an offer to "hit a guy" (this apparently means that he had an offer of money to kill another person); he said the payoff would be $3,000, but he did not intend to go through with it. He also informed me, however, that if he were "driven to the wall" by his financial problems, he might reconsider the offer.

Still another client who had been peaceful for many years described to me his urges to hurt a physician who had apparently not done a good job of treating his wife. He also described an episode of verbal expression of hostility in a supermarket with an Asian teenager who was employed packing groceries. My client refused to pay for the groceries that were touched by the teenager, and marched out announcing that he would never shop in the store again. When I think about this particular man (and about many of my other clients), I realize that he has a value system and expectancies and dispositions that are absolutely foreign to me. In my optimistic moments I think we can whittle away at these if we continue working together. In my more pessimistic moments, I think that I, or the client, will be dead long before much change is made in many of these domains.

Some clients fade away completely for years, usually changing addresses, and becoming impossible to contact. Frequently they reappear, in trouble, after a few years. Usually the trouble is not with violent behavior, but with depression, or an interaction of life stresses with physical illness. I find that after a few sessions over a few weeks, I can slowly decrease the scheduling to once every three months.

In 2006 I am not as close to many of my clients as I was in the 1970s and 1980s. While many more clients and much more group work have led to much less individual work, I am very fortunate that I had the opportunity to do intensive individual work. It enabled me to learn a great deal about how to do any sort of work with these clients.

Part Five

Self-Regulation Training with Other Populations

16: Working with Male Clients in Groups: An Overview

Since 1989, our ideas and methods for helping our clients, including our violent clients, have changed as a result of increasing numbers of referrals and the need to follow-up on the individual treatments of an increasing number of clients. At present, if a new violent client is to be worked with individually, the individual assessment and ongoing assessment strategies are similar to those described in Chapter 12. There are two exceptions: We most often begin with the group assessment format described in Chapter 8, and we do not routinely use the extensive and relatively formal psychophysiological assessment described in Chapter 12. A psychophysiological assessment is generally done in conjunction with the interview, but it is usually quite brief and much less structured. The data sheets shown in Chapter 12 are still used, as is the record-keeping form shown in Chapter 12. If I am working individually with a violent client, I will most often use compressed versions of phases 2 and 3 described in Chapter 12. The results of such work continue to show the positive outcomes described in Chapter 12, with the physiological results continuing to show the same level of reduction in resting baseline.

The violent clients who have completed individual treatment are followed up in two settings. The first is an ongoing weekly support group for very long-term clients, most of whom were violent at the time of referral. The majority of these clients have previously been treated individually, using the methods described in Chapter 12. Group sessions are two hours long, with minimal psychoeducational content, the focus being on support, relapse prevention, and crisis management with a solution oriented approach.

The second setting is a weekly, 90-minute group program that is modeled loosely after Linehan's work (1993). Violent clients are included in this group, along with clients who have a wide variety of diagnoses, but no history of violent behavior. This group is known as "the stress and anger management group" or "the dialectical behavior therapy (DBT) group." I will come back to this group in the next chapter. Now we will consider some important issues that have become clear to me since I began spending more time with groups.

Group Work with Males in Northern New England

As I consider the challenges suggested by the phrase "psychology in the trenches," I am confronted with the realization that the trenches we work in are probably quite different from those where many other psychologists do their work. The northern New England males we work with are typically men of few words. Data from group testing indicate that our sample has a higher verbal intelligence than the national average, but has rapid access to fewer words and is likely to be alexithymic (without words for emotions). As will be described in subsequent chapters, some standardized (and even manualised) treatment formats have had to be modified in order to be useful with this sample. Finally, it is possible that some of the new formats I describe may be unnecessarily detailed, and more concrete and repetitive than is needed with some other populations.

Some time ago I heard about a study carried out in the greater Boston area comparing men and women who sought mental health treatment. The data indicated that the women sought treatment at an earlier age than men, and when their suffering had been going on for a shorter time than was the case for the men. It was also observed that the women used a richer vocabulary to describe their psychological and emotional difficulties than did the men. Since that time, a great deal has been published on important considerations for working with men in the psychotherapeutic endeavor (Mahalik, Good and Englar-Carlson, 2003). Excellent summaries have been written by Cochran and Rabinowitz (2002, 2003).

Cochran and Rabinowitz (2002) mention difficulties males have with gender role conflict, depression, anxiety, low self-esteem, and negative attitudes toward help seeking. The importance of considering the effects of masculine socialization on men is emphasized. While primarily focusing on individual therapy, they emphasize the importance of using certain specific strategies with men early in therapy. They recommend the use of "action oriented language, shared storytelling, positive connotation of the client's masculine behavior" and "respect for defenses designed to moderate emotional vulnerability." These considerations may be even more important when men are treated in groups. The concept "the culture of cruelty" that is experienced in groups of adolescent boys (Kindlon and Thompson, 1999) is important here.

In our groups we frequently see the culture of cruelty rear its head among adult clients. In individual sessions we can cope with the macho tradition and the pressures to be a "real man," but there is something about the group setting that makes these difficulties more powerful. There seems to be a demand characteristic which leads many of our group members to posture in manners that indicate they are very tough and very quick to pass judgment, that they are doing quite well already and don't need any help. We have called this the "machismo factor"; this factor goes hand-in-hand with an aggressive attributional style, and a history of frequent violent behavior (see McNiel, Eisner and Binder, 2003). These behaviors present difficulties the first time a group meets, and often at the beginning of subsequent group sessions. We have evolved some strategies for dealing with these difficulties, but still struggle at times. At the end of a recent DBT group meeting, a co-leader said, "That was an easy group because it had a low narcissism factor." I knew exactly what she meant.

Yalom (1985), writing about group therapy, has provided useful suggestions with regard to such problems. In Chapter 13 of this book, he describes his strategies for dealing with nine types of problem clients. These types of problem clients include the narcissistic, as well as several other others we frequently deal with.

During the past decade I have had the good fortune to occasionally help out in the group therapy training program at the Dartmouth Department of Psychiatry. A psychologist, Bruce Baker, conducted this program with great expertise and energy. His primary text was the classic *Experiences in Groups* (1961) by W. R. Bion.

The ideas of Baker and Bion led me to sketch some cartoons (see Figure 16.1) depicting my clients in various modes that have been identified in group work. The modes that I focused on were the work mode (working on a clinical problem in the here and now), pairing to work (somehow joining together to focus on a clinical problem), the flight mode (fleeing from work or ignoring a clinical problem by talking about something irrelevant), pairing to flee (joining together to avoid focusing on a clinical problem), the fight mode (somehow resisting pressures to work on a clinical problem or fleeing in some angry way; I depicted two subcategories of the fight mode, one being "righteous rage" and the other "trash talk"), and the passive or dependency mode (looking to others, usually the group leaders, to do the work).

I have been able to use these cartoons, and the ideas behind them, to guide groups out of many of the binds they get themselves into. The cartoons have been particularly helpful in dealing with the machismo and narcissism problems, usually by guiding people toward the work mode and toward pairing to work in the here and now. It is also worth noting that I have occasionally encouraged or even initiated the flight mode to help with the work of pairing, and to give the group a brief rest from consideration of a particularly difficult problem. An example of this is finding an opportunity to say something like "How about those New England Patriots?" or "How about those Boston Red Sox?" A brief discussion of a sporting event or team, or of some details of a particular occupation, such as logging, carpentry, or operating a tug boat, can bring people together, raise the level of trust, and sometimes provide a brief respite from necessary work on a particularly unpleasant topic. It is also worth noting that I have consistently discouraged any flights that focus on politics or religion. These topics generally have the effect of isolating some members of the group and creating unnecessary factions. These topics also can lead quickly to episodes of "righteous rage." The concept of righteous rage is worthy of a brief comment. I have noticed that some group members seem to enjoy the expression of righteous rage. Their faces become animated and flushed, eyes glisten, the voices rise in volume and the pace of speaking increases. When expressing rage my clients are often taking an extreme fundamentalist position that moves them to a simple world of right and wrong, black and white. They shut out shades of gray and create primitive and clear meaning where there was confusion. They no longer feel ordinary, and certainly no longer feel any culpability for previous misbehavior. Suddenly they are special, and at center stage. Their problems drop away. They suddenly feel obligated to heap scorn on some despicable monster. This is the monster Horowitz was talking about, and this state of righteous rage, for many of my clients, is the "hoped-for self" that Markus and Nurius referred to.

Figure 16.1. *Cartoons depicting Bion's modes of group behavior.*

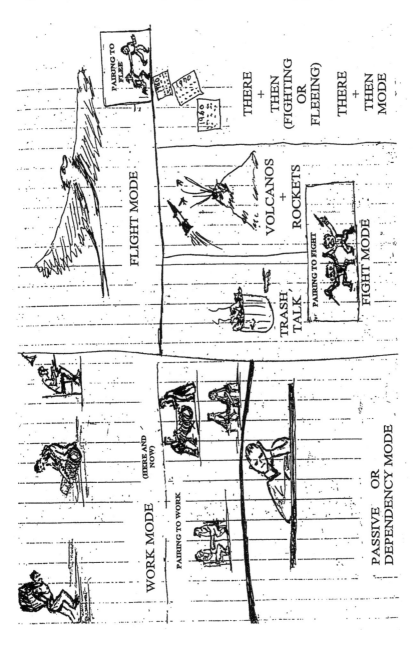

Some General Lessons about All Mental Health Work

My work with groups has led me to realize that I need to think a lot more about the interaction of individual differences and social pressures, particularly those pressures I have labeled "compelling situations." I have noticed vast differences in social pressures, as expressed in group norms, rules or cultures (some would call these group personalities), even in DBT meetings that only run four sessions per cycle. These group experiences remind me that our clients go from our sessions into sub cultures that are characterized by a wide variety of norms. The subcultures that our clients return to can present various difficulties, not only after group meetings, but even after an individual outpatient therapy session, to say nothing about returning after prolonged hospitalization.

I will illustrate my point with an embarrassing story. Around 1967, when I was working as codirector of the behavioral therapy unit at the Allan Memorial Institute in Montreal, a 40-year-old man was referred for extreme shyness and lack of assertive behavior. He had been in the hospital for several months with no notable improvement. His insurance was running out, and someone referred him to us to see if we could help him. We did a rapid assessment and developed a case formulation and treatment plan, both of which were carefully discussed with him. The treatment plan involved shaping his social behavior using role-playing situations and a variety of guiding signals. In seven sessions he was surprisingly improved. He was able to look people in the eye, state his wishes, and stick to his principles. He appeared ready to become a functioning member of society, rather than a submissive pawn at the mercy of anyone who noticed him. However, he had to return to a home many hundreds of miles to the east of Montreal, and face a set of norms in a culture about which we knew very little. A particularly important element of his outpatient environment was the specific set of expectations that his wife had about his role in the family.

He arrived home late at night. He crept quietly into his bedroom and found his seven-year-old son, who had apparently abandoned his own bed after a nightmare, sleeping in his place beside his wife. He woke his son and tried to guide him into his own bed. His wife woke up and said something along the lines of "leave him alone—go sleep on the couch." Our client protested, apparently using strategies we had taught him—to no avail. He went out into the kitchen and had several cans of beer. Then he returned to the bedroom and loudly ordered his son to go to his own bed. His wife stood up (I understand that she was almost a head taller and about 40 pounds heavier than our client), remembering her role and the role of her previously submissive husband. Very soon he was in the kitchen again, alone. His son was still not in his own bed.

Our client then had a few more beers. He took his gun out of a drawer and loaded it. He went into the bedroom again, pointed the gun to his head, and said "I will shoot myself if you do not obey me." His wife said, "You don't have the guts." He then shot himself in the arm.

I found out about this when I gave a speech at a hospital about 150 miles east of Montreal. In the audience was a young psychiatrist who had been called in to consult on the case of a man who had shot himself in the arm. The psychiatrist learned the client's story, and that Dr. Corson was behind this tragedy. I think I handled the questions and comments fairly well, but confessed—and confess again now—that I had failed. This is a dramatic example of an important problem in mental health work. We usually don't have all of the important information about the situation the client will return to. I had only a vague idea about his family situation, and thought he was a social drinker who went many weeks without drinking any alcohol. I had a better idea about his workplace, the way other people treated him at work, the kind of work he tried to do, and his need to be assertive in his second job as a free-lance carpenter.

In my assessment and case formulation, I focused on only a part of his dilemma. The "compelling situation" presented by his wife's persona and behavior was not part of my case formulation. If I had assessed his case more carefully I might have found out about these difficulties, but I am not sure. Now that I am often able to work with clients for a longer period of time than just seven sessions, I frequently find out that my concepts of the client's proclivities and circumstances unfold, as if we were peeling an onion. This takes time and careful attention. In a group this work usually cannot be done. It is a crapshoot! Our individual clients often have difficulty in maintaining treatment gains, but many of our group clients have more difficulty. We are often unable to do much, if anything, to prepare them for their unique social milieu.

What Do These Group Observations Tell Us about Research on Treatments?

These experiences with groups bring me to the realization that the task of doing good research on mental health treatment strategies, and developing standardized treatments for various disorders is even more difficult than I had thought 15 years ago. I have recently come across a variety of opinions about the difficulties of doing this work. Yalom (2002), an analytically trained psychiatrist, suggests that we should create a new therapy for each patient. He says there is a paradox in contemporary psychotherapy research: In order to do research on a standardized therapy that will be uniform for all clients in the project, the therapy must be compared to another standardized therapy. Furthermore, both therapies must be described well enough so that future researchers and therapists can replicate both therapies. "And yet that very act of standardization renders the therapy less real and less effective. Pair that problem with the fact that so much psychotherapy research uses inexperienced therapists or student therapists, and it is not hard to understand why such research has, at best, a most tenuous connection with reality" (p. 33).

At the other extreme, we can find the same kinds of complaints in behavior therapy journals. There are reports of claims that go beyond the data (e.g., Corrigan, 2001), reports of flawed studies that claim to be randomized clinical trials, clients dropping out, failure to follow-up, the occasional follow-up study showing a loss of the majority of the clinical gains, etc. We find similar complaints from the middle of the road in psychotherapy. In this literature it has been pointed out that the few fairly long-term follow-up studies show a dramatic fading of any gains from therapy. It has also been observed that the criteria for admission to the typical randomized clinical trial have excluded really problematic clients, such as those with more than one problem, and that many clients drop out, the therapists are inexperienced, and the effects are small (DeRubeis, and Crits-Christoph, 1998).

Nevertheless, I am sure that we should continue attempts to gather data on the potentially effective treatments. Randomized clinical trials are certainly useful, but for the purposes of most therapies and most of the clients we see, those with several diagnoses and long-standing problems, the usefulness of published clinical trials is severely limited in terms of pointing to a definitive or stand-alone treatment method. We make use of the published clinical trials whenever possible, and use variations and parts of the established methods in working with many of our clients. However, in working with the majority of our clients it has become clear that we are a very long way from being able to conduct a randomized clinical trial with satisfactory specifications of who the appropriate clients will be and what the appropriate method(s) might be. We need more education, more time with clients, more careful thought and observation, more detailed stories about apparently unique clients and their case histories, more very long-term follow-up, more stories about our failures and partial successes, and more case studies of both individual and group therapy. Finally, we need more feedback from the trenches, an area of practice from which very few contributions to the research literature are made.

17: A Group Treatment Strategy Owing Much to Linehan's "Dialectical Behavior Therapy"

Of our group treatment programs the one that reaches the most clients is a weekly 90-minute group modeled loosely on certain aspects of Linehan's work (1993). This group is variously known as "stress and anger management group" or "dialectical behavior therapy (DBT) group." Our group format focuses on the self-regulation aspect of Linehan's work and has evolved quite far from Linehan's model. Because of these divergences, I am increasingly uneasy about retaining the DBT label. At this point it is worth noting that Linehan's program was designed for work with borderline personality disordered individuals. In our experience, the males who have a history of violent explosions and have been diagnosed with PTSD (other frequent diagnoses that these clients have been given are antisocial personality disorder and narcissism) show many of the same characteristics as individuals diagnosed with borderline personality disorder.

We conduct this group every Friday afternoon for the first four Fridays of every month. The following is a brief description, with some illustrations of observations and strategies. A detailed outline of each session is presented in an appendix.

DBT is a packaged set of cognitive and behavioral procedures that was put together by Marsha Linehan for work with women with borderline personality disorder. She and her colleagues have published data showing that her format is more successful than any other procedure that has ever been used with this difficult population.

Linehan's DBT program includes four stages. Stage 1 focuses on self-regulation/behavioral control. Stage 2 focuses on decreasing quiet desperation and increasing the capacity for emotional experience. Stage 3 focuses on coping with problems in living and developing a tolerance for variations between ordinary happiness and unhappiness without experiencing a meltdown. Stage 4 is aimed at moving from a sense of incompleteness to a sense of meaning in life and development of a capacity for joy.

In Linehan's format, the first stage includes five different components (some of which we have been unable to consistently apply). The components are: (1) psychoeducational skills groups focused on four sets of skills; (2) individual outpatient psychotherapy; (3) phone consultation ("coaching"); (4) therapist consultation and support group; (5) guidelines for structuring the therapeutic environment to support the client and therapist capabilities.

Since 1995 we have concentrated on Linehan's stage 1—self-regulation training format (stages 2, 3, and 4 are carried out, when possible, in individual sessions). We have made a number of changes to the Stage 1 program. Wording has been changed to accommodate northern New England male clients with a possibly lower educational level than Linehan's female clients. Other changes have been based on feedback from our clients. Because of problems with logistics, staff limitations, and difficulties in getting our clients to commit to attending a psychoeducational group for many months (as is done by Linehan) we have also experimented with changing the length of the program; at various times we have used sequences of 6,8,10 and 12 session groups. Now we are using cycles of four sessions each and inviting clients to attend several cycles.

Each session lasts 90 minutes. Sessions are run on the first four Fridays of every month except July and December. The four sessions are divided as follows: mindfulness; self-regulation; interpersonal effectiveness; distress tolerance/crisis management (details are presented in an appendix).

We work to convince clients to return to subsequent cycles once they have been through one cycle. One argument is that practice and repetition have been shown to be more helpful than a single exposure ("you get more out of it the second time"); another point is that returning clients function as highly effective cofacilitators; a third point is that clients know which module is offered on which Friday of each month, and can tailor their return visits to their individual needs; and the final point is that relapse is highly probable, and that relapse prevention is facilitated by return visits.

We analyzed long-term follow-up data gathered from 32 clients who went through a 10-session format we employed between 1995 and 1997. These data, with follow-up intervals ranging from 6 months to 2 years, show clear (statistically significant) positive impact of our version of DBT on self-report measures of mood, energy, irritability, and sleep.

Between 1997 and 1999 we experimented with different lengths of cycles. Our DBT work prior to 1999 was done with a relatively narrow sample of clients. All clients had to go through the group psychometric assessment described in Chapter 8. We used cutoff points for verbal intelligence (above 110 on the Ammons Quick Test) and abstract reasoning ability (above average on our shortened version of the Gorham Proverbs Test) as criteria for entry; and we attempted to have individuals begin at the beginning.

Since 1999 we have opened the DBT program to all clients. We no longer require psychometric assessment and use no cutoff points. Now all referred clients are immediately invited to the group sessions. We made this change for several reasons. First, a large part of our veteran population failed to make the previously used cutoff criteria, and second, we believe that it is often best to begin work as soon as possible after a referral is made.

In order to keep these groups somewhat manageable we have asked our referring agents to avoid referring decompensated psychotic or demented clients to this group. However, a few decompensated psychotic and some demented clients have attended, and some have appeared to profit from the experience. When an individual is referred they are told by the referring agent to attend the group beginning on the next Friday—even if it is in the middle of a cycle.

At the start of the first session a number of administrative details are covered. An overview of all four sessions is given, and the research element is described, along with the data we analyzed in 1997. We describe the consent form and the purpose for it, ask clients to sign it, and tell them that after the program we will occasionally contact them by telephone to discuss how they are doing and to ask for feedback on what elements of the program seem to have the most durable positive impact. Following this, we begin the psychoeducational work. This first session focuses on "mindfulness," staying as close to Linehan's terminology as possible. We describe Linehan's work, and define "dialectical" and give a general rationale and overview of mindfulness in the context of self-regulation. This session includes two forms of relaxation training, some developmental and biological psychoeducational material (focusing on functions of the amygdala, impact of head injury, impact of psychological/emotional trauma, the "culture of cruelty" experienced by adolescent males—and resulting difficulties in self-regulation), and a brief outline of self-management strategies for coping with "temporary attention deficit disorder" related to self-regulation difficulties. The first session emphasizes the value of slowing down reactions to any emotionally provoking stimulus. This concept is at the basis of all our work in this group. A model of the brain is brought to the first and second sessions, and the function of various brain structures is discussed. There is particular focus on the amygdala, and the general concept of the fast acting "reptilian brain" that has a very limited repertoire and can, in many situations, "hijack" the rest of the brain into behaving in a counterproductive way. This part of the program is discussed in the next chapter.

The second session is entitled "self-regulation." It begins with a review of the previous session and a reminder of the general rationale for self-regulation and the reasons for slowing down. Early in this session we discuss cognitive, emotional and behavioral signs, particularly early warning signals, of the need to regulate emotions. Strategies for monitoring feelings are considered, and the concept of anger as a frequent habitual or impulsive attempt to cope with painful emotions is presented. We emphasize that anger is a secondary emotion that rapidly follows a drop in self-esteem, frustration, a sign of disrespect, etc. A printed copy of "first-line strategies" for managing painful emotions, strategies to be used when there is little or no time to think, is covered in detail (see appendix).

The third session is entitled "interpersonal effectiveness." It begins with a review of the first two sessions, and some data and ideas that support the value of maintaining good relationship with other people. One important focus is the evidence of the positive impact of continuing relationships on health and longevity. During this session, the first-line strategies that had been presented in the second session are again covered. These are now being recommended as tactics for coping with difficulties in maintaining a relationship. A printed list of brief reminders of powerful strategies for mediation/conflict resolution is covered in detail. There is a discussion of strategies for anticipating difficult interpersonal situations. This leads to a discussion of "second line strategies" for use when there is some time to think about how to behave in difficult interpersonal situations.

An example of a first line strategy is the "minimal effective response," the idea of dealing with situations that require assertion by starting off with a clearly assertive, and informationally strong, but non-aggressive response. For example a client of mine (who had been in jail many times—and in handcuffs and leg irons at least 50 times since he got back from Vietnam—all for violent behavior), went to "Dunkin Donuts." He left his young daughter in the car and raced in to get her some hot chocolate and himself some coffee. When he got to the cash register with his purchases, the cashier and another woman were talking busily about an interior-decorating problem. He thought of doing his well-practiced explosion—with loud profanity, throwing the coffee and hot chocolate, perhaps kicking windows out, etc.—then he remembered the minimal effective response that I had been teaching him. He asked himself "how would that work in this situation." An answer came to him and he politely said something along the lines of: "if you are done paying for your stuff I would like to pay for this because my daughter is going to start making a racket out in the car unless I get out there quickly." The two women apologized—they were extremely ashamed—and one offered to pay for his purchases.

We tell such stories during these sessions to illustrate the use of many of the strategies.

The final session focuses on distress tolerance and crisis management. At the beginning, the first three sessions are briefly reviewed. Next we discuss the relationship between physical and emotional distress. Various strategies for managing crisis and distress are covered in this session, including brief descriptions and illustrations of many of Linehan's strategies (distracting, self-soothing, improving the moment, thinking of pros and cons). Toward the end of the session we review the relaxation strategies taught in the first session, and introduce some additional brief relaxation/meditation exercises. At this session we also describe a relapse prevention strategy we have labeled the "proactive strategy." It is a brief exercise (90-120 seconds) the client is asked to do periodically during the day, and includes brief relaxation, an image of a friendly mentor, and a mental rehearsal of a prosocial response to a difficult situation. (The strategy is described in more detail in Chapter 21.) This session, perhaps in part because it is the last of the four, stimulates a great deal of participation, with many helpful examples being offered by the clients of their own distress tolerance and crisis management strategies. They also frequently talk about those strategies from our program that they have high hopes for. At this session we again remind clients of the various reasons for attending additional sessions.

We have found that this program is surprisingly effective in some ways that we had not anticipated. For example, we have repeatedly observed a clearly therapeutic impact on a group member who spends some time helping another group member. Very frequently this therapeutic impact persists, and the new role of being able to help someone else out becomes an important part of that client's daily life. Also, quite surprisingly, we have seen that some clients who have been unable to get started in individual therapy have been able to make large gains as a result of attending only one cycle of this group. We have been able to track several of these people as they reenter individual therapy, and have found that they profit in ways that we had not initially anticipated. One of the changes that frequently takes place as they reenter individual therapy is that they will now collaborate with the therapist, instead of taking a passive or angry and resistant role.

The usefulness of this program has also been demonstrated in some ways we had anticipated. For example, quite a few clients have returned to the program after many months, or even several years of absence. Some have returned when in crisis, and have appeared to pull themselves together extremely rapidly after only a few more sessions in the group. Perhaps this utility is being demonstrated because the clients feel that they can reenter the group any time they want to, but to reenter individual therapy would be likely to involve delays, perhaps a different therapist, and perhaps a sense of failure. Returning to the group is possible after little or no waiting, and involves no inherent signaling of failure, since all participants have been enthusiastically invited to return, and have been told that we and the group members will profit from their account of their attempts to use strategies they learned in the group, whether the strategies have succeeded or failed. It is worth noting here that the literature on long-term maintenance of gains from various forms of mental health therapy is very disappointing (DeRubeis and Crits-Christoph, 1998). Furthermore, males have been shown to have negative attitudes toward psychological help seeking (Mahalik et al., 2003). These negative attitudes toward initial help seeking seem likely to be present when a male considers returning for help during a relapse. All things considered, we believe that the relapse prevention potential of this open cycling group format is excellent.

We now have some data to support this belief. We recently completed analysis of data from 20 clients with follow-up periods ranging from six to thirty months. The data show highly significant improvement in self-reported mood and energy (indexed by the affect grid instrument that was developed by Russell, Weiss, and Mendelson, 1989) as well as reductions in self-reported irritability, anger, anxiety and depression.

We have also found that this program can be very helpful as part of an inpatient program for clients with PTSD. Cohorts of five to eight clients from all over the east coast are admitted for stays of three weeks. The inpatient version of this program is delivered in six sessions, each lasting one hour. Exit interviews indicate that the clients value their experience in this group.

We have considered experimenting with some additional changes in the near future. One of the most intriguing possibilities is to select one or several particularly articulate clients, who have been through the group and have apparently profited, to serve as cofacilitators with us for one cycle. We have the hunch that this type of innovation could significantly increase the power of the program. It would also be rather easy to gather data that would allow us to evaluate the impact of this change. Another possibility we have considered is the inclusion in the group program of a brief period of biofeedback, arranged to convince clients of the value of the quick calming response. A few pilot efforts using biofeedback with the inpatient cohorts described above have been particularly promising.

18: Self-Regulation Strategies Used in Groups

In one way or another, self-regulation is involved in almost all of the work we do. Chapter 17 described our wide-spectrum group program for self-regulation, primarily aimed at stress and anger management, and included considerable focus on self-management in interpersonal relationships. We also run groups focusing on self-regulation for clients with chronic pain and for clients suffering from anxiety and depression.

Self-regulation has been considered from various points of view and several have been especially helpful in the development of the ideas and strategies presented in this book. Watson and Tharp (2002) have just published the 8th edition of their successful psychology textbook entitled *Self-Directed Behavior*. This book is a well-reasoned, learning theory-based presentation that includes guidance for the reader in conducting a self-direction project.

Bradley, a psychiatrist, has published a book entitled *Affect Regulation and the Development of Psychopathology* (2000) that presents a well-informed examination of genetic, developmental, parenting, learning, traumatic, and neurobiological factors influencing self-regulation. Schore has published a remarkable and highly acclaimed book entitled *Affect Regulation and the Origin of the Self* (1994) which covers issues that pertain to self-regulation from the molecular to the psychoanalytic level.

The present chapter, in accordance with the mission of this book, has a relatively narrow focus with regard to self-regulation. We first consider the details of one of the specific psychoeducational segments of our DBT group described in Chapter 17. This segment seems to be of considerable help to clients with urges to do violence or express hostile feelings. Many of these clients mention this set of ideas long after they have last attended any of our group meetings. Next we consider a psychoeducational strategy for clients suffering from transient problems with attention deficit that often accompany extreme agitation. These two procedures are usually presented in a group setting, and are regular parts of the group treatment format described in Chapter 16.

Self-Regulation Strategies—Violent and Hostile Urges

In the group work described in Chapter 17, as well as in individual work we frequently use a brief psychoeducational presentation concerning some of the neurological circuitry involved in violent behavior and a description of some "first-line strategies" (first-line strategies are outlined in an appendix) for use when a violent or hostile urge arises suddenly.

The presentation concerning the neurological circuitry involved in violent behavior is along the following lines:

Structures in the human brain have been developed over many centuries. An early evolutionary development is still with us and is frequently called the reptilian brain. The term reptilian brain refers to a large part of the lower levels of the brain and the top part of the brain stem/spinal cord. A small nucleus is intimately involved in the functioning of this reptilian brain—the nucleus is known as the amygdala. Research done by LeDoux (1986,1993,1995), and others shows that the amygdala functions as the key piece in detecting danger, feeling fear and responding quickly. The amygdala is a sort of sentinel—scanning all sensory inputs for any sign of danger. Once a sign of danger is seen, a response is rapidly executed. These responses are extremely rapid, and have been called manifestations of a "hot system." This system has its own memories and its own response strategies.

The "cool system," or higher brain structures such as the frontal lobes and the rest of the cortex, developed more recently in the evolutionary process. This is the system that allows humans to delay the tendency toward a rapid and impulsive response and to formulate responses to danger or fear that will be much more effective in the long-term. This system can also be called "the wise mind."

An individual who has been traumatized has developed a complex, danger related set of memories that are partly stored in the amygdala. In the event that the traumatized individual detects some danger similar to the original trauma there is likely to be a very rapid response that will often be counterproductive. Van der Kolk (1994) has studied many individuals diagnosed with PTSD. He has concluded that the memory systems of these individuals often fail to incorporate the traumatic experience into the autobiographical or narrative account of their lives. If it is incorporated at all, it seems to be incorporated only in a fragmentary form. It has been suggested (Metcalfe and Jacobs, 1996) that the use of narrative therapy could "reweave" these hot and fragmentary and troublesome memories into autobiographical memory and thus into a framework that would allow the "cool system" to help prevent rapid, impulsive and often counterproductive responses to any form of danger or fear. Another way to say this is that narrative therapy can help engage the wise mind or cool mind, and allow a traumatized individual to take the necessary time to formulate a relatively productive response.

The traumatized person is also typically highly aroused, even when sitting still. In this state, the amygdala and the "hot system" are likely to be in a state of high readiness—poised to leap into action. In many cases the memory of the traumatic event is a "state dependent memory." It is retrieved when the body is aroused to the high level that the trauma originally caused—thus reinstating or replicating the trauma state in many of its details. Thus, the traumatized person is likely to be tormented by flashbacks and a general uncomfortable emotional state. At this high level of arousal, the cool system or wise mind is sidelined. One way to assist an individual in dealing with this set of problems is to train them to calm down. We have had considerable success using biofeedback and forms of relaxation and self-hypnosis to help individuals lower their resting arousal level, and decrease the amplitude, duration and frequency of episodes of very high arousal.

When two individuals with a history of being traumatized are interacting, there is the possibility that a hot system response from one will elicit an equally unwise hot system response from the other. We have repeatedly seen in a married couple with one or both members having been traumatized, that an argument takes the form of a skirmish, with each taking turns firing increasingly cruel verbal responses at the other. In a sense their reptilian brains or "hot systems" are doing the arguing. Frequently— sometime later—each will realize that they have said things that were unwise, and even some things that they did not mean at all. However, it often seems impossible for our clients to heal from, or apologize for, these statements. We have developed a set of strategies (called "first-line strategies") to help these individuals avoid arguing with the reptilian brain.

Recently a client was describing to me an argument with his wife. This argument followed a pattern that began with relatively low level insults exchanged between the two of them—the argument quickly escalated to a loud and raging conflict. I used the client's description of this episode to delineate a pattern that seems to characterize most of their arguments. I went on to identify some choice points in any typical argument where he could bring his "wise mind" to bear. I gave him a copy of the above paragraphs along with a diagram depicting brain function—highlighting the role of the amygdala in fear-driven and angry conversation. Using some of our "first-line strategies," I explained that in order to engage the higher levels of brain function one needs to slow down. It is a good idea to speak slowly and softly and to avoid swearing, since rapid and loud speaking and swearing tend to go along with high levels of biological arousal and with activation of the amygdala and the associated reptilian brain—leading to increasingly impulsive and often counterproductive utterances.

He brought this discussion up again in our next session. Apparently the pattern I had identified made good sense to him, and he had used two of the first-line strategies in an argument with his wife the night after our last session. His wife was surprised, and said that he seems to be changing, and that his therapy must be doing some good. Since that night they have not argued again, even though they have continued to talk about the problems that had previously triggered arguments.

We present the first-line strategies as tools to use when there is no time to think. The best of these appear to be strategies that slow the client down, such as speaking softly and slowly. (Avoiding swearing is also important, and seems to be less likely when the client speaks slowly and softly.) In order to help them put one, or several, of the strategies into play whenever necessary, we talk about categories of emergency signals. A person who suddenly detects danger experiences a variety of changes. These changes function as signals that reverberate through three classes of variables, and feed back on each other. There are changes within the self—in covert behavior—these variables may range from the cognitive level, with a sudden flood of memories about similar situations, to salient bodily sensations, with a sudden feeling of a knot in the stomach. There are changes in overt behavior—these may include bodily movement, swearing, etc. Finally, there may be changes in the other person. These may include raised voice, swearing, and visible bodily changes, such changes in facial expression and body language. Voice, face, and body language changes could indicate a cowering/submissive or aggressive/ dominant attitude. In our first-line strategies, we make use of signals from each of these three sources (within the self, overt behavior of the self, responses of the other person) to initiate self-regulation plans. Initiation of one of these plans (e.g., talk softly and slowly, with no swearing) can actually prevent (or sometimes abort) the cascade of responses initiated by the amygdala. In order to help counteract the speed of transmission to and from the amygdala, we ask clients to practice a simple first-line strategy repeatedly, and in a variety of situations. When a client is successful we can see that the first-line strategies have enabled the "wise mind" or cool mind to overcome the tendencies of the reptilian brain.

Self-Regulation Strategies—Transient Attention Deficit

Five years ago we ran a one-week psychoeducational program for six severely-impaired adult males with attention deficit disorder. These sessions involved three 90-minute meetings and homework assignments. The format was based largely on the work of Barkley (1998), and emphasized "point of performance" signaling, primarily structuring the clients' day by having them do specific activities when signaled by the occurrences of sunrise and sunset.

This was a very interesting experience; it seemed somewhat like an attempt at "herding cats." Attendance was spotty and attention wandered. Six clients started this group. All were on medication that was presumed to be of help with attention deficit disorder. Of the three clients who attended all four sessions, one has been able to obtain employment appropriate to his educational level for the first time in 20 years and has held that job for over four years—the first time in his life that he has held a job for more than one year. This client presented a complicated picture, with attention deficit being combined with considerable use of alcohol (not to the level that I would call "alcoholic," but fairly close), and downward mobility. By downward mobility I refer to a considerable drop from the socioeconomic level of his parents, who were themselves downwardly mobile, apparently due to his father's excessive consumption of alcohol. I am also referring to his own drop from the socioeconomic level that he started out with after an excellent education. Both of the other clients who completed this brief group experience said they gained from it, but we have not been able to obtain clear evidence of their gains.

Because of the small size of our staff and the many demands on our time, we have not been able to conduct groups specifically for individuals with attention deficit disorder. However, we adapted the approach described above for use in the group format described in Chapter 17, and have invited individuals with attention deficit disorder to attend that group. We introduced this element into our group format because it appears that many clients who have not been diagnosed with attention deficit disorder show chronically high levels of arousal that frequently get to the level of severe agitation. During times of severe agitation, many of these clients complain that their ability to attend to their responsibilities is profoundly impaired. Early in our group program we include instruction on several types of rapid relaxation. We build upon these with the following instructions.

Temporary ADD—Multitasking Is the Signal

When you notice yourself multi-tasking mindlessly, (without a sense of priorities), or feeling agitated and ineffective, you are usually in a highly distractible state. It is as if you have a **temporary attention deficit disorder (ADD).** Use this multi-tasking/agitation as a cue to do the following:

1) When you notice that you are agitated and ineffective, immobilized or mindlessly multi-tasking—Stop! Sit down! Do the quick calming response. Next take a pencil and paper and list all the tasks you have been trying to work on, and all the problems you have on your mind.

2) Categorize the tasks into one of the following four classes: "do, delay, delegate, or dump."

3) Now—use the quick calming exercise again. Be in the moment. Quick calm serves two purposes: to help slow you down/decrease arousal, and to focus your attention on **one** thing that you might be able to do something about.

4) Consult your list again, and select the highest priority item on your list. If you have time, move on to the next step. Whatever happens, be mindful, stay in the present moment and stay focused. Use the quick calming response whenever you feel that you are beginning to lose it.

5) Make a deal—or **contract**—with yourself to do between one and five minutes worth of work on the top priority task before the next sunrise or sunset. From now on **Use Every Sunrise and Sunset as Signals** for you to alternatively plan work and do work for small, fixed chunks of time. It will help to **use a timer** while you work, to tell you when the work period has ended. The bell or signal when the timer goes off, will function as a reward. It will boost your spirits a bit and help you realize that you have kept your contract with yourself. Try to do this little bit of work every day. It is like whittling at the list of tasks. It will make a huge difference in boosting your mood and completing your tasks.

6) Be a **"personal scientist"**—think about, and write down, your priorities at one of your signals (at **Sunrise** or **Sunset**). Look at your record of priorities and work briefly on your top task at the other signal. Let one of those occasions (e.g., sunrise) be a signal for you to review what single task you will plan to work on. Let the other of those occasions (e.g., sunset) be a signal for the starting time for a short period of work (one to five minutes) on that task.

19: Self-Regulation Strategies Used in Individual Sessions

The two self-regulation strategies presented in this chapter are used for the treatment of panic disorder and sex offenses. We have attempted to do some of the work on both of these problems in group settings, but have not persisted. The basic reason for giving up, at least temporarily, on doing this work in group sessions is that the individuals with these difficulties seem to focus on the differences between themselves and other members of the group. Odd sorts of behavior occurred in the panic groups, the most disruptive of which was a form of competition between some members regarding who had the most severe symptoms of panic. In the sex offender groups, attempts to downplay the severity of one's own offenses were frequently more difficult to get beyond than would be the case in individual sessions.

Our panic disorder format is a biofeedback-enhanced and shortened version of an interoceptive exposure procedure developed by Craske and Barlow (1990; also see Barlow and Craske, 1994). On the other hand, our sex offender format, which is described in much greater detail, uses a strategy that seems to be completely new.

Panic Disorder

As mentioned above, the panic disorder format is a shortened and biofeedback-enhanced version of an already-published strategy. A major innovation of the Craske and Barlow system is the use of "interoceptive exposure," meaning that the client is exposed to the internal sensory correlates of a panic attack. To accomplish this, the client collaborates with the therapist to run through a series of exercises (e.g., a minute of hyperventilation) that are designed to provoke some of the physiological/subjective aspects of the client's panic attacks. The client is exposed to a menu of these provocations, and following each is asked to describe the interoceptive sensations that have arisen, to rate the level of anxiety reached during the provocation, and to rate the degree of similarity of this experience to the feelings that occur during a full panic attack.

Prior to being exposed to this menu of provocations, the client is trained in a rapid relaxation strategy, and collaborates with the therapist to develop a covert coping statement that would help the client put an attack into a non-catastrophic and manageable perspective. Early in this sequence the client will have been given a record-keeping outline that they are asked to fill out whenever a panic attack occurs. This outline is designed to elicit descriptions of any interoceptive sensations.

After exposure to the menu of provocations, the therapist and client select one or several of the provocations that the client can practice at home for one or two minutes each night. The client is given a homework assignment to practice this individualized provocation at home each day. Immediately after completion of the provocation exposure, the client is to rate the feelings, relax quickly, and use the covert coping statement to help accelerate the termination of the interoceptive sensation(s).

We shortened the Craske and Barlow format to six sessions after a large percentage of our clients began to miss sessions or completely drift away after six or eight sessions. When we had the opportunity to reassess one of them, we found that he felt he had learned what he needed in the first few sessions, and was now doing quite well. In other words the early sessions provided a level of improvement that was satisfactory to him. Two additional clients who dropped out after the first 5 sessions have said things along the same lines. (Interestingly, there is some literature that addresses the issue of some clients showing maximum gain at very different points in a manualized sequence. Otto, Pollack, and Maki (2000) have addressed such issues in the treatment of panic disorder.)

Biofeedback was added to the Craske and Barlow format at the outset of our work with this paradigm, on the basis of our very positive experience with this procedure. The biofeedback is introduced into our six-session format in the following manner:

On the first day, in conjunction with teaching a brief (five-minute) relaxation exercise, we make an audiotape of the relaxation instructions and do psychophysiological monitoring of skin conductance, heart rate and peripheral blood flow while the client is relaxing and listening to the making of the audiotape. We give the client the audiotape of the relaxation exercises, along with a photocopy of the graph of the physiological changes that took place during the relaxation session. We color code each of the monitored variables, and explain what it means and how it reflects the relaxation process. The client is then asked to practice relaxation daily.

On the second day we use psychophysiological monitoring to evaluate the client's use of the brief relaxation exercise. On the third day, which is the day when the interoceptive exposure provocations occur, we do not use biofeedback. However, we guide the client in use of the rapid relaxation exercise after each provocation. On the fourth day, after reviewing the panic log and the interoceptive homework data sheet, we discuss the client's experiences with use of the rapid relaxation and covert coping statement after the interoceptive exposure trials that were done at home.

At this point we usually discuss the escalation pattern typically involved in the panic attack, in which some stimuli, some of which are very likely to be interoceptive, lead to automatic thoughts and catastrophic expectations. We go on to discuss how this sequence can be disrupted or interrupted by using the covert coping statement and/or rapid relaxation. Although this sort of discussion will have taken place during earlier sessions, it now seems to engage the client more than previously, probably because of the experience with the homework exposures.

The psychophysiological monitoring is inserted following this discussion. The monitoring leads are attached, and the client is asked to go through the interoceptive exposure homework assignment and use the rapid relaxation and covert statement immediately upon finishing the exposure. The client is once more given a photocopy of the graph of the psychophysiological changes that took place during the exposure and the use of the relaxation and coping statement. This graph is compared to the graphs obtained at the first and second sessions. The client's attention is called to the dramatic impact of the interoceptive exposure, and the departure of the psychophysiological indices from the range seen in the first two sessions. The client's attention is also called to the rapid recovery that they have been able to produce by use of the rapid relaxation exercise and coping statement.

On days five and six, biofeedback/psychophysiological monitoring is not often used. On the sixth day we conclude with issuance of four weeks of panic attack record-keeping blanks and schedule a follow-up session after one month. We ask the client to choose whether or not they think they should continue with the exposure homework assignments during this four-week period, and clients most frequently choose not to do so. At the follow-up session we have been finding that the positive effects have been maintained. (A detailed outline of the steps in this sequence is presented in an appendix, along with copies of several prompts and record-keeping formats.)

It is worth noting here that we have not compared this six-session sequence to a procedure that does not involve psychophysiological monitoring, and have no intention of doing so. There are good reasons for this. We deal with widely different individuals, some of whom are likely to profit from this element, while others may not. Our clients tend to be quite interested in the graphs of the psychophysiological results, particularly the graph obtained on the fourth day. This relatively simple psychophysiological monitoring procedure seems to be a helpful component of our short format.

Sex Offenses

My clinical work with sex offenders and reviews of the published literature have left me with the impression that we are faced with almost insurmountable difficulties. These difficulties include wide individual differences among sex offenders, lack of data showing a truly powerful impact of any single treatment, the fact that most therapists do what they are familiar with, a low general level of accountability in the field, and problems in attempting to arrange long-term follow-up visits with these clients. Before describing our procedure for the treatment of sex offenders, I will briefly review some of the literature on assessment and treatment of sex offenders.

The most promising article I have seen on recidivism is by McGrath, Cumming, Livingston and Hoke (2003). They examined the recidivism rates of 195 inmates who had been referred to a prison based cognitive behavioral treatment program for sex offenders. They wrote "Over a mean follow-up period of almost 6 years, the sexual reoffense rate for the completed-treatment group was 5.4 percent vs. 30.6 percent for the some-treatment and 30.0 percent for the no treatment groups."

Raymond et al. (1999) addressed psychiatric comorbidity in pedophilic sex offenders. They studied 45 males who had been convicted of pedophilic offenses and found that 93% of these subjects met criteria for at least one disorder other than pedophilia. Hoyer, Kunst and Schmidt (2001) noted that there are heightened scores for social anxiety, and even social phobia in paraphiliacs. From these results it is clear that individual differences, such as the presence of untreated comorbid psychiatric disorders, play a very important role in treatment failure and recidivism. Grossman et al. (1999) also addressed the issue of individual differences. How do we know which offender is at greater risk of reoffending? How do we know which offender will profit from which treatment? How do we know whether the sex offender is proclaiming innocence while simply carrying on with the pattern of sex offenses, and is now escaping detection? On this latter point, Abel et al. (1987) reported that nonincestuous pedophiles who molested boys had committed offenses against an average of 150 victims. This statistic suggests that the average pedophile has frequently avoided detection before the first arrest, and probably expects to resume avoiding detection if he chooses to continue molesting children.

Unfortunately, it appears that the closest practical monitoring of an outpatient sex offender may not detect ongoing offenses. Furthermore, phallometric (penile plethysmography) and polygraphic detection formats are also fallible. For example, even with a highly selected group of subjects (homicidal child molesters), Firestone et al. (1998) were forced to resort to very cautious probability statements in their discussion of the utility of the penile plethysmographic data.

A recent paper on assessment concludes that specialized instruments for assessment of sex offenders have little empirical validity, while some research programs focused on risk assessment show promise (Lanyon, 2001). On the other hand this paper indicates a promising future for the use of multistep and decision-making models in improving the accuracy of assessment procedures for sex offenders.

Other recent reviews have concluded that multifaceted cognitive/behavioral programs show significant positive results with familial and nonfamilial child molesters and with exhibitionists (Marshall, Ward, Jones, Johnston and Barbaree, 1991; Marshall and Pithers, 1994; Marshall, 1996). These reviewers also strongly emphasize the importance of a relapse prevention approach. Weinrott, Riggan and Frothingham (1997) described an encouraging application of vicarious sensitization with adolescent sex offenders who showed deviant arousal patterns. However, in accord with points made by the above reviewers, it is important to note that this work was done as an adjunct to ongoing cognitive therapy. Finally, progress is being made in research on anti-hormonal and other medication treatments (e.g., see Bradford, 1998). Thus, it now appears that medication treatments should be included in the initial treatment of sex offenders, and that vicarious sensitization might also be a useful component in a multimodal program, featuring cognitive/behavioral interventions including social and life skills training, cognitive restructuring, victim empathy, and relapse prevention strategies.

From all of this rather confusing information, one message, at least for the near-term, can be distilled. A multimodal treatment format that attempts to match treatments (albeit blindly, given our current level of resolution) to individual differences among offenders is advisable. In colloquial terms, a "shotgun" approach is warranted. A second message is that clinicians and researchers need to continue to develop and test assessment and treatment formats for sex offenders.

A method that we have devised appears to be very helpful in the treatment of sex offenders. It is a self-regulation method that can be taught in a very short time, and focuses only on the elements of control and reduction of deviant arousal and relapse prevention. (It is important to note that I am describing clinical research done in a small practice, using a repeated-case, or single-group longitudinal design, with many confounding variables. It is also important to note that it is not being suggested that this method should be used alone. Other components such as those described above should be included in the treatment regimen whenever possible.)

Our brief focused treatment of sex offenders is distilled from a multifaceted format I used at the Veterans Administration Hospital in White River Junction, Vermont in the 1970s. This format included extensive assessment of sexual history, social history, sexual and social attitudes and proclivities, penile plethysmograph and polygraph assessment, biofeedback, and exposure to a wide range of auditory and visual test stimuli. The work was done both individually and in groups. The group sessions, conducted whenever there were two or more clients in treatment at the same time, included elements of perspective taking, victim empathy, sex education, and values clarification. One element in the treatment involved training clients to use hyperventilation to prevent and/or abort sexual arousal. It is on this element that I will now focus. This brief protocol has been used, essentially alone, with the offenders treated at this facility since 1981. Concomitant treatments were used with most of the clients, and these, since 1981, have generally been provided by outside agencies.

In the work that we did during the 1970s it appeared that individual differences rendered some of the elements of the larger program useless, or at least of dubious value. However, the hyperventilation element appeared to be a powerful feature for every client. Furthermore, the hyperventilation element could be properly taught, practiced, and evaluated in six sessions. The hyperventilation element and its rationale could be easily communicated to all government and legal agencies involved in the case. Finally, the hyperventilation element clearly places responsibility on the offender. At the end of the first session he should understand the immediate and powerful impact of the hyperventilation activity on cognitive and physiological aspects of sexual arousal.

The hyperventilation protocol is based on the following considerations:

1) Hyperventilation destabilizes the autonomic nervous system. The components of this system—the sympathetic and parasympathetic divisions—must work together in an intricate sequence in order to develop and maintain male sexual arousal (Wenger, Averill, and Smith, 1968; Walsh, 1998). More specifically, penile tumescence is developed by a series of shifts in dominance between the sympathetic and parasympathetic divisions. This subtle sequence is disrupted by hyperventilation, which produces a rapid surge in sympathetic dominance, soon followed by a change to parasympathetic dominance and a subsequent prolonged period (from one to several minutes) during which development of tumescence is unlikely, if not impossible (Walsh, 1998). Similarly, maintenance of a fully-developed erection depends on the maintenance of a particular stable relationship between the sympathetic and parasympathetic divisions (Walsh, 1998). Autonomic balance is disrupted by hyperventilation and detumescence is rapidly initiated.

2)   Hyperventilation dramatically changes the electrical activity of the brain and disrupts the train of thought. Fisch (1991) reported that hyperventilation triggers EEG responses that "consist of generalized slow waves which begin soon after the onset of hyperventilation," and the disruption in an individual with normal brain function "ends within one minute after the patient stops hyperventilating." It is clear that brain function and train of thought are important factors in most occasions of sexual arousal. If the reader doubts that hyperventilation influences train of thought, the proof is only a little over a minute away. Select a topic and think about it for 15 seconds. Then hyperventilate vigorously for a minute while attempting to maintain this train of thought. At the end of the minute, notice the degradation in the thought pattern, clarity of images, perhaps total loss of memory for details of the thought that occurred over the first 15 seconds, and in some cases loss of even the topic that had been selected for consideration. Also notice that many seconds go by before one can resume a train of thought approximating in all aspects those prevailing before hyperventilation.

3)   There is some evidence that the type of instructions and the demand characteristics of the situation can influence the affective impact of hyperventilation. However, when no expectation is provided to subjects regarding the sensation that will be produced (Salkovskis and Clark, 1990), hyperventilation is aversive. Hyperventilation has been aversive for all individuals we have studied, and is profoundly aversive for many. Consistent pairing of an aversive stimulus with a particular pattern of thoughts and behaviors produces an emotional reaction which should decrease the probability of thoughts of illegal sexual acts in the future and should decrease the probability of sexual arousal in the presence of a potential victim.

4)   In the event that the conditioning process does not have a reliable automatic impact on sexual arousal in inappropriate circumstances (in the presence of an under age person, or a non-consenting adult), the offender, on the occasion of noticing sexual thoughts or tumescence, can initiate hyperventilation (functioning as an

"operant," in learning theory terms) to abort sexual arousal and attendant thoughts. In other words, this procedure is portable.

5)   In some cases the convergence of some or all the above factors can lead a motivated client to a pattern of self control which appears to contain classically conditioned elements (or to function as a "respondent," in learning theory terms). Our best example is a college student who had been previously convicted of a sexual offense. Prior to going to college this young man had been extensively treated using other procedures. Finding himself continuing to be attracted to young boys, he volunteered for therapy at his student mental health center. He was then referred to us. We used the format described here and found that he could interrupt the train of thought and prevent development of tumescence with two to five hyperventilating breaths. When he realized that this was occurring, he became much more confident in his self control and a moderate to severe depression went into remission.

There were 20 clients in our study and all were male. Nineteen of these were military veterans, ranging in age from 27 to 71. One of our clients was a 20-year-old college student from an urban area, and all of the others were residents of small towns or rural areas of Vermont or New Hampshire. The college student was treated by the author at the Dartmouth Hitchcock Medical Center, and the other 19 participants were treated by the author at the Veterans Administration Hospital in White River Junction Vermont.

The group included two exhibitionists and 18 pedophiles (15 of whom molested only female children, and three of whom molested primarily male children). All but one had a criminal record, with at least one sexual offense included. Three of the participants volunteered for treatment and were not currently under investigation for, or mandated to seek treatment for a crime. None of the participants were currently incarcerated, although many lived in supervised quarters, and were under the supervision of probation and parole agencies.

Before beginning treatment, we insure that the client has had a recent physical examination. When the client has a clean bill of health in terms of neurological, cardiovascular and respiratory functioning, the one-minute hyperventilation assignment presents no risk. In the event of neurological, cardiovascular, or respiratory problems, a physician is consulted. When there have been health concerns, reduction of the duration of the hyperventilation assignment from 60 seconds to 15 to 30 seconds has been found to be safe.

The treatment protocol consists of six weekly sessions, with follow-up sessions scheduled over the following two years. The follow-up sessions are separated by one-month intervals at the beginning of the follow-up period, and by three-month intervals at the end. The six treatment sessions involve assessment, contracting, training in the use of hyperventilation (using biofeedback to verify the biological impact of hyperventilation), and a daily homework assignment, with the homework exercises tape-recorded.

The first session begins with a clarification of the client's situation regarding type of offense, any pending charges, and so forth. Next, we provide the client with a full text of our assessment and treatment format, and encourage discussion. The document describes the use of polygraphy during assessment and includes a section promising full disclosure of all details of sexual and social history. A self-referred offender who is not facing charges is immediately informed of our professional and legal reporting obligation.

Following this phase, the client is asked to sign a statement at the bottom of the document describing the format that says, "I have read the above description of planned assessment and treatment and agree to participate in, and comply with, all aspects of the program." (A copy of this document is available from the author.) Then the client is asked to sign a release of information form for each individual and agency (e.g., state's attorney, probation officer, client's attorney) involved in the referral of this client to us. These forms specify that all details of assessment and treatment can be transmitted to any individuals representing government and legal agencies involved in the case (a copy of the document that we send to government and legal agencies explaining our procedure is available from the author). We do not start treatment unless the client is willing to sign the above-mentioned documents. Finally, the client is asked to read over a consent form that, if signed, will allow us to aggregate his data with data from other people undergoing the identical treatment so that we can do further evaluation of its effectiveness. The client is told that even if he refuses to sign this consent form, treatment will continue. None who have signed the release of information agreements have refused to sign the consent form allowing us to do the aggregation of data.

In some cases an offender will suddenly seek treatment when he realizes that government agencies have recently been or will soon be notified of his illegal behavior. Most of the offenders seem to do this in the hope that the government and legal agencies will treat them more kindly if they have begun to seek help. It is important that the therapist make clear to the offender and to the government and legal agencies that this program is not a substitute for due process.

It should also be noted that many individuals will seek treatment at a Veterans Hospital in order to avoid the expense of obtaining private treatment. It seems advisable to prevent them from using this alternative if there is any possibility for them to pay fees to a community mental health center or to a private practitioner approved by the court, since the payment of private fees would probably increase the motivation of many individuals.

After the documents have been signed, the polygraph leads for monitoring skin conductance, peripheral blood flow from little finger of the right hand, and heart rate are applied. At this point the two purposes of the polygraph are explained: first to help ensure full disclosure, and second to demonstrate the biological impact of hyperventilation to the client. Next, a brief sexual history is obtained. Resistance can be expected at this stage. Several focusing tactics can be helpful. One tactic is to request information regarding the first sexual experience and the most recent sexual experience. The client can be encouraged to describe legal sexual experiences if it appears that this might help him get started. Another tactic is to ask about the first time the client was ever offended against. Some clients deny any such experience, while confessing to numerous occasions of being the perpetrator of illegal sexual acts. It is worth noting that one client who testified to having been involved by older boys in repeated sexual activities, beginning when he was seven years old, insisted that he had not been victimized, that he enjoyed the experiences, and that his subsequent offenses against others were not due to his having been a victim of sexual assault. It is also worth noting that this man re-offended after going through our treatment program (more details on his case are presented below).

When the therapist obtains a description of the first illegal sexual act and the most recent illegal sexual act, it is important to search for the details of antecedents, behaviors, and consequences in the attempt to understand the various incentives, beliefs and values influencing the behavior of the client. Even though this work is compressed into a short period of time, it can be highly valuable in developing a case formulation. A good case formulation is essential in evaluating and guiding the homework assignments.

After the sexual history has been completed, at least 20 minutes is spent describing and demonstrating hyperventilation, and explaining the rationale for its use. First the relationship of thoughts to sexual arousal is explained, and then the ability of hyperventilation to interrupt both thoughts and sexual arousal is spelled out. Finally, hyperventilation is demonstrated, and the client is engaged in a brief hyperventilation practice session immediately after being asked to think about their most recent sexual experience. The physiological changes produced in the client by hyperventilation are clearly shown on the monitoring screen. At this point the client is asked about the impact of the hyperventilation on his thoughts and feelings. All have mentioned dramatic changes, including loss of train of thought, and most have mentioned feeling dizzy and confused during and after the hyperventilation.

Clients must be made aware that they are being trained in use of hyperventilation to prevent and/or abort unwanted sexual arousal. It is important to emphasize to them that the key is motivation to avoid illegal sexual activities and that they will have the ability to do this, using hyperventilation, if they choose to do so in the future.

Following this explanation, the client is instructed in the format for daily homework practice of producing and aborting sexual arousal. The homework assignment is clearly explained on a record-keeping sheet that is presented to the client to aid in the instruction. The instructions specify that the practice must be carried out each day, and that the whole exercise must be tape-recorded. The client is instructed to become sexually aroused using his typical fantasies, or images of a typical episode or a desired episode of sexual activity. He is instructed to describe his fantasies aloud, so that the tape recorder will pick them up. Once he has achieved his peak sexual arousal, short of orgasm, he is to rate the sexual arousal (using the scale from 1 = "just noticeable" up to 10 = "highest ever"). He is then to start a stopwatch and begin hyperventilating for the prescribed time (usually one minute). When the hyperventilation period is over, he is to rate his sexual arousal again. Copies of this homework data sheet are used to guide and monitor homework between each of the subsequent sessions, and between the final session and the first follow-up session, which is scheduled four weeks after the end of the six treatment sessions. At this point, the client is also told that he should now begin using hyperventilation to prevent or abort occasions of sexual arousal in the presence of anyone other than a consenting adult partner.

Clients often complain that we are attempting to produce an effect that will prevent them from indulging in legal sexual activity in the future (e.g., with their spouse). It is important to address this complaint immediately, emphasizing that the use of this procedure depends upon their own choice and their motivation to use the strategy. If they are motivated to use the procedure to prevent illegal activity it will work, and will have no impact upon their legal sexual activity.

Another common complaint is that the request to indulge in sexual fantasies about illegal acts is against the work they are trying to do, or is against their religion. (One client brought his pastor to a session to help support this complaint.) Again, it is important to address these complaints carefully, and in some cases it is necessary to point out that sexual activity is a normal human function, and if they prefer not to indulge in fantasies involving illegal sexual activity they may be able to use fantasies of legal activity in order to develop sexual arousal. This approach will encourage them to start practicing the procedure for developing erections and then aborting them by the use of hyperventilation. It must be emphasized that this practice will enable them to use hyperventilation to abort sexual arousal when it occurs in inappropriate, illegal, or immoral situations. Clients making such complaints are reassured that the use of the hyperventilation is always a matter of their own choice, and that it will not interfere with normal sexual activity. (Interestingly, some of these clients have expressed extreme indignation at being asked to even consider an immoral act. As I mentioned in connection with our group work, some clients seem to enjoy the expression of righteous rage; they seem to be taking an extreme fundamentalist position that moves them to a very simple world of absolute right and wrong. In this simple world they see themselves on the side of goodness and right, with the privilege, or even the responsibility of heaping scorn on some despicable monster. For example, the sex offender may focus on a police officer who made a mistake in writing up some small aspect of the findings. They speak of this event as if it were a sin worthy of extreme punishment. As they speak it appears that they suddenly feel little or no culpability for their own misbehavior. It is as if their problems have vanished, or at least have become relatively unimportant in comparison to the horrible sin they are righteously describing.)

A frequent complaint from older clients is that they no longer experience erections. In such cases the homework assignment is phrased to focus on sexual imagery, particularly concerning memories of the sort of behavior that brought them to us. The basic idea here is that this client is in trouble because of his own behavior, which can apparently occur in complete absence of erections. We instruct these clients to focus on memories and images of the behavior that got them into trouble, and then rate the clarity of those images (instead of sexual arousal or the degree of erection) before and after hyperventilation.

As mentioned above, each homework session is to be tape-recorded to insure that homework is completed properly. The client is told to leave the tape recorder on throughout the sequence, from the beginning of fantasizing out loud, to the final rating of sexual arousal. The client is asked to bring both the tape recording and the completed homework record-keeping sheet to the next session. (If there are any clicks or other indications that the tape has been turned off and on during the sequence of a homework session, the therapist should be suspicious regarding compliance, and should again instruct the client to leave the tape recorder on throughout each homework session. If the client has no tape recorder, the therapist should make available an inexpensive tape recorder and tape for the client to take home. In such a case, the client can be required to sign a contract to return the tape recorder at the end of treatment.)

The second session and the remainder of the six treatment sessions are scheduled a week apart. At the second session, the homework data sheet is reviewed, and the tape is spot checked in the presence of the client. Any omissions or odd sounds are discussed in detail. It is frequently necessary, even with people of above-average intelligence, to repeat all instructions and the rationale on the second and third session, to forestall, or cope with, any failure or pretense of failure to understand the instructions.

The polygraph/psychophysiological monitoring system is again used in the second session. The purpose of this is to monitor use of the homework assignment. Accordingly the client is asked to describe his sexual arousing imagery, rate sexual arousal, hyperventilate, and rate sexual arousal again following the hyperventilation. Skin conductance is a particularly useful index, since it provides a dramatic and rapid means of showing that hyperventilation quickly leads to a large increase in skin conductance, which is accompanied by a rapid loss of the subjective sense of sexual arousal and by the disruption of related cognitions. It is important to note that whenever the review of the tape at the outset of any subsequent session indicates that an individual does not understand the procedure, a second demonstration, using skin conductance biofeedback during practice of the homework assignment, is advisable.

Once the client has clearly understood the instructions and has properly completed a homework assignment, subsequent sessions simply involve a review of the homework sheets, combined with spot-checking the tape and issuing a new homework sheet and tape. During these sessions, time is available for brief discussions of value systems, and work on perspective taking, victim empathy, social skills training, sex education, and cognitive restructuring. Whenever a particular need is identified that is not likely to be addressed in sessions that have already been scheduled with other agencies (e.g., severe social skills deficit), we either arrange for a referral to another provider, or do this work ourselves when the six sessions of hyperventilation training have been completed.

During the sixth and final hyperventilation session the client is given homework record-keeping blanks for four weeks, and is scheduled for a follow up visit one month later.

The results of application of the hyperventilation format are very promising. Only two of the 20 clients re-offended (the shortest follow-up period is three months, and the average follow-up period is over six years). This result is particularly noteworthy, since 13 of the clients have continued living in the relatively rural setting in which the crime was committed. They have been under very frequent, if not constant surveillance, by police, community and/or family members. Several of the clients lived for many months in a location that was run by the correctional system. Several others live in a sheltered living situation; these individuals would have been quickly reported to the legal authorities and eventually to us if a re-offense had occurred. (It is worth noting that we are in frequent communication with many of the attorneys and the probation, parole, and police officers who know these clients well and see them frequently.)

Of the two re-offending clients, one had previously molested many male children, and had spent five years in federal prison, where he had participated in various forms of therapy. Upon his release, the rehabilitation department of the prison contacted us because of our proximity to the client's hometown, and because of their concern that he would re-offend. After completing our six-session program, he continued to report powerful urges to seduce young boys. We worked with him for an additional 20 sessions, over fourteen months, of cognitive-behavioral therapy, with continuing practice of the hyperventilation strategy, before he re-offended. He was on an antiandrogen medication regimen, beginning with the third session of our work with him, and was on this regimen at the time of the re-offense. He was able to abort this offense (touching the penis of a nine-year-old boy he was baby sitting) after a few seconds by using hyperventilation and reported the offense to the therapist within 48 hours, knowing that he would be once more incarcerated. Following his release, he completed four booster sessions. During one of these sessions he said he did not want to damage any more children. He said that he is now avoiding dangerous situations (e.g. no longer "babysitting"). He also stated that, when tempted to re-offend, he would use the hyperventilation routine and leave the situation as quickly as he could. He has been closely observed by the police in his town, and by other citizens. He is currently attending follow-up visits with us approximately every three months, and as far as we can determine, he has not re-offended during a 10-year follow-up period.

The second re-offending client was an exhibitionist. He completed the protocol prior to committing another offense (an obscene phone call that was traced). Since he was still on probation for previous offenses, he was imprisoned for over one year, and while in prison he joined a church. He has been in occasional contact with us since his release. He has remained involved with the church he joined while in prison, and as far as we can determine he has not offended again.

The reader may wonder why only 20 clients have been through this protocol in over two decades. One factor is obvious. We are located in a relatively rural area where fewer clients with any particular problem are seen during any fixed period of time. Workers in an urban setting will be able to amass large numbers of subjects far more quickly than we can. A second factor has to do with engagement in therapy. During the period covered by this report, 28 sex offenders were referred to us. Of these, one was organically impaired, from a severe stroke, and another was mentally retarded, apparently from birth. Both of these clients failed to grasp the basic elements of the program. The other 6 clients did not engage with us. Several refused to sign the release of information agreements allowing us to communicate with legal authorities involved in the case, and some failed to return for subsequent sessions. Most of these individuals were self-referred, but two chose to put themselves at the mercy of the legal system rather than go through our procedure. (It is worth noting that the author, with a relatively confident, authoritative manner of presenting this program, has had much greater success at getting clients to engage in therapy than have several other members of our team.)

The hyperventilation format has produced convincing positive results with our clients. The format has numerous advantages, including short duration of treatment, placement of responsibility on the client, and ease of communicating the method to the client and to other interested parties. Furthermore, this format can easily be included in existing multimodal treatment programs. Our results strongly suggest that hyperventilation might be a powerful tool for reducing sex offenses.

Part Six

Working with Life Stories, Self-Concept, and Available Selves

20: Learning the Client's Story—Narrative Work as Both Assessment and Therapy

In Chapter 9, I mentioned the use of a brief narrative therapy interview that we use to help with development of our case formulation; and in Chapter 2 and some other chapters, I mentioned elements often associated with narrative therapy. I believe that learning the client's story is at the basis of most successful therapeutic work. Some clients have been surprised when I bring up a part of their story that they might have told me many years before, and apply it to something going on their current life. The surprise has always been accompanied by positive affect. The positive affect seems at least partly due to the realization that they are in the presence of someone who knows their story and cares enough about them to recall a particular aspect of the story that pertains to their current life. Another way to say this is that the client expresses positive affect as a result of feeling validated.

There are other important reasons for knowing the clients story. Knowing the story helps us to understand the powerful incentives in the client's life, the situations the client has found particularly compelling, and the meanings the client attaches to those situations. Knowing the story also helps us to appreciate some of the details of the essential audience, and the shifts in the working self that demonstrate the range of available selves. Thus, knowing the story is essential for the development of a good case formulation and therapeutic strategy. Furthermore, as mentioned in earlier chapters, when dealing with an individual suffering from PTSD, narrative work can help "reweave" or develop a coherent narrative history and serve as an important therapeutic activity.

Finally, in individuals without a diagnosis of PTSD, narrative work can yield other benefits. Pennebaker (1999) has summarized the results of many years of research into the benefits of telling or writing about a powerful negative or traumatic emotional experience from one's earlier life. In short, he and his colleagues have found that writing about distressing events, and about the emotional impact of those events, produces a number of very helpful changes, including enhanced immune system function, reduction in symptoms of asthma and rheumatoid arthritis, greater sense of well-being, reduced frequency of physician visits, reduced absenteeism from work, and improved academic grades. There is a clear relationship between Pennebaker's research and many of the strategies I have described in this book, such as the use of homework assignments to keep records of the most emotionally powerful experience each day, and the retrospective strategies of developing life charts (described in chapter 2).

An appreciation of the value of learning the client's story is not at all new. Many experienced therapists, of differing theoretical positions, have noted that essential aspects of the successful therapeutic process include providing an accepting environment for the client to enable and assist the client in telling her or his "story." An excellent example has been provided by a psychoanalyst with 30 years of clinical experience.

In a paper entitled "Does technique require theory?" Lindon (1991) reviewed his experiences with four different impulsive clients that he treated at different times in his career. These clients were treated with four different strategies based on the four different theories he favored at various stages of his career. He concluded that the primary elements in the positive impact of the therapy were working "to understand the patient from his or her point of view and conveying my understanding of the patient's psychic reality." At another point he indicated that he worked to establish what Winnicott (1965) called a "holding environment," and that he was trying to understand his client's "story." One could easily argue that the crux of the work he was doing was essentially "narrative therapy."

A brief digression will help. A 77-year-old friend recently told me about a decision that one of her grade school classmates has made. She was recently widowed, and was being pressured to move to a retirement community. After considering it carefully, she finally decided to stay in her home of many years. Her reason for not going to the retirement community was stated as "they don't know my story."

As described in chapter 9, I begin work on case formulation with a fairly rapid assessment that includes some parts designed to elicit the client's "story" and "psychic reality." With some clients I have scheduled a 90-minute visit on the first or second session to allow me to use a form of brief narrative work as a step in assessment. Following this, if I decide to work with the client individually instead of in a group, I generally use a highly-focused intervention that either solves the "presenting problem" or brings it under considerable control. This generally takes between 6 and 18 sessions. In some cases I have noted that even though the "presenting problem" appears to be under control, the client is still somehow "stuck" with a very negative attitude and experiencing a very low quality of life. If I can identify another clearly circumscribed problem, I consider contracting for another highly focused period of work. However, it is often the case that I do not identify such a circumscribed problem.

Occasionally I have referred these clients to other care providers, who generally use some kind of psychodynamic supportive strategy, and sometimes continue to see the client for a very long time. However, I have recently been resorting to using a more extensive attempt at getting at the client's "story"—a form of narrative therapy—at this stage of treatment. I have found that this narrative work has been surprisingly successful in getting these clients "unstuck," and moving toward termination of our therapeutic work and a better quality of life. I have also used narrative work, with surprising success, early in my work with several clients who have been extensively treated by other therapists, and who remained "stuck," and were eventually referred to me for an assortment of reasons. An example: a client was referred to me who had been seen over 100 times by another therapist who was leaving our facility. That therapist had focused on the diagnosis of depression and had written excellent progress notes. From these notes it appeared that the client was stuck. My first visit with the client supported this impression. Accordingly I used a brief narrative assessment/therapy procedure that was completed in three sessions. During these three sessions it became apparent that obsessive-compulsive disorder (OCD) was at least as important in this client's life as depression. Application of the Yale Brown Obsessive-compulsive Scale supported the OCD diagnosis. In eleven sessions we focused on

OCD and found that the problems of both OCD and depression were dramatically reduced in severity.

Narrative therapy has many ancestors and many variations. Instead of presenting a detailed history and rationale for the variation I favor, I will give a brief, selective history and then sketch out the steps that I have found useful in helping clients develop a narrative (i.e., tell their story).

In earlier chapters of the book I have mentioned some Adlerian concepts. One strategy I have occasionally used is based on Adler's statement roughly paraphrased as "ask what the symptom or problem does for the client." This can be treated in a variety of ways, including questioning what power or control the problem, or problematic behavior, gives the client. Power and control issues related to problematic behavior and problematic aspects of the self-concept are central to the current narrative work of White and his colleagues. This work has recently been reviewed in an article that presents a narrative therapy approach to brief treatment (Kelley, 2002).

As part of the narrative assessment/therapy work we have also used Adlerian strategies in examining early memories. It has been very helpful in my work with violent clients to ask about a client's first memory, or their first happy, sad, or fearful memory, or their earliest memory of being comforted. Since 1989 I have come across the work of James Mann, and I now realize that many of his strategies are also of the sort I had been attributing to Adler. I am pleased to see that Mann's time-limited method, with its story-related elements of early life experiences with important relationships, was recently evaluated in a randomized controlled outcome study with long-term follow-up. The results show very significant improvement and excellent long-term maintenance (e.g., see Shefler, Dasberg, and Gershon, 1995).

In Chapter 2 I mentioned that I had made use of George Kelly's ideas. I wrote that "Kelly (1955) and others have noted that we are all personal scientists in the sense that we work, and even struggle, to make sense of the world, of our impact on the world, and of our possible roles within the world." Kelly used some very interesting strategies to develop understanding of crucial aspects of his client's stories, and one of these will be elaborated in the next chapter.

I also mentioned in Chapter 2 another excellent narrative device, Almy's "life chart." The life chart relates the events in a person's life to various gastrointestinal and other medical symptoms, and allowed Almy to simplify and to relate to each other various behavior patterns, symptoms, and experiential events so that the complex symphony of life of a person in various situations would become more clear.

Since 1989 I have frequently used a combination of these approaches to get at a client's recollections of periods, or milestones in their personal history. Among the important milestones that help bring the story to life are periods of being at emotional peace or in emotional turmoil, of feeling respected or disrespected, of being victimized, or being valued and comforted. I am sure that use of these narrative-based strategies has helped me to know people better and to observe the origins, natures, and functions of the client's usual patterns of behavior and thought. Some would call these typical patterns of behavior and thought "aspects of their personality." Throughout this book I have called them "available selves." Finally, it is worth noting that Meichenbaum (1994, 2000) and other cognitive and behavioral therapists have made use of narrative therapy.

A Narrative Strategy

The narrative strategy presented here has seven simple elements that I have presented in several different ways. I have compressed the basic elements into a 90-minute session, spread it over five to seven sessions, or worked with the client in a series of sessions to complete each step. (A voice-activated typing system allows me to create a manuscript very quickly, often as the client speaks. This procedure enables the client and me to edit the account in real time.) A few clients have found it possible to complete some of the steps between sessions. In such cases, the subsequent session is spent discussing the homework product and editing what has been completed so far, before moving on to the next step.

There are many points in these seven steps where lengthy digressions, and even complete departures, can be expected, and generally encouraged. As one of my colleagues put it, in using these sequential steps "I would allow the therapeutic moment and the needs of the client to dictate the 'road taken' within the therapeutic session." The sequence of steps may seem amusingly rigid and restrictive compared to the artistic, humane and flowing narrative work of someone like Michael White (e.g., see White and Epston, 1990).

I offer three reasons for the use of these steps: (1) I am dealing with clients from northern New England who often fit the folklore about them—they are not very talkative; (2) I am a clinician who works much of the time in the relatively structured mode of behavioral and cognitive behavioral therapy; (3) I have often been able to get a wonderful conversation started using the first one or two steps, and when this happens we may not need the rest of the steps.

1) First step: Begin with sketching out the "life chart." The instructions for the life chart are easy to follow. I typically use the following system: Put the date of the client's birth on the left edge of a large page and put today's date on the right edge of the page. Put down the approximate dates and episodes of each of the following in the approximate positions where they would fit on a timeline that is arranged across the page, phrased in terms similar to those used to instruct the client: **the places you lived; the schools you went to; the jobs you held; your military career (including training, duty assignments, duty stations, etc.); the physical illnesses and injuries you suffered.**

2) Second step: On a separate paper, the client, or the therapist being dictated to by the client, writes one or several paragraphs responding to this: **"Recall the first time—an episode—when you felt comforted, loved and protected. Enter a representation of this important relationship on your life chart, indicating the timeframe during which it occurred."** (Note that this part of the procedure is likely to provide cues to the members of the positive essential audience.)

3) Third step: On a separate paper, the client or the therapist being dictated to by the client, writes a piece responding to this: **"Recall the first time—an episode—when you felt afraid, or rejected, or abandoned, or betrayed. Enter a representation of this important event on your life chart, indicating the time frame during which it occurred."** (Note that this part of the procedure is likely to provide cues to the members of the negative essential audience.)

4) Fourth step: The client is told something along the lines of **"Look at your life chart. Consider the high points and low points of your life. Notice that many of these are related to beginnings and endings of relationships. See if you can sketch out/describe the**

high and low points of your life and the beginnings and endings of your important relationships on your life chart. You could put the high points above the horizontal midline and the low points below the horizontal midline of the chart."

5) Fifth step: The client is told something like **"Look at the following words and tell me about individual episodes—or write paragraphs (or make outlines of paragraphs) for any two or three of these that seem important for depicting the depth and range of the narrative of your life: valued; honored; loved; respected; comforted; traumatized; disrespected; victimized; uncertain; confused; worried; powerless; dissatisfied; anxious; resentful; deprived; jealous; shamed; blamed; guilty; self pity; embarrassed; fear; feared; angry; rage; sad; sorry; depressed; procrastinating; perfectionistic; full of pride; innocent; adequate; effective or competent; joyful; loving; forgiven; forgiveness; generosity; fulfillment; courage; satisfaction; powerful; certain; clear thinking. (Add any other words describing feelings, sensations, thoughts or perceptions that have been related to important episodes in your life.)"** (Note that this part of the procedure is likely to provide cues to the nature of the client's various available selves.)

At this point I sometimes conclude the work with the development of a "document" (along the lines of work done by White and his colleagues), in collaboration with a client that somehow puts a positive "frame" or theme to all or part of a client's story. I put this document on a three-by-five card and encourage the client to carry it with him and think of it, or even touch it, whenever feeling stuck, demoralized, lost, or alone. This has worked quite well in some cases. An example of such a document is "My sons love and respect me." Also, at this point some work of the sort described by Pennebaker (1997) will have been completed, and the client may actually appear to be "unstuck" without further work being done.

With other clients I have found it useful to carry on with at least two additional steps:

6) Sixth step: the client is told something like a **"Sit back now—take stock. See if you can observe at least two sides of your personality, or "available selves" that have characterized you during the course of your life. It may help to ask yourself "what would my best friend say about me if asked "what are the two sides of ...'s personality?" See if you can identify one side of your personality that you are particularly pleased with, and another that you are less pleased with. Think about the situations that brought the more pleasing or positive "available self" into play. On a separate page write down a brief description of one or two situations that trigger this more pleasing or positive available self and describe some of the behaviors we would see if that available self were responding to those situations."**

7) Seventh step: the client is told something like **"Can you imagine any way to maximize the probability that this side of your personality or available self will be in control all the rest of this day, and through the date tomorrow? If you come up with ideas on this, write them on a separate page."**

This simple system for eliciting narratives has served us very well. It has helped us formulate effective treatment strategies for some clients, and to get some clients unstuck from a passive and negative mode of living. In some clients it has led to development of a sense of agency. In a few cases this work seems to have even led to the development of something that looks like psychological mindedness or an observing ego. Furthermore, all of the clients with whom we have used this system seem to be buoyed up by realizing that someone now knows their story. Most of our clients need all the buoying up they can get.

21: Putting It All Together and Making It Last: Working with Life Stories and Optimizing Available Selves

In ordinary conversation we sometimes hear statements such as "part of me wants to," "that wasn't me," or "I can't believe I did that." The notion that there are different self-states has been considered from many points of view. One of my favorite passages on this topic is from Tyler's (1965) textbook on individual differences. She wrote, when addressing the sudden changes sometimes observed in human behavior: "...things like religious conversion, the response to the challenge of a new and demanding position, or the pervasive effects of a genuine commitment to a movement or an ideal. These phenomena must be studied if individuals are to be understood." She went on to say "The possibility of such a psychology was envisaged long ago. One of the earliest and perhaps the greatest of America's psychologists, William James, assigned a place of fundamental importance to the individual selective process we have been considering. He expresses the idea in this way:

> ... the mind is at every stage a theater of simultaneous possibilities. Consciousness consists in the comparison of these with each other, the selection of some, and the suppression of the rest by the reinforcing and inhibiting agency of attention....
> The mind, in short, works on the data it receives very much as a sculptor works on his block of stone.

> In a sense the statue stood there from eternity. But there were a thousand different ones beside it, and the sculptor alone is to thank for having extricated this one from the rest.... Other sculptors, other statues from the same stone! Other minds, other worlds from the same monotonous and inexpressive chaos! (Tyler, p. 507)

Or again:

> I am often confronted by the necessity of standing by one of my empirical selves and relinquishing the rest. Not that I would not, if I could, be both handsome and fat and well dressed, and a great athlete, and make a million a year, be a wit, a bon-vivant, and a lady-killer, as well as a philosopher; a philanthropist, statesman, warrior, and African explorer, as well as a "tone-poet" and saint. But the thing is simply impossible. The millionaire's work would run counter to the saint's; the bon-vivant and the philanthropist would trip each other up; the philosopher and the lady killer could not well keep house in the same tenement of clay. Such different characters may conceivably at the outset of life be alike possible to a man. But to make any one of them actual, the rest must be more or less suppressed. So this seeker of his truest, strongest, deepest self must review the list carefully, and pick out the one on which to stake his salvation. All other selves thereupon become unreal, but the fortunes of this self are real. Its failures are real failures, its triumphs real triumphs, carrying shame and gladness with them. This is as strong an example as there is of that selective industry of the mind on which I insisted some pages back. Our thought, incessantly deciding, among many things of a kind, which ones for it shall be realities, here chooses one of many possible selves or characters, and forthwith reckons it no shame to fail in any of those not adopted expressly as its own.

Perhaps at long last we are now ready to build a structure of research and practice on the foundation William James laid" (pp. 507-508).

In Tyler's quotations from James we are considering a single career choice point, when a possible self for the long-term is put into place. However, some of the shifts among clinically important self-states occur repeatedly in response to situational demands.

Such shifts are exemplified by another of my favorite passages on possible selves, this from the novelist Patrick O'Brian (1991).

In a historical novel about the British Navy in the early 1800s, O'Brian is describing his hero, Capt. Jack Aubry, who had just finished speaking encouragingly to his troops after a battle.

> He hoped the words sounded cheerful and that they carried conviction, but he could not be sure. As it usually happened after an engagement, a heavy sadness was coming down over his spirits. To some degree it was the prodigious contrast between two modes of life: in violent hand-to-hand fighting there was no room for time, reflection, enmity or even pain unless it was disabling; everything moved with extreme speed, cut and parry, with a reflex as fast as a sword-thrust, eyes automatically keeping watch on three or four men within reach, arm lunging at the first hint of a lowered guard, a cry to warn a friend, a roar to put an enemy off his stroke; and all of this in an extraordinarily vivid state of mind, a kind of fierce exaltation, an intense living in the most immediate present. Whereas now time came back with all its deadening weight-a living in relation to tomorrow, to next year, a flag promotion, children's future-so did responsibility, the innumerable responsibilities belonging to the captain of a man-of-war. And decision: in battle, eye and sword-arm made the decisions with inconceivable rapidity; there was no leisure to brood over them, no leisure at all. (pp. 43-44)

This passage, relevant to the experiences of many of my clients who are veterans of military combat, brings out several extremely important points. One is that in battle, or in any form of compelling situation, the difficulties and responsibilities of daily life, the "deadening weight" of mundane details, are not in the conscious mind. Another is that the sense of time is altered, and in battle the body reacts as if being controlled by extremely rapid and highly-trained psychobiological subsystems, instead of the subsystems that work to deal peacefully and deliberately with the demands of daily life. Finally there are the potentially intoxicating and even addictive elements of the vivid state of mind, the fierce exaltation, the intense living in the most immediate present. I believe that these factors play a large role in the maladaptive behavior shown by many of my clients.

Working with Shifts in Self-State

Some attempts have been made to develop interventions to address these problems in the clinic. Ryle and his coworkers have taken an interesting approach to these issues with what they call the "self states sequential diagram." The therapist works with the client to construct this diagram. Eventually the client is able to apply the concept of multiple self states to their own experience and behavior, and thus to develop some understanding of the circumstances that pull for a particular self state. Ryle and Marlowe (1995) write that in their borderline clients the extreme shifts between self states "can best be explained and managed by identifying and characterizing the two or more more-or-less discrete and dissociated self states which alternate in these patients, and by tracing the switches between these states." Initially these switches are seemingly automatic or unconscious movements from one state to another, with a few triggering situations identified as likely precursors to a shift. Later in therapy the client would ideally be able, on the basis of new insights, to manage difficult experiences without dramatic and counterproductive shifts in self-state.

Willful Induction of a Self-State

While I deal with some clients who need that sort of work, I also deal with many clients who are well practiced at self-observation and self-management, and who often choose to induce self-states that are extremely problematic, both to themselves and others. In the example of willful induction of a self-state by Mr. B., he was instituting a very powerful state of himself that would be clearly dominant and threatening in a social situation.[1] It often seems that such willful inductions of a self-state occur in anticipation of a challenge, or in response to a drop in self-esteem or sense of

---

[1] In a letter Mr. B. wrote to me he added a postscript saying "I might add: self-induction of mania, together with willful intent, was part of my dysfunction for many, many years."

efficacy – often in response to a sign of disrespect. The induced self states in my violent combat veteran clients often function as a form of armor, and are well-practiced responses to fear that were learned sometime between childhood and military service.

With some clients I have been able to use strategies that help the client develop an ability to induce a prosocial self-state, or available self. Frequently this process has taken the form of small experiments in fixed-role therapy. In order to begin with these experiments, we need to know how the client sees himself. In Chapter 9, I described a number of strategies for gaining this understanding, including the technique of asking clients to write descriptions of themselves that might be written by their best friend, their worst enemy, and by themselves. This strategy owes much to Kelly (1955). Kelly's strategy of fixed-role therapy used several procedures to arrive at an understanding of the role, or roles, that an individual has become accustomed to, and has been typically falling into. Kelly saw one of the primary tasks of clinical psychology as being to understand the way in which clients interpret and give meaning to their various life experiences. The starting point for fixed-role therapy is exploration of the present self-characterization of the client. Kelly's first principle runs (similar to a strategy of Adler): "If you don't know what is wrong with someone, ask him: he may tell you." The self-characterization is an example of this principle and the "credulous approach" in action. The carefully-worded instructions invite the person to tell the therapist about himself. (Fransella, 1985).

Quoting Kelly: "I want you to write a character sketch of (for example) Harry Brown, just as if he were the principal character in a play. Write it as it might be written by a friend who knows him very intimately and very sympathetically, perhaps better than anyone ever really could know him. Be sure to write it in the third person. For example start by saying, 'Harry Brown is....'" (Kelly, 1955).

Writing in the third person apparently lowers anxiety and gives the client maximum room to decide what to share with the therapist. It is also helpful, in the early stages of therapy, to ask the client to write such a passage about themselves as they are now, and then as they will be when their problem has been eliminated (Fransella, 1985). Use of these procedures has made it possible to identify potential roles (that approximate a hoped for possible self, or a best available self) that the client might profitably practice. Kelly's fixed-role therapy employed enactment techniques to help clients approach a specific problem situation in a different manner.

Script Theory and Affect

In his script theory, Tompkins (see Demos, 1995) developed a number of concepts that can be used in connection with Kelly's techniques. Among the most important of these is the notion that affect selects scripts (containing something like a role and at least one affect and a thought linked to the affect). In other words, a particular emotion calls forth a particular script or role (or persona or available self, with an attitude). In our clients there are certain highly probable and very powerful emotions that reliably call forth certain maladaptive scripts. These may not occur as thoughts, accompanied by words, but may be expressed as sequences of actions (for example, a negative mood may lead to drinking and/or searching for someone to "knock the chip off my shoulder"). While some of the scripts or roles may have been adaptive in risky or cruel playground situations, or later in combat situations, they are profoundly maladaptive in most low-risk, everyday civilian situations that adults find themselves in.

In our clients it seems that a particular script (or role, or available self), selected by one emotion may lead to a very different emotion. In other words, a particular script may transform affect—for example from intolerable to tolerable. Could the client be doing this on purpose? When one considers the many possibilities inherent in planful or directed use of scripts to transform affect, one can envision a continuum ranging from a pathological, antisocial, or destructive use of script to a more healthy, even, therapeutic or constructive use of script (this is essentially what Kelly was working on). One is able to glimpse some of the complexity of possibilities presented by this way of viewing human behavior by considering the ample evidence that a person can experience "mixed emotions," or more than one affect in any single moment.

A Case Vignette

One way to manage this complexity is to consider emotional antecedents and consequences to any particular script. A case vignette will illustrate use of this strategy. Ted is a Vietnam combat veteran who has problems with alcohol (occasional binge drinking) and anger. His anger has often been expressed, and violence has often occurred, in both sober and intoxicated states. Ted was brought up in a non-drinking, strict, apparently humorless and highly religious northern New England farm family. Ted was an above-average student, and a promising athlete. However, his father thought that both athletics and education beyond high school were wastes of time. Therefore he forbade Ted to spend time on college preparatory courses or athletics. Instead, Ted was required to take practical courses, with little or no homework, and was to go directly home after school to work with his father on the farm.

Ted went into the Marines immediately after graduation from high school. He remembers feeling anger much of the time before he went into the Marines, but, prior to boot camp, he recalled only behaving in a violent manner on one occasion. Ted says—"It was when a kid in my high school kept mouthing off at me—I told him to back off. He didn't so I let him have it. We were going at it hot and heavy when one of the teachers broke it up."

In boot camp and in his military career, both in combat and out, Ted recalls appreciating and thriving on the military system of discipline and structure. However, he expressed no respect for the commissioned officers he served with. Ted said "only the non-comms were out with us, where they should have been—they ran the real show—the lieutenants and captains were all college boys and they stayed out of the line of fire."

In his subsequent civilian life, Ted was unhappily married, with five children ranging in age from the lower teens to the mid-20s. He worked as a construction supervisor and was rated partially disabled (50% service connected) for post-traumatic stress syndrome and diabetes. We learned a good deal about Ted by using variations of Kelly's format, and the approach to script theory described above. We learned that Ted apparently detested his employers (calling them "yuppies," "liberals," and "college boys") and many of his coworkers (calling them "yes men," "free loaders" and "clock punchers"). He had never come to physical combat with any of these individuals, but frequently made threats of physical harm to employers and coworkers. He believed that there are two reasons he still had the job—Ted said, "I'm a damn good worker – and they know if they ever tried to dump me I would fight back legally with all the energy I put into my work."

Whenever Ted felt that he had been let down, when he felt confused or ashamed of something (**antecedents**), he was very likely to fly into a script that we call "righteous rage" (**behavior**). He was very well-practiced with this script. The words would flow without interruption, and the facial and body language were clear in communicating that violence was inevitable if anyone disagreed. The script typically led Ted from feelings of confusion and perhaps internalized blame to simplification of the situation, empowerment, comfort and externalization of blame (**short-term consequences**). This was Ted's desired state and his preferred reality. He wanted desperately to have the moral high ground, and rejected any suggestion that he was cowardly, lazy, stupid, disorganized, or in any way unworthy of the highest regard. If his opponents or audience showed respect for his position everything would be fine. They usually did not dispute him, but simply withdrew, and there usually was no violence. However, when this occurred he felt somehow disappointed,   even   somehow   disrespected   (**long-term consequences**), and at this point he had to struggle with the urge to begin drinking again.

Here one might ask what Kelly or Tompkins would suggest as methods to help us conduct more detailed assessment and develop a case formulation for Ted, and what would they suggest about how we might proceed with Ted's therapy? Would it help to explain the apparent relationship between affect and script selection to Ted? Was Ted's righteous rage script so "ego syntonic," or natural and comfortable for him that we would be wasting everyone's time? Could we try to get Ted to see what's in it for him to work toward tolerating the uncomfortable feelings, and perhaps developing new scripts for responding to them? Would he listen?

Here is what has happened so far: Prior to 1997, Ted attended two cycles of our 10-session stress and anger management/dialectical behavior therapy program (as described in Chapter 17, this program has now been changed to a four-session format). During this program it became clear that Ted had difficulty tolerating sloppiness and hypocrisy, and had a very negative attitude toward individuals who do not have his work ethic or his political beliefs. It was also clear that rage and violence, and concepts of character, commitment, strength, and even "firepower" were at the center of Ted's concept of himself and his preferred reality. On the other hand, Ted was at least partially aware of the toll being taken on his family and his coworkers by his behavior. After a brief discussion we decided to begin individual therapy to address problems of anger management.

The individual anger management program we contracted to use was a six session cognitive and behavioral program that includes many of the elements described in Chapter 12, and employs rapid relaxation exercises and carefully fashioned (in collaboration between client and therapist) internal dialogue to help the client learn to perceive and control the autonomic precursors and correlates of anger episodes.

Over the next eight months we were not able to complete the six-session format. There were four occasions when Ted asked for timeout. On two of those occasions he said things along the lines of, "this is eating me up, I need a break. I will call you when I am ready to start again." On the other two occasions he needed to be away, once for a vacation and once for a work project.

Finally, I decided to attempt narrative therapy. The beginning steps took place in two 90-minute sessions, during which we covered, albeit in a somewhat sketchy manner, the first six steps described in chapter 20. During these sessions it became obvious that Ted was beginning to understand his situation. He knew he had a very positive available self, and that committing himself to that role would have very positive effects on his family, and on all aspects of his life. However, he also faced choices that he was not completely ready to make. At that time it was clear that Ted's armor of the warrior persona, and his ego syntonic and highly-practiced scripts that we had noticed during dialectical behavior therapy were probably not going to be completely dislodged or replaced using any therapeutic format we had thus far selected.

What next? Perhaps we could use the exact procedure authored by Kelly. One can imagine asking Ted to write the script for a play with himself as the lead character—first as he is now, and later as he would be if his problems were solved. One can also imagine that Ted's visualization of his problems being solved would highlight the ego syntonic role of rage and violence in his preferred reality. Would Ted consider with us the progression from the short-term consequences of righteous rage to the longer term consequences? Would he appreciate the trajectory from empowerment, comfort and clarity in the short term, to disappointment, loneliness, and feelings of being disrespected in the longer term? In Ted's case, the answer for over a year was "no." He stopped the narrative work after two sessions. During the next several months he was apparently weighing the pros and cons of staying with the known defenses, to keep his warrior self close at hand.

This case, to this point, represents the downside, the powerful secondary gains that many clients get from their presenting problem. I am pleased to report that Ted is now doing much better. I am not completely sure what role we had, but he has now taken many of the important steps toward letting the secondary gains go. He no longer presents himself as the armored warrior. I have observed him being particularly peaceful and supportive with other very troubled combat veterans. His support is now prosocial and constructive. Instead of joining an angry and combative veteran in his rageful state, he is able to calmly and constructively help him work on identification of the problem and on brainstorming through possible solutions. I still see him about once every several months, in the hall, or in a group setting, and it does seem that the work with narrative therapy and the clarification of the presence of his available selves had something to do with his improvement.

Relapse Prevention

In many cases it takes years to do this work to the extent that the gains will last. The pattern of work that I have described in other parts of this book, carrying out 6-18 individual sessions, and/or a psychoeducational group, has permitted us to do the initial work reasonably quickly. Exploration or testing of various forms of internal dialogue, roles and scripts (as noted in item No. 14 of the summary of Chapter 2) can begin quickly, but often proceeds very slowly. Accessing an adaptive and nonviolent available self is frequently fairly easy. However, solidifying that adaptive and nonviolent available self so that it will serve as the permanent working self often involves long struggles with secondary gains, and may take a very long time. The consolidation of much of the work, and the realization of real gains, as in the case with Ted, frequently goes on outside our treatment setting. However, even for individuals like Ted it seems that follow-up is essential. Follow-up, in the relatively formal, relapse-prevention sense, is certainly important. However, there also seems to be some important contribution of feeling that he is known and valued by us. Having collaborated with us, and having been told that we have seen something in him, an available self that is particularly positive and worthy of respect, gives us a special role in his life. We have become a positive essential audience. Seeing one of us, or hearing us over the telephone now and then seems to help maintain, and even enhance the positive effects of therapy.

We are now addressing the formal follow-up and longer term relapse-prevention tasks with invitations to return to our four-session group, telephone follow-up, and scheduling of occasional individual sessions. Without this follow-up and relapse prevention work, and without the reminders of the work we have done together, I am sure that many of our clients would fall back into their old ways.

Putting It All Together

Now I will attempt to pull together many of the things you have read in this book. Here I see my job as giving you a clear view of what overall approach I think works best in the trenches. Many of the details of the strategies I have described are presented in the appendices. As you look through these, you will see that I have used pieces and variations of many cognitive and behavioral strategies developed by others. Some of these strategies have been tested and proven in controlled clinical trials. Some of what I have presented in earlier chapters, and what I will present below is new, as far as I can tell.

Directing the Symphony

Ekman and his colleagues have shown that emotion—specific activity in the autonomic nervous system—can be brought about by "constructing facial prototypes" of emotion when subjects are cued to use various facial muscles in certain specific ways (Ekman, Levenson and Friesen, 1983). Other workers, using this general paradigm, have presented convincing evidence that emotion and thought can be triggered by a simple postural change. Such findings suggest that we have a potential handle on our emotions that is quite simple to use. Handles on emotions, as well as thoughts, memories, etc., are essential if we are to do a good job of directing the symphony. Our approach to working with available selves makes extensive use of such techniques.

What Are Some of the Handles or Tools Available to the Self as Conductor?

I have used the term "reciprocal determinism" throughout this book. Research of the type that Ekman and his colleagues have carried out provides clear and simple examples of reciprocal determinism. Here we see again that the human system, the symphony, can be directed or shifted by making use of a change in any of its components. At the basis of the strategies described in the book is the idea that each of the following acts, memories, emotions, or thoughts can access, or at least pave the way for, the occurrence of every other one of the following set:

A behavior (such as a smile)

A memory (such as a thought of an old supportive friend—part of a positive essential audience)

An affect or emotion; these can be accessed by way of a script or role (such as used by Kelly and Tompkins)

A situation (that might include the behavior of another person).

Any of the above can be used to trigger an available self. We have made use of a "proactive strategy" to increase the probability that a positive available self will be in place at all times. The proactive strategy is tailored to each individual client. The client uses a watch with a timing and signaling function (such watches can be obtained for between $15 and $40) to provide a signal for using a four-part strategy that takes about 90 seconds to go through. A signal can be set to occur every half-hour at the beginning of use of this strategy, and the time can be extended to two to four hours later.

The four-part strategy is as follows: the first piece is the "quick calming response" (described in appendix to Chapter 17), which takes about 15 to 20 seconds and ends with an out breath and a smile; the second piece is the image/memory of a person, or an interaction with a person who has been a particularly important member of the positive essential audience; the third piece is a repeat of the first piece—the quick calming response; and the fourth piece is the image/memory of a time when the positive available self coped with a difficult situation.

Some clients, after using their version of the proactive strategy for a while, have realized that they can keep the positive available self in place simply by using the quick calming response every time they hear a telephone ring, or go to the bathroom. Other clients have managed to keep the positive available self in place, even in particularly difficult circumstances, by simply using the image of a member of the positive essential audience.

A brief case vignette perhaps best illustrates this latter strategy. In the early 1970s I received a telephone call from a high official in the Catholic Church. He described a very promising young man who was studying to be a priest. This young man had one very serious fault which came out when he played ice hockey. He was a member of an adult hockey league, and had been having trouble controlling his temper. On the day before the telephone call this young man had become so violent in a hockey game that police were involved, and, although charges were not pressed, he was given a very stern warning.

I was asked to work with the young man to see if we could develop a way of preventing violent explosions, while allowing him to continue to play hockey. During the initial session it became clear that the primary member of this young man's positive essential audience was Jesus. At the end of this session I walked out to the hall with this young man. We had agreed on the date and time of our next session and said goodbye. As he walked down the hall away from me an odd idea came to me. It was the idea that the image of Jesus sitting in the stands of the hockey arena could help him keep his positive available self in place even when severely provoked. I ran after him and asked him to use the strategy of imagining/visualizing "Jesus in the stands" at every hockey game between then and our next session.

When he came to the second session he was smiling broadly. He said "this is a miracle." He could clearly visualize "Jesus in the stands," and he described him sitting alone in white robes and looking on attentively. He also described several severe provocations to do violence in the games that he had played since our last visit, and on each occasion he was completely calm. We had several more visits, and I taught him some additional self-regulation strategies, but it was clear that the most effective work was done in the first session. I was able to follow up with him several years later, after he had become a priest. He greeted me with a smile, and said, "it works as well now as it did on that first night. Jesus is still in the stands."

On the other hand, some clients don't seem to be able to put strategies to work that will lead to the maintenance of a positive available self. I sometimes think about the concepts of observing ego, psychological mindedness, and the conductor of the symphony as possible labels for what might be missing in these clients. However, I don't have a good answer as to why some people seem to be able to make use of the strategies and others do not. It does not seem to be a function of intelligence or motivation in any simple sense. We have made progress with some of these particularly difficult clients by teaching them some of the many self-regulation strategies that have been described in this book. When we are fortunate, they are able to pick up on one or several of them and put them to work. With these clients relapse prevention seems to be more problematic than it is with the clients who can make use of something along the lines of a proactive strategy.

What about Managed Care?

Mental health care providers are under constant pressure to spend only a few sessions with any individual client. I believe that one useful key to doing the sort of work I have described here in the context of managed care is the cycling psychoeducational group format described in Chapter 17. In fact, this group approach appears to be particularly helpful in dealing with the clients described in the preceding paragraph. The firm invitation to return occasionally to that group, after going through a single four-session cycle, appears to be our best hope for maintaining the gains made by these individuals. Another cycle through the four sessions, or even attendance at one session in a calendar year may have a very helpful effect.

Another case vignette will help illustrate this effect. Recently a young man, with whom I had briefly worked individually and in a group in 1998, returned to the group. Prior to our first 1998 visit, he had been in jail many times, most frequently for alcohol-related episodes of violence. My first step in 1998 was to work with him for six sessions using the tactics described in chapter 12. Following that he attended this group for five sessions, with some gaps between them. He then dropped out of treatment.

Several weeks before his recent return to our group, he began using alcohol again, and there was another episode of violence. The courts and correctional personnel reviewed his record and found that he had maintained sobriety and avoided violence for the longest period since his middle adolescence during the four years after his attendance at our group. They mandated his return. Upon his return to the group, he testified that there had been several self-regulatory strategies that had stayed with him. The one that he could describe to us was a variation of the "quick calming response" (described in the appendix to Chapter 17).

What about Diagnoses?—Who Can Profit from This Work?

The strategies described in this book have been used with clients who have been given most of the diagnoses listed in DSM-IV, including such particularly difficult-to-work-with diagnoses as paranoid schizophrenia, senile dementia, and bipolar disorder. In fact, one of my clients has been given 6 different psychiatric diagnoses (including bipolar disorder, PTSD, and panic disorder) and a wide assortment of medical diagnoses (including diabetes, hypertension, and obesity). Furthermore, this client is currently prescribed more than 10 medications. He has worked with us in 15 individual sessions, including six sessions and a follow-up session using the panic disorder protocol described in Chapter 19, and six sessions of brief narrative therapy along the lines described in Chapter 20. He now continues with occasional group attendance. He attends about eight group meetings per year. All of his care providers agree that he has profited immensely from his work with us. My point here is that diagnoses do not amount to much in doing this sort of work in the trenches I have been working in.

Final Words about the Essential Audience and the Best Available Self

Many clients have told me that they can imagine what I would say about various situations. Some say they can hear my voice when they need it. I am not alone in receiving such comments. At a recent workshop, one participant said something like "I recently ran into one of my former patients and he said 'I was about to go crazy the other day, but then I heard your voice talking to me.'"

Along these lines, I had an amusing experience several years ago. In one of our stress and anger management groups, a long-term client said something like "I was about to deck this guy and then I heard the Corson bird on my shoulder telling me to start using my wise mind." One of the other members in the group, a very accomplished artist and wood carver, came back the next week with a five-inch tall rendering of my bespectacled, bald, and bearded head atop the body of a rather stout and bandy-legged bird. This bird sits in a place of honor in my office, and many clients who were not involved in the group sessions where the idea of the bird was hatched have looked at it and indicated that they recognize what it means. To use my jargon, I had become a part of their essential audience, apparently with a prosocial influence.

One more story will demonstrate that the development of an essential audience with a positive, or prosocial influence does not necessarily require individual work with clients. A Vietnam combat veteran, diagnosed with PTSD and several other disorders, recently informed a long-term group of his sporadic use of the proactive strategy. He realizes that whenever he is using the proactive strategy he has no problems with violence, and absolutely no brushes with law enforcement officials. On the other hand, when he puts aside his watch and does not use the proactive strategy he is very likely to become extremely violent. (His proactive strategy takes about 90 seconds and involves the following sequence: the quick calming response; visualization of a deceased uncle who was always kind to him; the quick calming response again; finally, visualizing a time when he coped calmly with a situation in which he had initially sensed that he was being disrespected.) This client is clearly the director of his own symphony, and he now realizes that his choices regarding use of the proactive strategy determine the quality of his life.

At a subsequent group meeting several weeks after this disclosure, the group was listening to a very agitated Vietnam combat veteran, also diagnosed with PTSD, as he described his inability to do any sort of self-regulation. The first client again described his proactive strategy to the group and urged the agitated client to try it. The agitated client quickly gave a series of reasons why this strategy would not work for him. One of the reasons he gave was that he never had a friendly mentor, or even a good friend. Fortunately, members of the group recalled that the agitated client is a devout Christian fundamentalist. The group designed a proactive strategy for this agitated client, as follows: the quick calming response, visualization of Jesus looking down on him, the quick calming response, and finally a brief prayer. As the group ended one of the members said to this agitated client "we are your friends." Tears came to the eyes of the agitated veteran, and I had the sense that this group was well on the way to becoming a very positive part of this man's essential audience.

Final Thoughts about Doing Psychology in the Trenches

In some ways this work is terribly difficult, sometimes horrifying, and in other ways it is magnificent. As I said in the acknowledgments in the 1989 book, "The people who have been my clients have been tormented, and they have tormented others. Many have killed other people. Most who were killed were killed in wartime combat or paracombat situations, but some were killed in peacetime. The misery, fear and unfairness in their lives and many of the lives they have touched make this whole project a sad burden for me and for my clients. I am thankful that they have had the energy, ability and motivation to join me in this project."

As I look back on their lives now, 12 years later, I feel less sad than I did in 1989. The remaining problems experienced by most of these clients, as well as those I have met since 1989, illustrate the need for continuing development of new assessment and treatment procedures, and for very long-term therapy and follow-up of deeply troubled clients.

Personality and Society—Some Possibilities

More general problems remain in the society that gave rise to such terrified and terrifying people. A great deal has been written on these broader issues. I will not add much more. The problems in our society range from child-rearing practices to the examples set by many of our leaders and models. Many of us revere violence, as shown by the popularity of boxing, wrestling, and movies such as *Rambo*. Throughout recorded history there have been wars, and the tradition of the warrior persists. Many problems stem from this tradition. Most of the clients described in this book were explicitly trained to be warriors.

Some of the clinical procedures that have been described here might also be used in mainstream educational settings to assist children in considering a range of alternative responses to situations that are likely to be highly stressful and that frequently provoke anger and violence. There is some evidence that programs targeting aggressive behaviors can be added to the educational curriculum and help counteract some of the negative effects of the warrior tradition (Wilson, Lipsey and Derzon, 2003). We might even move closer to Freud's ideal (see Chapter 11) of enlarging the population of those we see as potential friends and thus reducing the population of those we see as potential enemies—a most worthy goal.

I have no final solutions to offer. Many possibilities come to mind. One of my favorite possibilities is a central theme of this book: Let us try to empower the individual by helping him or her to develop a sense of agency and the attitude of the personal scientist/theorist.

Appendices

App. 1: Pertains to Chapter 5: A handout used with families

App. 2: Pertains to Chapter 7: Attention—a story about its power

App. 3: Pertains to chapter 8: Questionnaires and tests used in group assessment

App. 4: Pertains to chapter 17: Outlines for four session group DBT anger/stress management program

App. 5: Pertains to chapter 19: Outlines for six session individual panic disorder program

---

APPENDIX 1

Addendum to Chapter 5—a handout used with families.

The Family as a Team

The team approach to family organization can be used with any family. The goal of the program is to promote a wealth sharing team concept and to give more control to the family members, particularly to the children, than is typical in North American society.

A short description of the program, as it would work in a two-child family, follows:

- an "allowance" or salary level is determined for each child;
- a list of necessary chores for each child and a list of unacceptable behaviors is established;
- an approximate baseline level (i.e. the level already occurring) of unacceptable behaviors and failures to do chores is determined;
- a penalty is assigned based on the estimated baseline rate of these problems, so that during the first several weeks the child would earn about half of the possible top allowance level (if the baseline rate of the problem behaviors continues as it did prior to the onset of the program);
- whenever an unacceptable behavior occurs the mark (the first one or several letters describing the unacceptable behavior – e.g. H for hit, T for tantrum) is put on a chart posted in a visible place (e.g. on the door of the refrigerator), and the child is informed of the mark;
- in the list of chores a deadline point is established for each chore; parents should check to see if each chore is done by the deadline point, and a mark "C" is put on the chart for any chore left undone; the child is notified when that mark goes on the chart;
- each morning one child should have between 30 and 45 minutes alone with one of the parents (alternating which child is with each parent on alternate days), during which time no mention is made of negative behavior; this is a time for undivided positive attention devoted to discussing, or participating in things that the child enjoys;
- a brief review of the previous week's problem behaviors is conducted on Saturday morning, and payment is made (a sample program is presented at the end of this document).

Primary components of the program are:

1. A specific family-unit contract regarding the duties and privileges of all members.
2. A method for systematizing parental attention.
3. A method for systematizing, monitoring, and eventually matching rewards and punishments to real-world schedules—so that as children grow to adults they are prepared to face the adult world.

Methods

This document spells out methods that have been tried and proven in over 30 years of work (detailed description of methods and results are presented in other publications—Corson, 1976; 1989).

The Family Meeting and Contract

First, the whole family should gather together and talk about the idea of the family unit as a team. This is a team where the parents are the coaches and leaders, at the same time as being team members, and children are the team members who are learning from the coaches. Everyone in the family shares in the wealth of the family team. Positive behavior and completion of necessary jobs and chores is expected, and when chores are done and no negative behavior occurs the children earn a salary (the old word for salary is "allowance").

It is important for all members to know their privileges and responsibilities and to stay away from behaviors detrimental to themselves or to other family members. The family meeting should lead to development of a contract—as follows:

1. The parents and children list the responsibilities and privileges of each family member (it is more simple when the parents and children simply list the responsibilities and privileges for each child—leaving the parents out of the reward and punishment aspect of the program).
2. The parents and children list any behaviors of any family member (including themselves) that have previously bothered them or other family members.
3. The parents and the children list the rewards and punishments currently used in the family.
4. Discuss and edit these lists in collaboration with all members of the family.
5. Make the lists into a contract (a sample contract for a 13-year-old boy is shown at the end of this document).

Parents' responsibilities are understood to include earning money, preparing most meals, and being consistent and controlled in observing behavior and in delivering rewards and punishments. Parents also have the responsibility to be the leaders and primary decision-makers, to be fair, and to be the judges of what is fair. The parents must take the lead in reconsidering contract details at regular intervals (preferably every Saturday morning). The children, as developing members of the team, also have responsibilities, and some of their behaviors should be charted by the parents. Children should receive some of their usual rewards and punishments in accord with the contract. (See the sample contract in Table 1, at the end of this document.)

All family members should bear in mind two primary obligations of all members: (1) to notice when changes in the contract are needed (for example—in order to increase responsibility and privilege as children grow), and (2) to take an active role in considering and discussing possible changes.

Systematic Parental Attention

It is important to schedule some parental attention by means of a simple procedure. Every morning at breakfast, for the five days of the work week, one child should be in a separate room (such as a den) with the father alone, and without sibling(s) or mother present. This should last for about 45 minutes, and in a two-child family each child would receive father's attention every other day. On alternate days, the child would be with the mother. This can be seen as programmed parental attention that does not depend (is not contingent) upon the occurrence of bad or good behavior of the children. Parental attention should be paired with part of the daily routine to ensure its occurrence, and it is intended to partially satisfy the children's urge for (addiction to) individual parental attention. If it is not practical to do this in the morning the family should work out a method for combining parental attention with some other part of the daily routine.

Rewards and Punishments

The technique for managing punishment and reward is more complex. The family should tape to the refrigerator door, or kitchen wall, a chart on graph paper with days of the week blocked out on it (a sample chart is shown in Table 2 at the end of this document). Each incident of behavior that the contract specifies as being detrimental (unacceptable) should be immediately entered on the chart in the form of the first letter of the descriptive term (e.g., a tantrum is denoted by a T, hitting by an H, and failure to do chores by a C). The child should be notified immediately when the mark goes onto the chart. The scheduled daily periods of parental attention should generally avoid mention of unacceptable behaviors, but should instead be used as a time for the child to receive individual positive attention. (Most parents have decided to only review the chart on Saturdays, and to have the attention on the other six days of the week be totally positive.)

All of the marks have a long-term consequence. Each Saturday morning, the parents should review the previous week's behavior with the children. A salary, or allowance is an important part of this program. In all families that have previously used allowance as an incentive, the marks have been assigned monetary values to roughly match existing allowance rates. (The allowance is now treated as a salary—paid to people who contribute to the well-being of the team.) For example, in some families each negative mark costs the child five cents. Each negative mark would subtract five cents from the week's total possible salary, which in these cases was $1.40. (Remember this program was designed before 1970. Today more money will be involved.) In all cases the week's minimum was set at zero rather than having a child incur a debt for a particularly bad week. (One family had not previously used allowance or monetary incentives, but had instead used family outings; for example, bowling on Saturday afternoons had been withheld when the child had misbehaved. In this family, we systematized the delivery of various types of family outings in a manner similar to that used for money in other families.)

A timeout should be administered only when a child has indulged in three consecutive incidents within the same category of unacceptable behavior, or in five incidents across categories. The timeout should be administered immediately after the final mark is obtained (three or five). As mentioned above, the chart entries should be made when each incident of unacceptable behavior occurs. The child should be told of the mark being put on the chart and this announcement (or the timeout when necessary) should signal the end of the attention gained by the child for the unacceptable behavior. In cases where a child continues to be dangerous, destructive, or intensely disruptive, he or she should be removed, isolated, and ignored for a "time-out" period of no more than five minutes. This additional step is rarely necessary, since the entry of a mark on the chart generally ends such behavior. (Some families have elected to use a timeout from certain activities—e.g. access to video games, instead of using a timeout chair or room.)

Each timeout is noted on the chart with an asterisk. After a timeout, the child starts anew, in the sense that the next single unacceptable behavior is the beginning of a new series. Children also start with a clean slate each morning, in that no marks for unacceptable behavior from the previous day will count toward a timeout on the subsequent day.

[Note that the rewards and punishments are delivered in accord with the actual real-world schedules that psychologists have observed, with punishments on a high-ratio, short-interval schedule and with certain rewards on a low-ratio, long-interval schedule. Note also that this scheme is very different from the typical "token economy" approach (Atthowe, 1973).

The scheme is in fact opposite to the token approach in some respects (such as attention to rapid delivery of negative incentives and long delays of material and non-routine positive incentives).]

Table 1: Sample Contract for a 13-year-old boy in a two child family

Tom's responsibilities:	Unacceptable behaviors:
Brush teeth	Hitting brother
Make bed	Destroying things
Clean up room	Teasing brother
Feed dog	Untidiness
Get along well with brother	Disobeying
Complete homework	Arguing
Take your laundry to the laundry room	Irritating
Go to bed at 9:30	Yelling
Mow lawn when asked	"Blowing up"
Shovel walk when asked	Failure to do chores

Examples of Privileges and Limits for Tom:

1. Tom's maximum allowance/salary is seven dollars per week.
2. If Tom does all his chores and commits no unacceptable behaviors during a week, he will get all seven dollars on Saturday morning.
3. Tom's baseline rate of problems (unacceptable behaviors and failures to do chores) before the program started was about seven per week.
4. Each negative behavior costs Tom 50 cents; if he keeps on having problems at the same rate, he will get seven negative marks in the week and he will have earned $3.50 by Saturday morning.
5. If Tom gets 3 marks of the same category in a row on any one day, he is given a timeout immediately after he receives the last mark in the sequence.
6. Whenever a mark for unacceptable behavior is entered on the chart, Tom is notified about it, and whenever possible, this will be the only attention Tom receives for the unacceptable behavior.
7. No matter how many marks of any category Tom gets, he can spend time alone with one of his parents each morning.

[Adding privileges to the mark system has sometimes been done which increases the complexity. The following is an example of the privileges and limits that could be established for Tom:

1. If Tom gets no bad marks on any one day, he may watch two hours of TV programs of his choice the following night.
2. If Tom gets only two bad marks on any day, he may watch one hour of TV of his choice on the following night.
3. If Tom gets no bad marks in any week, he receives seven dollars that Saturday; he may pick his choice of dessert for two suppers in the following week; he may stay up until 11 on Friday and Saturday nights.
4. Each bad mark costs Tom 50 cents. If Tom gets only 2 bad marks in any week, he loses one dollar and he receives six dollars of salary on Saturday morning, and he may pick his choice of dessert for one support the following week.
5. If Tom gets seven bad marks in any week, he will not go bowling with Dad on Saturday morning; he may not watch TV all of the following week; he may not get to pick his choice of dessert; and he gets $3.50 allowance/salary for that week.]

At the end of the contract, a signature section should be included along the following lines—each member of the family should sign:

_____   _____   _____

Table 2: Sample Chart

Saturday	Sunday	Monday	Tuesday	Wednesday	Thursday	Friday
HDD	HG	HG	DG	GG	DH	GG

Bads/Goods	$
8/7	$3.00

APPENDIX 2

ATTENTION: a STORY about its power *(with a few learning principles and behavioral strategies noted in italics)*

The First Hospitalization: the Power of Attention

In the Fall 1974 I moved back to New England and started a new job. The job combined work as a professor at Dartmouth College in Hanover, NH, and the Chief Psychologist position at the Veterans Administration Hospital in White River Junction, Vermont.

When I had been at work for a few days I found my way to the hospital cafeteria. In the line in front of me at the cashier a nurse turned around and spotted my name tag. She exclaimed "Aha! A psychologist— just what we need." "We have a patient on my ward who for some reason insists on defecating in his bed. Everyone is sure it's a psychological problem. We have done every test imaginable to find a physical cause for this. Nothing!"

This sounded interesting and I asked her to sit down with me, and tell me the story about this man. As the conversation went on I learned that they had been recording every time this patient does a bowel movement and it was adding up to at least two per day that were ending up in his bed. I asked "What is he here for, and how long has he been here?"

She answered, "Well, I think he has been here for at least a month, but it seems like a year! He was in rough shape when he came in, actually still is in a lot of ways. He had such severe frostbite from his service in Korea that two weeks ago he had his left leg amputated from the knee down. They may have to take more off. His other leg is in bad shape too."

"We have to keep him here for physical therapy and education. We're trying to teach him how to take better care of himself."

"He lives alone in a trailer way out in the country on a dirt road. He doesn't see anyone for a week or two at a time, except for somebody who brings him a few groceries now and then."

During the conversation she told me this patient not only does bowel movements in bed, but he is also a "nasty man". I asked her about that. She explained: "Well, he's mean to the staff, and yells at us with the most disgusting language. He's mean and nasty to every one of us. Naturally nobody wants to be in the same room with him."

I said, "That is not good news. My proposal may sound very strange and might be quite difficult to get you folks to go along with. The basic idea is that maybe he wants companionship or attention. Maybe he just doesn't know how to ask for it, or to keep it once he gets it."

The nurse just laughed.

I said, "I know it sounds strange, but I have some data on the power of attention in all sorts of situations. I think you might be able to use it to manage this problem. You're already gathering the data to test a method and the ideas behind it. You're counting those B.M.s he does in his bed." *[Regarding learning principles and behavioral strategies: attending to the bowel movements provides a focus or "pinpoint" and the counting of bowel movements that end up in his bed provides a "baseline" against which to test the method I was about to propose.]*

She said, "Well we have to count the bowel movements anyway. So what's this magic method you have in mind?"

The plan had two components. First we would use a form of extinction. I told Nancy that she would need to have her staff give his client minimal, perfunctory attention whenever he did a B.M. in his bed. "Just go in, clean it up, and get out of there. Don't engage in any social interaction beyond what is necessary to do the cleanup job." *["Extinction" is a fundamental principle of learning—it means decreasing the frequency of a behavior by withholding the incentive—in this case I was assuming that it was the attention—that appears to be maintaining the behavior.]*

"The other component—and this may sound strange, relates to what I call the addictive power of attention. What you need to do is set your watch so that it signals you on every even hour. When that signal goes off someone from the nursing staff must go into his room and spend at least 10 minutes with him. You could talk about the weather, the news, the World Series—whatever you feel like talking about. You could even talk about things that he doesn't seem to be interested in. Do these two things and let's talk in about a week." *[In summary—I was hypothesizing that attention was functioning as an incentive. The procedure involved, on the one hand, extinction of the attention that had been linked to the bowel movements; on the other hand, it involved provision of "clock contingent" attention every 2 hours. It was as if he was addicted to attention and had found a counterproductive way to get it. We needed to get rid of the counterproductive behavior and provide for his addiction at the same time.]*

Of course the conversation went on for a while, because I had to do quite a bit of selling on the ideas and the method. She eventually agreed and we parted.

After a week I spotted the same nurse in the cafeteria again. She smiled when she saw me.

"It worked! He is cured. After the first 3 days, he hasn't done it at all."

"Great!" I said, but then I noticed I was going to be late for a very troubled client if I didn't move on quickly. "I'm sorry, I have to go. Keep up the good work. See you soon."

I should have let myself be late. Rushing off was a big mistake. A few weeks later I saw the nurse again and this time there were no smiles.

"What's happening with your nasty patient?"

"Back to the same old tricks. He's just as bad is he ever was."

"Have you been keeping on with the program?" (I was asking if they had continued to do the two things I had suggested.)

"No! We don't have time to keep on going in and putting up with his abuse every 2 hours. He's right back to doing two B.M.s a day in his bed."

Then I realized that I had done a "hit and run" consultation. I had forgotten an important lesson. I watched the nurse buy a sandwich and followed her out of the cafeteria. As she walked back to the ward we talked.

I told her I was sorry that I had not kept in touch, and that I realized that I should have been much more clear about the program and the theory. I also told her that I should have gone to the ward with her so that I could have tried to sell her colleagues on the program. At first she seemed irritated with me, but as we walked I was able to begin convincing her that this man really does seem to be addicted to attention. I also was beginning to be able to convince her that in order to keep him from causing trouble the staff will have to continue to spend time with him.

By the time we got to the ward she was ready to try again. I talked with the other nurses that were on that shift and I promised to come back the next day, to brainstorm more about the problem and my proposal.

When I got back to the ward the next day I was greeted with smiles. I was surprised to learn that the nurses had restarted the program on their own. The client had again stopped doing bowel movements in his bed. I decided it was my turn to go to his room and visit with him.

He was indeed a nasty man. His third word to me was profanity, and about every third or fourth word was also profanity. "Who the xoxo are you, and what the xoxo are you doing in my xoxoing room?" I realized that this man was one of those people who was able to use the same word as an adjective, a verb (both active and passive), a noun, an adverb, and for every other purpose imaginable. It was easy to see why the nurses didn't want to be in the room with him. I spent a few minutes there and then went back to the nurse's station. They were all standing there grinning.

"You see what you been putting us through? He's the worst we've ever seen. Most of these guys are nice to us."

Even though he was a nasty man, the nurses agreed to persist. This client left the hospital a few weeks later without having done another bowel movement in the bed.

Some Reflections

This hospital stay provided an experiment that can be framed as an ABAB reversal design (A= baseline, B= intervention for 1 week, A= second baseline, B= resumption of intervention). Prior to my first meeting with the nurse, baseline data on the number of B.M.s in the bed were being recorded. This was the first A. After the intervention, the first B, was begun it only took 3 days for the rate to drop to 0. The rate stayed at 0 until the nurses decided they didn't have time to spend with the patient with when he was not having a problem. When they stopped the program the second A was in effect. Finally, when they restarted the program, the second B, and kept it going until he was discharged from the hospital the complete cessation of further B.M.s in the bed provided a rather convincing proof that the intervention had been working.

The fact that we tested the application of two principles simultaneously produced a confound. Nonetheless, my data on other cases show that the application of clock contingent attention is worthwhile whenever anyone is left alone for long periods of time and begins to develop a behavioral problem.

The Second Hospitalization—Trapping Flies with Honey

It was October 1978 when I got a call from the new head nurse on the same ward where I had met the fellow who did the BMs in his bed. "Dr. Corson," she said, "we have one of your old patients back. I saw your consult reports in the chart from 4 years ago. Do you remember Joe L. who had a problem with bowel movements in the bed?"

"I sure do! He was unforgettable. How is he doing with you?"

"Terrible! Right now, as I am calling you, he's yelling obscenities at the staff, and he did a B.M. in his bed this morning. He came back in for another amputation and some additional work on the first one. We are going to have to deal with him for a while because the treatment plan includes bilateral prostheses and at least several weeks of physical therapy."

I said "I'll be over in about 30 minutes and we can talk about getting him back on the program that worked the last time he was here. We used the program of extinction and clock contingent attention; as long as we kept up the intervention he stopped defecating in his bed."

"Great!" She said, "I'll get his other nurses to join us."

When I met with the nurses I recognized the nurse I first spoke with 4 years ago. She didn't seem very pleased to see me again. We looked at the notes from the 1974 visit and I described the method, rationale and outcome. As soon as I finished my old friend spoke out "haven't you got anything better to suggest than for us to go in and spend time in that bastard's room?"

"Everything else I could suggest would be even more labor-intensive. With the other approaches, you'd have to spend even more time with him to change the behavior."

They reluctantly agreed to try the plan for a week, but just a few days later the head nurse called me. "Dr. Corson, we are going crazy with Joe. He won't stop his behavior, and the staff are refusing to start the program because they don't want to spend the extra time with him. We have some very sick people here now and it's much worse than usual. We really are too busy to do this."

I thought of the psychiatry ward, where I had been working with a group of nurses to develop behavioral programs for use with a series of challenging patients. I picked up the phone and called Pat. I sketched out the details and asked if she thought we could transfer Joe to her ward. She agreed and the transfer was completed.

On the psychiatry ward we kept the two original procedures (extinction and clock contingent attention) as the "boilerplate condition." Over the 12 weeks that Joe stayed on the psych ward we added several other conditions.

First we added "differential reinforcement." Using attention as the incentive, the staff rewarded or reinforced any appropriate or polite behavior by providing Joe with additional attention, by commenting on how nice it is when he is polite, and by more animated conversation. At the same time they worked to extinguish his vulgarity and rudeness by ignoring him when he was carrying on in his old manner. [The basic idea here is that a desired or adaptive behavior is rewarded while maladaptive behavior is extinguished or, in some cases, punished. In this case the differential reinforcement procedure involved rewarding one class of behavior and extinguishing another.]

At this point Pat and I decided to explain to Joe what we were up to. By explaining our plans, we gave him an opportunity to immediately "rule govern" his behavior. [Regarding the learning principle of rule governed behavior, B. F. Skinner described it as "behavior that is controlled by descriptions of the contingencies (i.e. the relationships) between specific responses and specific reinforcers." (By reinforcer he meant incentive. This terminology can be confusing, and my use of it is spelled out in Chapter 4 of the text.) The concept of "internal dialogue", or covert speech is part of this picture. Skinner also said "presumably these self-presented silent verbalizations of contingencies act as stimuli that evoke behavior which obeys the rules."]

In response to our explanation Joe said "I don't give a shit." (His choice of words amused everyone, but he did not seem to understand our amusement.)

It turned out that Joe did "give a shit." He became very attached to Pat. After about a week Pat went on a few days of annual leave. Joe realized this about 2 hours into the shift when Pat would have been working with him. He asked for her and was told that she was on leave for 2 days, and another nurse would be working with him.

"None of you measure up to her—I don't want any of the rest of you in my xoxoing room! Xoxo you all!" Still, he did not return to doing B.M.s in bed during her 2 days away.

When Pat returned Joe was again vulgar and rude to her. She stuck to her guns and left the room immediately, *a penalty*, in effect, for Joe was very fond of her.

Within hours, Joe began to interact with Pat in a more pleasant manner.

During the weeks that Pat worked with Joe we continued to employ the previously described procedures of extinction, clock contingent attention and differential reinforcement, along with the rule governing opportunity we had spelled out for Joe. Now we had added a new principle—penalty, cutting short visits when Joe spoke rudely.

Soon I saw that Pat was adding other contingencies. She began verbally punishing Joe's vulgarity and rudeness, by telling him that it upset her, and she was going to leave his room earlier because of it. [Regarding learning principles, we now had two types of punishment in place-penalty, when Pat left the room early, and the verbal punishment that Pat was administering when she scolded Joe for being rude.] Pat was also using a behavioral technique called "modeling". Pat would tell Joe the exact word she wanted him to use to express something he had already expressed with vulgarity. Then she would ask him to repeat the words back to her. He resisted at first, but then began to go along politely. [Regarding learning principles, modeling involves learning by imitation, and getting Joe to practice the modeled behavior is known as "positive practice".]

For example, one day Pat came on her shift and spent a very long time in a staff meeting before she had a chance to go to Joe's room. When she finally went to his room he said "Where the xoxo have you been—what the xoxo is going on here?"

Pat said "Joe, you know I don't like that sort of talk. It makes me think you don't want to see me at all! I would rather you say, 'hello my old friend, I've missed you. What kept you away so long?'"

"Why don't you try saying that, right now Joe?" Joe was reluctant, but he went along with the plan—paraphrasing liberally, but leaving out the swearing. Pat laughed, and repeated her original statement and asked Joe to try again. He eventually complied. The last few times he repeated it, it sounded quite natural. Pat used this procedure frequently, and would always ask Joe to repeat it a couple of times, just to "stamp it in." *Repetition helps with the learning process.* Eventually Joe's greetings did change, and the swearing dropped out of most conversations.

Pat was also doing a form of incentive assessment while she was interacting with Joe. She found out that he wasn't interested in current events, politics, or many things that other people of his age group were interested in. However, he was very interested in baseball, particularly in the Detroit Tigers. So Pat began talking with him about baseball. In order to do this, she had to do some homework, since she had not been a baseball fan prior to this. Pat also discovered that Dick, one of the nurses on the night shift, was a baseball fan who had some affection for the Detroit Tigers.

Pat introduced Joe to Dick—thus laying the ground work for "generalization." [Regarding learning principles, in this case the "generalization" was from appropriate, polite interactions with Pat—primarily over baseball—to appropriate, polite interactions with Dick during the night shift. It worked.]

I occasionally visited with Joe during this time and the transformation was remarkable. He used less profanity, made more eye contact, and occasionally expressed interest in other people.

One day Joe winked at me after talking over the change in his behavior, and he said, "you can catch more flies with honey than you can with vinegar—right Doc?" *[Regarding learning principles, here he showed that he was "rule governing" his behavior and perhaps he was also using the image of flies and honey in his "internal dialogue."]*

When he said that I realized that there had been a shift in his self-concept, and that he was in the process of changing his whole life situation. By chance, one of his grown children dropped by—just expecting to spend a few seconds—and spent a few hours. (Joe's wife had taken the 4 children and left their trailer in 1968. There were divorced in 1970. Joe had seen his children only a few times since then. By 1978 the youngest child was almost 20 years old.) Apparently this was the first time that any of Joe's children had enjoyed spending any time with him.

A few weeks later both Dick and Pat were going on annual leave at the same time. Pat had warned me, "Brace yourself, Dr. Corson. Both Dick and I are going on leave next week."

I was afraid that in their absence we might drop back toward the original baseline condition. Late on the second day of the week I was passing the physical therapy department, on the way to the ward, when I heard Joe's voice. (Joe was being trained to walk with artificial legs.) I stopped and eavesdropped for a few seconds. It was an interesting conversation.

"Did you see the xoxoing big guy hit that xoxoing record long homer last night? It went right the xoxo out of the stadium. "

"No, xoxo! I was asleep by then. The xoxoing TV was on, but with this xoxoing medication they give me I can't stay awake for the xoxoing games. But I heard about it on the radio. I figure that puts him ahead of the xoxoing homerun record pace for this point in the season. He's ahead of Maris, Mantle, and even xoxoing Babe Ruth!"

Well, xoxo! I'm really sorry you missed that one."

Joe was talking with one of the other patients about baseball. I heard plenty of vulgarity, but the conversations seemed to be enjoyable for both men. I went in and spoke to Joe. He seemed happy. I asked him how he was dealing with the absence of both Pat and Dick.

"Hell, it's okay if they're not around. Most of the people around here know baseball. I never knew that before. I just found out that xoxoing guy right here probably knows baseball even better than I do. He's a regular xoxoing historian."

It is worth noting that Joe never did a bowel movement in his bed while he stayed on the Psychiatry ward.

The last time I saw Joe he again said, "Doc, remember, you can catch more flies with honey."

The transition back home, to the small trailer in the back woods turned out to be difficult, but he eventually sold the trailer and moved closer to the town in which one of his children lives. Follow-up a few years later indicated that Joe had been doing reasonably well.

Some Reflections

I realized what good work Pat and Dick, and the other nurses had done with Joe. They used all of the learning principles I have mentioned, and they employed crafty "shaping" strategies that involved successive approximation of the desired behavior. They also progressed from using relatively primitive incentives, such as I had started out with when managing attention and the extinction process on the first ward, up to using more complex incentives, including some activities and interactions, which had apparently never previously functioned as incentives for Joe.

The work they did with Joe is an outstanding example of what has been called "behavior trapping." In this case the natural contingencies were always available out in the "real world", but Joe could not access them because of his negative expectations and nastiness. Now, with the help of Pat and Dick, the "behavior trap" had been sprung. Joe's new self-concept and repertoire allowed him to interact with other baseball fans, and eventually to build a social support system that he valued greatly. Another way to look at this is that Joe's self-concept had shifted, and he had developed some skills, and some new tastes, and-very importantly-he had stopped doing some counterproductive things that had isolated him. Said in still another way—the various elements of our program enabled him to be exposed to new incentives (also known as reinforcers), to develop what could be called "new tastes" and to develop new behavior/incentive (or reinforcement) complexes.

Joe's case also demonstrates the limitations of an analysis strategy called the reversal design, or ABA design. As mentioned earlier the first hospitalization fit the format of the ABAB reversal design. Gathering baseline data and then employing an intervention, and later returning to a baseline can show "stimulus control." We might predict that whenever the situation is returned to the baseline condition the behavior will drop back to the original (preintervention) level. This was the case during Joe's first hospitalization.

During the second admission we have an ABA reversal design, which leads to a different conclusion. In each case the B phase is an active intervention. The second A phase involves return to baseline. It is important to note that during the last A phase of the second hospitalization, and after discharge from the hospital, Joe had shown maintained performance, instead of complete stimulus control that depended upon the presence of the contrived intervention.

In describing this case we have come a long way from considering the power of attention. It is important to remember that the power of attention is what allowed us to get started.

APPENDIX 3

Questionnaires and tests used in group assessment

1. A questionnaire requests information about the presenting problem, living situation, social support, social and physical activities, physical and psychological health, sleep, memory, moods, emotions, thoughts, locus of control, quality of life, pain, substance use/abuse, memory, concentration and attention. The questionnaire also includes items that assist us screening for PTSD and in risk assessment. Most of these items were taken from a National Institutes Of Health Questionnaire (D. R. Hill, personal communication, June, 1994).

2. The Zung Depression Scale (Zung, 1965). This scale and the following scale are presented in language that most clients easily understand.
3. The Zung Anxiety Scale (Zung, 1971).
4. The Dartmouth Pain Questionnaire (Corson and Schneider, 1984) is a device that incorporates the McGill Pain Questionnaire (Melzack, 1975) and adds items that ask about participation in a number of activities of varying difficulty in the presence of pain, and the impact of pain on several aspects of self-perception.
5. The Hooper Visual Organization Test (Tamkin & Jacobsen, 1984) is a test of non-verbal abstract reasoning.
6. A few key questions that are particularly easy for clients to understand were selected from the Yale – Brown Obsessive Compulsive Scale (Goodman, Price, Rasmussen & Mazure, 1992), a device exploring elements of obsessive compulsive disorder.

    [All of the above are included in a self-administered packet with the questionnaire. Clients typically take about 1 hour to finish with this packet. When the packet is finished in the following items are presented. This phase takes between 60 and 90 minutes.]
7. A story recall test. Initially we used a short-term story recall test (Bayles and Tomoeda, 1993), taken from the Arizona Battery for Communication Disorders of Dementia, to assess auditory comprehension and logical and contextual verbal memory. Now we are using a more complex story that has about 10 ideas in it. The story is read to the clients, and immediately after the story is read the clients are asked to provide answers to 10 carefully worded questions about the ideas in the story. Two of these questions are multiple-choice, and the rest are short answer essay questions. Delayed recall of the story items is again tested at the end of the session.
8. The Memory for Designs Test (Graham & Kendall, 1960) is a test of memory for designs and constructional ability, where 15 simple designs are presented for five seconds each and the client is required to draw the designs from memory. Delayed memory for these same designs is tested using a recognition test at the end of the testing session.
9. A brief test of attention in which the client hears a series of letters mixed with numbers. In the first part of the test the client is asked to listen to a string of letters mixed with numbers and to count to the number of letters heard. In the second part of the test the client must listen to strains of letters mixed with numbers and to count the numbers of numbers heard. (This was obtained from David Schretlen Ph.D.. Psychological Assessment Resources, Inc., 1997)
10. A digit span test, modeled on the Wechsler Digit Span Test (Wechsler, 1981), that requires forward and backward repetition of strings of digits

presented via audiotape and responded to in written, rather than spoken form.

11. An executive function test. Three items are added to the end of the digit span test (permitting us to use the numbers written down during digit span assessment) examining calculation ability, and the form of executive functioning that is required for listening to and following multistep instructions. These three items progress in difficulty from one to three step tasks.

12. A memory for melodies test (Denman, 1984) was used for the first 300 clients, but did not yield useful information. It was replaced with the FAS, a restricted word search/verbal fluency test (Tuokko & Woodward, 1996). This is a test requiring the client to write down in one minute as many words as possible beginning with a particular letter. The test is called the FAS because it requires clients to write down the words beginning with F first, for a minute, then A, then S. (This test has also been referred to as the COWAT, or controlled word association test) This test is said to be sensitive to frontal and temporal lobe impairments.

13. The Ammon's Quick Test of Verbal Intelligence (Ammons & Ammons, 1962) requires the subject to match a printed word with one of four pictures. This brief test correlates very well with more detailed and multidimensional tests such as the verbal score on the General Aptitude Test Battery (Nash and Schwaller, 1985).

14. A shortened version of the Gorham Proverbs test (Gorham, 1963) presents five items that require verbal abstract reasoning. The client is asked to read a sentence, such as "Where there's a will there's a way," and to write down a sentence that makes the same point, such as "When you really want to do something you can get it done."

15. A shortened version of the Wechsler Adult Intelligence Scale similarities test presents six items that require some verbal abstract reasoning. For example the client is asked "in what way are a chair and the table alike?"

16. A verbal memory recognition test (Iverson and Franzen, 1994) uses a forced-choice format and examines both memory and the possibility of malingering.

17. A version of the Stroop test has been adapted for group administration by my colleague R. F. Elliott. (This was adapted from the Stroop format for individual administration published by Delis, D.C., Kaplan, E. and Kramer, J. H. (2001) available from the Psychological Corporation.) The test is given at four different levels of difficulty. The first level is presented in black and white, with the words red, green, and blue appearing in random sequence. The client is asked to write

down the initial of the color name (red=R, green=G, blue=B). There are 90 items and the client is given 60 seconds to complete as many items as possible. The second level is presented in color, with red, green, and blue squares appearing in a random sequence. The client is asked to write down the first letter of the color of the square. There are 90 items and clients are given 60 seconds to complete as many items as possible. The third level is similar to the first in that the words red, blue, and green are seen again. But, in this trial the words are printed in conflicting colors; clients are now required to ignore the word and write down the first letter of the color the words are printed in (for example the word red might be printed in green letters). There are 90 items and clients are given 60 seconds to complete as many items as possible. The fourth level is similar to the third, but some items are enclosed in a box. Those inside a box require the client to write down the first letter of the printed word; those outside a box require the client to identify by first letter what color the words are printed in. There are 90 items and the client is given 60 seconds to complete as many items as possible. This test examines some aspects of executive function, including the ability to follow directions and the ability to deal with complex and shifting decision rules. Also, we are able to get a sense of processing speed and how this is influenced by more complex task demands.

[Test forms, normative data, local norms and correlation matrices are available from the author.]

APPENDIX 4

Outlines for four session group DBT anger/stress management program

DBT ANGER/STRESS GROUP*

(*Dialectical Behavior Therapy. It is important to note that much of this was taken from the book by Linehan, which is cited in the references. It is also important to note that much of this, with our adaptations for male veterans, would perhaps horrify Linehan—and I hereby apologize, in the event that she might read this and be horrified.)

A 4 session cycling group

Where: Building 8, Room 208
When: The first four Fridays of each month
(except July and December)

Facilitators: John A. Corson PhD; R. Fred Elliott, MA, Debra Scott, MA

ABOUT DBT: STRESS & ANGER MANAGEMENT GROUP

A.   WHAT IS DBT?

What does "DBT" mean?
➢ A theory of reality: comprised of opposing forces; the opposing forces
   are resolved to a middle ground, by–
➢ A process of change: where a new balance is worked toward, between
   the opposing forces in one's life.

The history of this work.
Cognitive behavioral source of ideas.

B.   HOW WILL WE PROCEED?

The group meets four (4) times each month, on the first four (4) Fridays of
each month (except July and December). Each meeting is 90 minutes long.

A different set of skills is emphasized at each of the meetings.

C.   ASSESSMENT FORMS (Two Types)

1.   **In session:** Asks you to describe how you feel "right now"; this helps
     us evaluate and improve the work we do;

2.   **At Home:** Daily record keeping. This will help you to become a
     "Personal Scientist" and will also help us evaluate the impact of the
     work we do in the group sessions.

D. GROUND RULES

1. **Confidentiality:** "What you hear here, stays here". Please don't talk about group members or events that occur within the group when you are outside of group meetings!

2. **Be Here Now!:** You (in a role similar to that of an athlete) are asked to accept the task of identifying and taking away from these session new strategies that are likely to work for you. One way to think of this is that, as you consider these potential strategies, you are faced with a huge salad bar or smorgasbord. We (in a role that is similar to that of a coach, or a chef) will do our best to put out a huge number of potentially powerful strategies—you will need to pick out what in this array might work for you. There will be a printed outline for each session, and we request that you take the session outlines home with you. In most sessions we will not be covering every item on the outline. We request that you make notes on the outlines and keep them together, as a sort of textbook, that you can study at home and consult when you would like to refresh your memory about the strategies we have touched on.

E. **Our Research Results**: We have evaluated the results of this work when done in a 10 session group format, as well as when done in this four session group format. (The length of follow-up that we evaluated ranged from 3 months to 2 years.) In both versions in the results show statistically significant positive effect. In the four session group format results showed significant improvement in mood and energy, and reductions in depression, anxiety, irritability and anger (see the figures that follow).

The figures show data from telephone follow-up of 20 clients who had been through at least one cycle of this program. The interval from the end of group attendance to the follow-up contact ranged from 3 months to 2 years. The results compare self-reported status prior to treatment with self-reported status at the time of follow-up. The results were analyzed using a two-tailed Wilcoxon test, and all results were statistically significant, indicating that this program is helpful in the areas we examined.

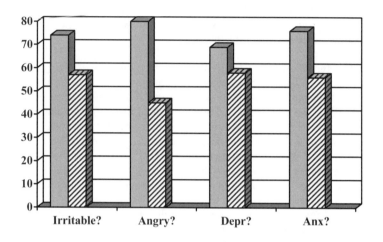

Pre-Treatment = gray
Post-Treatment = striped

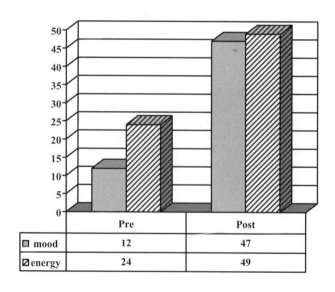

	Pre	Post
□ mood	12	47
▨ energy	24	49

Day 1 (of 4)—Mindfulness

1) **What is the wise mind?**

2) **Why use wise mind?**
  ➤ understand the forces working upon you.
  ➤ promote self-regulation.

3) **What prevents us from using the wise mind?** (Some observations about neurology)
  ➤ There is a high speed system in the brain that can detect some kinds of danger and fire off some kinds of responses, before the wise mind can do its work.
  ➤ Functions of the amygdala.
  ➤ Vulnerability of the amygdala, and other structures, to head injury (particularly if post injury amnesia lasted more than 15 minutes).
  ➤ Amygdala function is permanently changed by trauma.
  ➤ Amygdala function can be changed by training—by the age of 6 you knew that roads and cars are dangerous and you had learned "stop, look and listen."
  ➤ The amygdala was further trained to react rapidly to specific signals during basic training.

[More details on the amygdala are given toward the end of this outline.]

4) **How to help the wise mind:**

  *The what skills:
  ➤ Be in the present moment; this is the essence of mindfulness. Being mindful has a lot to do with calming yourself down—slowing down your body and mind.
  ➤ Observe the present moment—some people have helped themselves factor out negative feelings by focusing on some small aspect of their environment.
  ➤ Describe your present moments to yourself. Some people have been able to get into the present moment by describing to themselves what is going on.

  *The how skills:
  ➤ Focus on what is—not what should, or ought to be.
  ➤ Take a nonjudgmental stance - try not to think in black and white terms (accept what is, independent of whether it fits our beliefs or

conforms to our likes or dislikes). Try to stay away from alternating between reverence and devaluation in your relationships with yourself and others—always bearing in mind that nothing is perfect, and that there is some good in all of us.

➢ Focus on the current moment—don't split your attention among several activities.

➢ Be effective—do what is needed, or effective, rather than what would be "perfect" or "right"—or satisfying to your impulse to act out of anger.

5)   The "Quick Calming Response":

1.   **FOCUS ON YOUR BREATHING**: Take a little bit deeper than normal breath.

2.   **BREATHE OUT slowly** and think the word "**CALM**" on the out-breath.

3.   **DO IT AGAIN**: Take in another little bit deeper than normal breath; on the out-breath think the word "**CALM**"- this time while **SMILING TO YOURSELF**.

4.   **NOTICE** the warm, comfortable sensation developing in your hands and stomach.

Each breath takes about 10 seconds; the whole exercise takes about 20 seconds. At the end of this quick calming response notice how much better you feel. Try to do this at least 12 times per day.

Some people have reminded themselves to practice this response by doing it each time they look at a watch or clock, each time they enter a bathroom, or each time they hear a phone ring.

6) **"Sampling the senses". (Demonstrate)**
    [To Sample the Senses: first focus only on what you can hear for about a minute (or 10 to 15 breaths). Next look up above you and pick a spot to focus on. Focus on that spot for about a minute (or 10 to 15 breaths). Finally, gently touch together the thumb and forefinger of your dominant hand. Move these softly and slowly back and forth against each other. Note how the fingerprint lines move past each other. Focus on producing this movement, and the sensations the movement produces for about a minute (or 10 to 15 breaths).]

7) **Arousal.** Physiologic arousal interferes with our ability to attend. When we are highly aroused we become distractible. The mind flips from one thing to another—we try to do many tasks all at once and keep forgetting things.

8) **Temporary Attention Deficit Disorder (ADD).** When you notice yourself multi-tasking you are usually in a highly distractible state. It is as if you have a *temporary ADD*. You are not functioning in the present moment. You can learn to use this confused state as a cue to do quick calm. We are giving you a handout. If you read this carefully you will learn to take a brief timeout when you notice yourself multi-tasking or getting confused, feeling frantic and forgetting things. You'll also learn some other self-management strategies that can help with temporary ADD.

MANAGING TEMPORARY ATTENTION DEFICIT

> Agitation and confusion are the signals that you are in this state.
> When you notice yourself feeling confused, multi-tasking mindlessly (without a sense of priorities), or feeling agitated and ineffective, you are usually in a highly distractible state. It is as if you have temporary attention deficit disorder (ADD). Use this confusion/multi-tasking/agitation as a cue to do the following:

1. Stop! Sit down! Do the quick calm response. Next take a pencil and paper and list all the tasks you have been trying to work on, or feel that you should work on.

2.   Categorize the tasks into one of the following four classes: "do, delay, delegate, or dump".

3.   Now—use the quick calm exercise again. Be in the moment. Quick calm serves two purposes: to help slow you down/decrease arousal, and to help you focus your attention on one thing that you might be able to do something about.

4.   Consult your list again—pick the top priority task—then, if you have time, move on to the next step. Whatever happens—be mindful—stay in the present moment and stay focused. Use the quick calming response whenever you feel that you are beginning to lose it.

5.   Choose two signals that make sense for you; for example: Sunrise to start planning and Sunset to do a short piece of work. Make a deal—or contract—with yourself to do between one and five minutes worth of work on the top priority task before the next Sunrise or Sunset. From now on Use Every Sunrise and Sunset as signals for you to alternatively plan work and do work for small, fixed chunks of time. It will help to use a timer while you work. The bell or signal when the timer goes off, to tell you that the work period has ended, will function as a reward. It will boost your spirits a bit and help you realize that you have kept your contract with yourself. Try to do this little bit of work every day. It is like whittling. You will whittle away at the tasks and eventually you will notice that you have made a lot of progress. It will make a huge difference in boosting your mood and you'll be getting things done.

6.   Be a "personal scientist" 24 and 7. Think about your priorities at every Sunrise and Sunset, or at two of your mealtimes each day. Let one of those occasions (e.g. Sunrise) be a signal for you to review what single task you will plan to work on, and let the other of those occasions (e.g. Sunset) be a signal for the starting time for a short period of work (1 to 5 minutes) on that task.

9)   **Record-keeping.** Hand out forms for daily record-keeping. [If you choose to do this record-keeping, it will help you with an important aspect of mindfulness—becoming a "personal scientist".]

The following two sections should be reviewed outside the session, at your leisure.

The Reptile Brain Versus the Wise Mind

Structures in the human brain have been developed over many centuries. An early evolutionary development is still with us and is frequently called the reptilian brain. The term reptilian brain refers to a large part of the lower levels of the brain and the top part of the brain stem/spinal cord. A pair of small structures is intimately involved in the functioning of this reptilian brain—the structures are known as the amygdala; there is one in each temporal lobe of the brain. Research done by Ledoux (1986,1993,1995), and others shows that the amygdala functions as the key piece in detecting danger, feeling fear and responding quickly. The amygdala is a sort of sentinel—scanning all sensory inputs for any sign of danger. Once a sign of danger is seen a response is rapidly executed. These responses are extremely rapid, and have been called manifestations of a "hot system", or the reptilian brain. This system has its own memories and its own response strategies.

The "cool system" or higher brain structures such as the frontal lobes and the rest of the cortex, developed more recently in the evolutionary process. This is the system that allows humans to delay the tendency toward a rapid and impulsive response and to formulate much more skillful responses to danger or fear, responses that will be much more effective in the long-term. This system can also be called "the Wise mind".

An individual who has been traumatized has developed a complex, danger related, set of memories that are partly stored in the amygdala. In the event that the traumatized individual detects some danger similar to the original trauma, there is likely to be a very rapid and patterned response that will often be counterproductive. Van der Kolk (1994) has studied many individuals diagnosed with PTSD. He has concluded that the memory systems of these individuals often fail to incorporate the traumatic experience into the autobiographical or narrative account of their lives, in anything but a fragmentery form. It has been suggested (Metcalfe and Jacobs, 1996—PTSD research quarterly) that the use of narrative therapy could "reweave" these hot and fragmentary and troublesome memories into autobiographical memory and thus into a framework that would allow the "cool system" to help prevent rapid, impulsive and often counterproductive responses to any form of danger or fear. Another way to say this is that narrative therapy can help engage the Wise mind or cool mind, and allow a traumatized individual to take the necessary time to formulate a relatively productive response.

The traumatized person is also typically highly aroused—even when sitting still. In this state the amygdala and the "hot system" are likely to be in a state of high readiness—poised to leap into action. In many cases the memory of the traumatic event is a "state dependent memory", that is retrieved when the body is aroused to the high level that the trauma originally caused—thus reinstating or replicating the trauma state in many of its details. Thus the traumatized person is likely to be tormented by flashbacks and a general uncomfortable emotional state. At this high level of arousal the cool system, or wise mind, is relatively dysfunctional. One way to assist an individual in dealing with this set of problems is to train them to calm down. We have had considerable success using biofeedback and forms of relaxation and self-hypnosis to help individuals lower their resting arousal level, and decrease the amplitude, duration and frequency of episodes of very high arousal.

Practical Considerations: Lessons from Clinical Work

When two individuals who have been traumatized are interacting, there is the possibility that a hot system response from one will elicit an equally unwise hot system response from the other. We have repeatedly seen in a married couple with one or both members having been traumatized, an argument takes the form of a combat-like skirmish, with each taking turns firing increasingly cruel verbal responses at the other. In a sense their reptilian brains or "hot systems" are doing the arguing. Frequently—sometime later—each will realize that they have said things that were unwise, and even some things that they did not mean at all. However, it is often impossible for our clients to heal from, or apologize for, these statements. We have developed a set of strategies (called "first-line strategies") to help these individuals avoid arguing with the reptilian brain.

EXAMPLE:

Recently a client was describing to me an argument with his wife. This argument followed a pattern that began with relatively low level insults exchanged between the two of them—the low level insults quickly led to a raging argument. I used the client's description of the argument to describe a pattern that seems to characterize most of their arguments. I went on to identify some choice points in any typical argument where he could bring his "wise mind" to bear. I gave him a copy of the above paragraphs along with a diagram depicting brain function—highlighting the role of the amygdala in fear driven and angry conversation. Using some of our "first-line strategies," I explained that in order to engage the higher levels of brain function one needs to slow down. It is a good idea to speak slowly and softly and to avoid swearing. This is because rapid and loud speaking, and swearing tend to go along with high levels of biological arousal and with activation of the amygdala and the associated reptilian brain—leading to increasingly impulsive and often counterproductive utterances.

He brought this discussion up again in our next session. Apparently the pattern I had identified made good sense to him, and he had used two of the first-line strategies in an argument with his wife the night after our last session. His wife was surprised, and said that he seems to be changing, and that his therapy must be doing some good. Since that night they have not argued counterproductively again, even though they have continued to talk about the problems that had previously triggered arguments.

More Details on the Reptile Brain vs. the Wise Mind

Transmission of a signal from the ear to the lateral nucleus of the amygdala takes about 12 milliseconds. (As a comparison, a fairly fast bullet goes about 4 inches in 12 milliseconds.) On its way to the amygdala the signal goes through only one synapse, in the auditory segment of the thalamus. This signal, if perceived by the lateral nucleus as dangerous, initiates a rapid cascade of responses. This cascade of responses can be seen in behavior by changes in facial expression, posture, skin color, gross body movements and vocalizations, often including loud swearing. At the physiological level there are changes in heart rate, respiration, regional blood flow, skin conductance, and endocrine function, as well as massive changes in brain function, easily detected by the most primitive of EEG systems.

The signal that went through the auditory segment of the thalamus also was forwarded to the auditory cortex and then back to the lateral amygdala. However this took about 24 milliseconds, and was much too slow to prevent or abort the complex of emergency responses that had already been triggered.

From the point of view of the excited person there is a form of reciprocal determinism in these changes—reverberating through three classes of variables, and feeding back on each one. Within the self—in covert behavior—these variables range from endocrine shifts to salient bodily sensations; from the self—in overt behavior—these variables include bodily movement, swearing etc.; from others these variables include visible bodily changes, such as facial expression, perhaps swearing, perhaps clenching fists and standing and moving toward or away from the excited person.

More Practical Considerations

In our first-line strategies we make use of signals from each of these three sources (within the self, overt behavior of the self, responses of the other person) to initiate self-regulation plans. Initiation of one of these plans (e.g. talk softly and slowly, with no swearing) can actually prevent (or sometimes abort) the cascade of responses initiated by the lateral amygdala. In order to help counteract the speed of transmission from the lateral amygdala we ask clients to practice a simple first-line strategy, repeatedly, and in a variety of situations. When a client is successful we can see that the first-line strategies have enabled the "Wise mind" or cool mind to overcome the tendencies of the reptilian brain.

Breathing Meditation: Counting Breaths

A Mindfulness Practice: about seven or eight minutes. (You can put this on a tape with your own voice to guide you in doing these exercises. *The italicized sections suggest the length of quiet pauses*)

"Get as comfortable as you can. Let the surface you are resting on support you fully. Let your legs be supported fully. Let your feet be flat on the ground. Let your arms be supported, your hands in your lap, or supported by the arms of the chair.

Let your eyes close softly.

Many thoughts, or feelings might come up as you quiet yourself down. Sometimes your mind will create distracting thoughts or feelings. They tend to pull your attention away from this practice. This is to be expected. When this happens just notice the thoughts, or the feelings, or the sensations. Notice them, but do not follow them, or evaluate them. Just notice them as you would clouds passing in the summer sky. Then gently bring your attention back to your practice. If your attention wanders many times, that is ok... Just gently bring it back every time. Bring it back without frustration... without judging.

Now, focus your attention on your breathing. Let your breathing be slow and rhythmic. Let it be easy ...like the slow, relaxed breathing you notice just before drifting off to sleep.

Notice your stomach rise as your lungs fill with air.

Notice how your stomach flattens out as you slowly exhale.

Notice how cool the air feels as it enters.

Notice how warm the air feels as you exhale.

Let your attention settle on this simple process...noticing the rise and fall of your stomach, the gentle, slow passage of air ...in......and ....out.

If you notice your attention has wandered from this process, that is ok. Gently bring it back to your breath. ... [*about one minute*].

On the signal to begin start to count the breaths. Do it this way. As you breathe in count one. As you breathe out count two... in three...out four...in five...out six... and so on up to ten. When you reach ten start over...one in...two out...three in...four out... and so on back up to ten. Continue this cycle of breathing and counting for a few minutes. If you get distracted and lose count, gently bring your attention back to breathing and counting. Anytime you lose count, or get distracted begin again at one in...two out... OK? Ready? Begin... [*five minutes*].

All okay the five minutes are over. Open your eyes.

Stretch.

You are now prepared to reenter your daily routine with a new sense of calm."

DBT (Dialectical behavior therapy) GROUP

Day 2 (of 4)—EMOTIONAL REGULATION

Facilitators: John Corson Ph.D.; R. Fred Elliott, MA; Debra Scott, R. N., BSN, MA

Contents:
Overview of the emotional regulation session.
Early warning signs of emotional upset.
First line strategies.
Transcript of a meditation and relaxation strategy.

1) Review the details of the program and briefly review the first session (demonstrate "The Quick Calming Response" and demonstrate "Sampling the Senses").

2) Record-keeping
   a)   Do affect grid record-keeping
   b)   Review any record-keeping done since last session.

3) Emotional Regulation: Are You Often Agitated and Confused? Is it as if you are sitting at a stop light with your engine running at full speed?:
   a)   We know that emotional turmoil, and emotional and physical pain are inevitable.

b) We know that we will have stormy times and emotional pain. We also know that emotional pain can cause interference with thinking and attention.

c) Can we recognize the signs of emotional pain early? Among the signs could be swearing, talking loudly and fast, irritability, anger, impulsivity, confusion, loneliness, a feeling of emptiness, a sense of your life having no meaning, tears of unknown source, lethargy, sleepless nights, muscle tension, dry mouth, tunnel vision, suicidal thoughts, sweating hands, racing heart, tense jaw, feelings of helplessness, physical pain, agitation, flushed face, a feeling of impending doom.

d) Have you noticed that many impulsive attempts to cope with painful emotions can make the situation worse?

e) Anger is a powerful emotion. Anger is usually a secondary emotion. Often anger works like this: Self satisfaction or self-esteem, or sense of self suddenly drops because of something we have sensed. Perhaps it was a put down, perhaps it was a sign of disrespect, perhaps it was being ignored, perhaps it was a challenge, perhaps someone trespassed somehow on your feelings. Within a fraction of a second that hurt or anguish is translated into hate or anger—and the original emotion is lost.

f) Think of sources of emotional pain: a sign of being disrespected or ignored; thinking about lost opportunities; thinking about things that you wish you had done—or left undone; feelings of shame or guilt; memories of times when you had been taken advantage of or disrespected.

4) Can we do anything to help ourselves regulate emotion?
  a) What about an anger explosion—can it help?
  b) Sometimes—in most people's lives—anger has paid off.
  c) Many times expression of anger leads to at least a short period of relief, or even pleasure.
  d) Most times, for mature people who care about other people, the relief or pleasure that occurs for a few moments after anger expression, turns into disappointment or sadness after a while.
  e) For most of us anger, and the related emotion of depression, are the two most powerful emotions or feelings. (Even these powerful emotions can be managed, at least to some extent.)

5) Can distractions or pleasant experiences help us regulate emotion?
  a) Distractions that can help: Perhaps you could say something to yourself along the following lines: "I'll use mindfulness—I will

Stop what I'm doing—use the quick calming response—sample my senses [stop, look, listen and feel] I will use the things around me in this moment, to distract myself from this emotional pain".

b)   Sources of emotional pleasure that can help: Can relaxation—the quick calming response help? Can mindfulness help? Can music help? Can exercise help? Can reading the newspaper help? Would telephoning a friend help?

6)   Can any behavioral strategies help us regulate emotion?

a)   Yes, we can learn new ways of managing the behavior we do in response to our emotions.

b)   One of us has had success with the following method—when I am angry I say something along the lines of: "I'm upset; right now I'm too upset to think straight. I need to take a timeout. Maybe we can finish this discussion at another time (e.g., after two hours have passed; at this same time tomorrow)." To myself I say "this too shall pass—I will use the quick calming response—I will be able to think clearly about this later."

c)   There are Early Warning Signals that can tell us of the need to begin to use some simple and effective strategies [these are described below].

d)   There are First Line Strategies for when there is little or no time to think [these are described below].

First Line Strategies and Signals of Trouble

***The first line Strategies are for when there is no time to think, when you suddenly find yourself in a situation where you feel hurt or anguish or fear or rage or hate or anger.

There are **signals** you will notice as you realize **that you are in trouble**.

*Some signals may come **from your memory**—memories of having trouble in a particular situation, or with a particular person in the past. These can help you prepare yourself to use a first line strategy in advance, and perhaps even to practice so that you will increase your chances of managing the situation well, in the event that you suddenly experience one of these negative feelings (hurt, anguish, fear, rage, hate, anger).

*Some of the signals are **from inside yourself**—internal signals such as the following: dry mouth, muscle tension, tunnel vision, sweating hands, racing heart, tense jaw, feelings of helplessness, tears of unknown source, agitation, flushed face, a feeling of impending doom, feeling lethargic, thoughts of running away or attacking, suicidal thoughts, homicidal thoughts.

*Some of the signals are **from your own behavior**—behavioral signals such as the following: speaking loudly, speaking rapidly, swearing, clenching fists, pointing, shaking your finger.

*Some of the signals are **from the other person**—signs that you can pick up from their behavior such as the following: they are speaking loudly, speaking rapidly, swearing, clenching their fists, pointing at you, perhaps they look afraid or angry, perhaps they jump up from a seated position, perhaps they come toward you—or move quickly away from you.

*You can actually **plan ahead** for the unexpected. You can see any of these signals as presenting you with a "golden opportunity". Here's how you might go about it. **Select a strategy** from the following list to **rehearse** here today, and for the next week each time the sun comes up. When one of the signals comes along that is your golden opportunity to experiment with the new strategy. (Better yet, if you can anticipate an interaction with a difficult person, or a troublesome situation, you can do some extra rehearsing so that you will be able to remember the rule more clearly.)

First Line Strategies: Pick one (or several) of these and think about it and practice it so that it becomes automatic for you; use it as a plan or rule to guide your behavior; keep it in the forefront of your mind at all times so it will be ready for use. This is one way to retrain the brain and keep the amygdala from hijacking your brain and behavior. Use of one of these strategies will help you buy time, and slow things down so that you are able to think about the situation before you react.

*Talk softly—or even whisper.
*Speak very slowly; this can help you stay away from habitual angry emotional reactions.
*No swearing.
*Smile and say "it's complicated isn't it."
* Use the "quick calm" to slow things down.
*Refocus using coping self—statements ("this too will pass"; the serenity prayer).
*Another first line strategy—Minimal effective response, or "how to avoid swatting a fly with a sledge hammer."
*Another first line strategy—Be sure to select a simple goal and pursue it peacefully.
*Another first line strategy—If the other person is rude—don't be distracted.

*Another first line strategy—If the other person shifts ground or changes topics—don't be distracted.

*Another first line strategy—If necessary—be a "broken record"—repeat the simple topic to keep the conversation on track.

*The hyperventilation routine (changes brain waves, train of thought and arousal level).

*The "turn signal" (this has two versions—one is the actual use of the turn signal when someone is tail gating you, or somehow aggravating you in traffic; the other is a turn signal in conversation—saying to the other person—"I have to be on my way now—maybe we can talk about this some other time."

*Other plans/rules to help you avoid angry emotional reactions:

no obscene gestures,

no finger shaking/pointing;

avoid all rudeness;

avoid threatening.

*If all else fails remember to use the "timeout" strategy—say "I need a time out—I'm getting upset and I don't think straight when I'm upset. Maybe we can talk about this some other time."

*At the end of it all say to yourself "this is passing—it was only temporary—it was an experiment—I will use the quick calming response—I will be able to think clearly about this later."

****There is a remarkably powerful strategy that can be used even before the first line strategies. It can help us **stay** in the wise mind state. Here it is: we have made use of the **"proactive strategy"** to increase the probability that the wise mind or a positive available self will be in place at all times. The proactive strategy can be tailored to each individual. The individual uses a watch with a timing and signaling function (such watches can be obtained for between $15 and $40) to provide a signal for using a four-part strategy that takes about 90 seconds to go through. The signal can be set for every 30–120 minutes. *The four-part **proactive strategy** is as follows: the **first** piece is the "quick calming response," which takes about 15—20 seconds and ends with an out breath and a smile; the **second** piece is the image/memory of a person, or an interaction with a person who has been a positive mentor, or mature and helpful guide (perhaps this would be a kind relative, neighbor or teacher); the **third** piece is a repeat of the first piece—the quick calming response; and the **fourth** piece is the image/memory of a time when the wise mind, or positive available self, coped with a difficult situation.*

The last two pages of this document include a 10–15 minute meditation and relaxation strategy that can be of great help in learning self-regulation.

Would anyone like a new record-keeping form for each day between now and the next meeting?

Breathing meditation with warming imagery/suggestion

A mindfulness practice: about 10-15 minutes. (You can make a tape of these exercises using your own voice. The *italicized sections* suggest the length of quiet pauses.)

"This is your time.
There is nothing else you need to do right now.
There is nothing else you need to think about right now.
This is your time to quiet down.

Get as comfortable as you can. Let the surface you are resting on support your body fully. Let your legs be supported fully. Maybe your feet are flat on the ground, or maybe your legs are supported as you recline. Let your arms be supported, your back, neck and head ……… all supported.

Let your eyes close softly.

Many thoughts, or feelings will come up as you quiet yourself down. It is natural for your mind to create thoughts, feelings. They tend to pull your attention away from this practice. This is to be expected. When this happens just notice the thoughts, or the feelings, or the sensations. Notice them, but do not follow them, or evaluate them. Just notice them as you would clouds passing in the summer sky. Then gently bring your attention back to your practice. If your attention wanders many times, that is ok… Just gently bring it back every time. Bring it back without frustration…….. without judging.

Now, focus your attention on your breathing. Let your breathing be slow and rhythmic. Let it be easy and without effort …like the slow, relaxed breathing you notice just before drifting off to sleep.

Notice your stomach rise as your lungs fill with air.

Notice how it flattens out as you slowly exhale.

Notice how cool the air feels as it enters.

Notice how warm it is as you exhale.

Let your attention settle on this simple process…noticing the rise and fall of your stomach, the gentle, slow passage of air ……in……and ……..out. *[About a minute.]*

If you notice your attention has wandered from this process, that is ok. Gently bring it back to your breath. About half a minute.

Can you feel your body relax?.........Can you feel yourself settling in?........ Quieting down? ....Continue to notice the rise and fall of your stomach ....the quiet rhythm of your breathing. *[About a minute.]*

Notice the warmth of your breath as you breathe out. ....When you breathe in, the air is warmed by your stomach. Notice how warm your stomach feels. ....Does it feel warm and relaxed? As you breathe out....let go of any tension you might hold in your stomach. ....Let your stomach relax. ....

Enjoy the easy rise and fall of your stomach as you breath. ....Does it feel warm and relaxed now? .... *[About a minute.]*

Your stomach is warm and relaxed. As you breathe out notice how the warmth travels along your airways. Use your imagination now. Imagine that as you breathe out.....the warmth of your breath is surrounding your body in a blanket of warmth ....Imagine it is sending warmth all the way down to your toes............down to your fingers. Imagine your whole body bathed in warmth. Notice how good it feels, the warming of your tight muscles....... easing the aches and the pains. Take some time to enjoy these sensations. The warmth of your toes, your fingers, your warm and relaxing muscles. *[About a minute.]*

As you breathe out think the word "warm" to yourself as you imagine warmth spreading to the tips of your fingers and toes..........each breath relaxing your muscles more and more. Imagine the muscles in the farthest reaches of your body relaxing to let warmth and relaxation spread further and more deeply. Think the word "warm" across each out breath and breathe warmth and relaxation to the smallest toe and finger. This is your time to luxuriate in these welcome feelings of relaxation and warmth. Take your time and enjoy these sensations. *[About five minutes.]*

In the future, whenever you feel tense, you can bring warmth and relaxation to yourself again. Simply, breathe deeply and naturally, perhaps close your eyes softly and think the word "warm" to yourself as you breathe out. Once again your body will be bathed in warmth and relaxation.

When you are ready you may open your eyes, stretch and continue with your daily routine—refreshed from this experience."

DBT (Dialectical behavior therapy) GROUP

Session 3 (of 4)— INTERPERSONAL EFFECTIVENESS

Facilitators: John Corson, Ph.D.; R. Fred Elliott, MA; Debra Scott, RN, BSN, MA

Contents:
The first part of this outline is an overview of the interpersonal effectiveness work.

The last part presents some key ideas in a general Mediation—Conflict Resolution Strategy.

Briefly describe the details of the program and review the first two sessions—mindfulness and self-regulation.

Do affect grid record-keeping

1) Briefly review record-keeping ; see if we can find several examples of successful use of a coping strategy (was there a single thing—a take home message—someone took away from last week—and what has the experience been with that take home message/strategy?). [remember the smorgasbord/salad bar idea.]

Day Three: Interpersonal Effectiveness - people are important to each other

EVIDENCE: Consider the following research: thousands of people who had major heart surgery were asked the following question "do you belong to any sort of a community or group, such as a bowling league or church group, or a poker playing group?" One year later the individuals who answered "yes" were seven times more likely to be alive and free of physical complications than those who answered "no".

EVIDENCE: The research shows that single people don't live as long as married people—this is more pronounced for men. From this, and many other points of view is clear that wise people value, preserve, and foster important positive relationships.

CONCLUSION: Wise mind and the emotional regulation skills are the foundation of learning effective interpersonal skills. (The quick calming response and a smile can help you get into "Wise mind.") The wise mind will help you remember (1) that we need each other; (2) that none of us is perfect; (3) that we all have our weak moments; (4) when confronted by a very difficult person, remember that Abraham Lincoln said something along the following lines: "the best way to deal with an enemy is to befriend him"; (5) when dealing with someone who seems to be your enemy, or at least is being very difficult at the moment, remember that we really do need each other and that your wise mind will help you value and preserve that relationship in spite of the difficulty.

DANGER: Beware—Habitual emotional reactions can harm -or end-relationships.

Be sure to **review the first line strategies** that were handed out on day 2. [The schmorgasboard/salad bar method involves work at home—both to select a strategy that might work for you and also to practice that strategy.]

*To help yourself avoid a habitual emotional reaction, **monitor your feelings and behavior carefully for early signs of feeling upset** (such as swearing or racing thoughts). Whenever you notice a sign of upset go to a first line strategy.

*Think about the potential emotional impact on you of any situations you can anticipate—anticipate situations that might cause you trouble (e.g. a visit from a critical relative).

****We Will Stop here—ask for an anticipated situation from a group member. *Both your feelings and details of the anticipated situation can work as early warning signals. These early warning signals can help you prevent a habitual emotional reaction, and instead use different strategies that save the day.

*Think about how you might prepare yourself emotionally and cognitively to cope well with an anticipated stressful event. (For example— "I'll talk very quietly and slowly," or "I'll smile through the whole thing." For more details review the first line hand out.)

[Ask each participant to select one of the first line strategies that he thinks might work for him in an anticipated stressful situation.]

*Some second line strategies**—for when there is more time to prepare a strategy:

*Refocus using coping self—statements. (Some examples: "I will do The Quick Calm. I function best when I am calm." "I don't need to be angry when other people are angry." "I don't need to prove anything here." "As long as I stay relaxed I am in control of myself." "I can't control other people and situations, but I can change the way I respond by staying calm." "Is there something new I can learn from this situation?").

*Use "the four walls" to identify the problem and a sensible solution. (This is a good tactic to help one or more people to brainstorm. When you want to figure out what is happening, or how to proceed with a problem or situation: throw an idea upon one wall. Toss an idea on the same topic up on another wall. Continue until all four walls have ideas on them. Then see if any of the ideas make sense for the long-term. Throw out all the others and use the blank walls to throw up new ideas. Continue until you have identified the problem, and have developed a good plan for solving it.)

*Use "the magic telephone" to identify the problem and a sensible solution. (This is another brainstorming strategy. It is a good tactic for use when you are in trouble, and are away from needed sources of support or advice. Imagine calling a friend or mentor who has a calming influence on you. You hear their voice. He or she asks four basic questions: 1) What's happening? 2) What do you think the problem is? 3) What are you thinking of doing about it? 4) No—hold on—for the long-term, what is the most sensible thing to do about it?).

*Remember that "win–win" solutions are best—let the other person "save face".

*Be sure to select a simple goal and pursue it peacefully.

*Give reflection or "playback"—describe what you think are the interests of the other person. [For example you could say "Let me see if I understand—I think I heard you say you need..................." (be sure to be totally polite and respectful when you give the playback. Also—very importantly—listen carefully to the other person's response to your playback, and continue in the polite and respectful mode.)]

*Ask for "playback"—ask the other person to describe what they think you want (again be sure to stay in the polite and respectful mode— even if the other person becomes rude or shows disrespect. You are guaranteed to gain their respect, in the long run, if you can stay in the wise mind mode and stay focused on your original goal).

*Use a mediation or conflict resolution strategy. [In the text below you'll find "mediation—conflict resolution strategies." These are strategies we have learned in long hours and days of mediation training—review these at your leisure. See if any hold promise for you.]

*If things get out of hand—if you do get upset and can't pull yourself back together using the quick calm and coping self statements— you can end the interaction in a constructive manner.

*Remember—avoid making important decisions when you're upset.

*Before acting, slow down; give your wise mind some time to size up the situation. Gently consider the future cost of any hurtful statement or action—then don't do it—then don't say it. Remember—to do this work well you must be polite and respectful.

    *Here is the bottom line strategy for getting out of the situation—You can use the routine: "I'm upset—I think I had better take a break—maybe we can discuss this some other time."

Mediation: Conflict Resolution Strategy—Some Keys

If a conflict comes up—ask yourself:
Is this issue worth a confrontation?
Is this relationship worth confronting this issue?
What is the problem?
How do we see each other?
How do we see the solution?
What possible solutions do each of us have in mind?
What are our needs?
What do we really want out of this?
What ideas or options might meet both of our needs?
What do I need to learn or understand from the other person?
Can I be clear about my goals?
Can I keep it simple?
Can I be flexible about how to reach my goals?
Can I choose a good time to talk?
Can I avoid talking when I'm too upset?
Can I calmly warn the other person that the discussion is coming?
Can I help the other person feel safe?
Can I remember the "minimal effective response"?
Can I help myself feel safe?
Can I use the "quick calming response"?
Can I be respectful?
Can I avoid threats?
Can I keep from interrupting?
Can I think calmly and stay on track if the other person is rude or interrupts?
Can I think calmly and stay on track if the other person changes topics?
Can I tune into the other person's emotions?
Can I help deal with these emotions before attempting to negotiate the problem?
Can I listen with empathy?
Can I ask questions with empathy?
Can I ask open-ended questions ("tell me more about...")?
Can I test my understanding or give "playback" ("are you saying that you need"...)?
Can I be respectful when I give playback?

Can I avoid saying put-downs ("you'll get over it..." OR "why don't you...")?

Can I ask for playback—ask the other person to describe my needs or wants?

Can I use neutral language and avoid making judgments?

Can I avoid placing blame?

Can I avoid absolutes?

Can I be willing to apologize?

Can I accept my contribution to the problem?

Can I accept an apology?

Can I find an opportunity to help the other person save face?

Can I focus on wants and needs and avoid talking of finding "solutions" or "truths"?

Can I build on small agreements?

Can I emphasize common ground?

Can I focus on the problem—not the person?

Can I take a break if I get upset?

Can I say "maybe it would be best to set up another meeting to discuss this further?"

Can I recognize a power imbalance?

Can I try to correct, or compensate for, a power imbalance?

Can I try to test a possible agreement?

Can I have time to think before making a big decision?

***Now—in keeping with the smorgasbord/salad bar idea—think over and select the best tactic or tool that has been considered today—find a "take home message."

Would anyone like to take a record-keeping form for each day of the next week?

DBT (Dialectical behavior therapy) GROUP

Day Four (of 4)—CRISIS MANAGEMENT

Facilitators: John Corson Ph.D.; R. Fred Elliott, MA; Debra Scott, R. N., BSN, MA

Briefly review the first three sessions.

Contents:
The first part of this outline presents some topics and ideas about crisis management.

This session includes:
1. Exercises to Help You Be in the Moment, and
2. Ten Things to Know about Anger.

1) **Do record-keeping.** Briefly review this and any weekly record-keeping done since last session; try to identify and describe any examples of successful use of coping strategies (e.g. a first or second line strategy, self talk).

2) **Today's topic:** **Crisis Management/Distress Tolerance**

*We all know that there will be times of crisis and pain—this part of the program focuses on how to bear pain with some skill and without making things worse.

*Distress can include emotional and physical components of suffering. Pain and suffering change over time. There is a trajectory, a beginning, a middle, a tapering off phase and an ending (although sometimes—when the distress is at its peak, or if it has remained constant for an extended period, it is hard to convince yourself that it will taper off).

*At the highest level of intensity the suffering may seem unbearable. To help yourself tolerate this suffering remember "this too will pass." Or—perhaps you can say to yourself "this is a signal for me to take a rest—take a timeout."

*Distress tolerance skills are aimed at helping you to hang on—to cope with distress until you start to feel better.

*This is **a progression from the mindfulness skills**:
-**accept** (self and situation)
-**perceive** (notice what is going on in the present moment—be mindful; these exercises can help you get into and stay in the present moment:
 * Half smiling-try it.
 * Notice positions of parts of your body.
 * Notice the sound of your breath.
 * Sample your senses.

Think "Re" on the IN breath and "lax" on the OUT breath—smile to yourself on every other out breath.)

-observe (sometimes it helps to focus in on some small detail of your present environment; sometimes it helps to describe that detail or write about it; sometimes it helps to try to sketch or draw that detail)

*Four sets of **skills for crisis management/distress tolerance** are presented below—(These pages are provided for you to review at your leisure. Now we will briefly present examples of each of these skills sets.):

-distracting
-self-soothing
-improving the moment
-thinking of pros and cons

Distress Tolerance

1.   What are the "DISTRACTING" skills?

- Activities—Some activities can distract attention, pass time, preoccupy the mind with memories, images or sensations that can override (or make more tolerable) the negative or distressful situation. (What are some examples?)
- Contributing to the well-being of others (helping someone, making them smile, saying hello, calling them up, sending a card) can produce distraction and help us to get through an UPSETTING SITUATION. (Volunteer work?)
- Comparison of our situation to a worse situation (from our past, from our fears, or from someone else's life) can help put the present UPSETTING SITUATION into different perspective. (What are some examples?) Walk through the hospital wards?
- Emotions opposite to the current negative emotion can help us manage an UPSETTING SITUATION. (Norman Cousins was ill—he used humor e.g., Marx Brothers Films—to help him through the crisis.)
- Pushing a situation away by stopping insistent thoughts and blocking insistent thoughts from the mind can help. (What are some examples?)
- Positive thoughts can sometimes be so powerful that they can block out negative thoughts and emotions and sensations. (What are some examples?)

- Sensations can sometimes be so powerful or compelling that they can block out negative thoughts, emotions and sensations. (Examples?)

2. What are the "SELF-SOOTHING" Skills?

- Sampling the senses (try this along with your relaxation practice) (Vision, Hearing, Smell, Taste and Touch)
- Review mindfulness.

3. What are the " IMPROVING the MOMENT" skills?

- IMAGERY can be used to rehearse new behaviors, to imagine new ways of coping - or even to imagine people being present (e.g. children) for whom you could improve the moment.
- MEANING can be created in your mind to avoid seeing the situation as a disaster - you can give it new meaning. (e.g. see it as a "character building experience" or "something to be learned from")
- PRAYER can help. (What are some examples?)
- RELAXING can help. (What sort of relaxation strategy can help most with your present (or most recent) UPSETTING SITUATION?)
- ONE THING IN THE MOMENT is a mindfulness skill that can help with an UPSETTING SITUATION. (sampling the senses can help us get into and focus on the present moment. Are there other tools or strategies to help with focusing on the present moment?)
- VACATIONS or TIMEOUTS can help us get through an UPSETTING SITUATION. (E.g. "Time out—I need a break—I'm getting upset—I'm not thinking straight—let's make an appointment to talk about this tomorrow".)
- ENCOURAGEMENT Talk to yourself as you would talk to someone you care about who is facing an UPSETTING SITUATION. This can help you manage your own upsetting situation, (e.g. think of how you might encourage and coach a child through an upsetting situation—or imagine this child is going through this upsetting situation with you—and is scared—and needs your encouragement.)

4.   What is "Thinking of PROS and CONS"?

- Think of the costs and benefits of dealing with this upsetting situation in your usual way (e.g. an anger explosion, sarcasm, giving in, substance abuse or some other form of self-harm)
- Now think of some other way of dealing with this situation—and consider the costs and benefits of this behavior.

A CRISIS CAN SOMETIMES LEAD TO ANGER

Because anger is very frequently a habitual emotional reaction to distress we will now consider Appendix 3—the last of the attached pages—entitled: "Ten Things To Know About Anger." This will help focus our thinking about "pros and cons" (some of these pertain to reasons to slow down and engage the wise mind so that the amygdala and other lower levels of the brain don't hijack you into unwise behavior).

Ten Things to Know About Anger

(From Burns, D. D. (1980). *The New Mood Therapy.* New York: Avon books.)

1.   The events of this world do not make you angry. Your "hot thoughts" create your anger. Even when a genuinely negative event occurs, it is the meaning that you attach to it that determines your emotional response.

2.   Most of the time your anger will not help you. It will immobilize you, and you will become frozen in your hostility to no productive purpose.

3.   The thoughts that generate your anger more often than not will contain distortions.

4.   Ultimately your anger is caused by your belief that someone is acting unfairly or some event is unjust.

5.   If you learn to see the world through the eyes of others, you will often be surprised to realize their actions are NOT unfair from their point of view.

6. Other people usually do not feel they deserve your punishment. Therefore, your retaliation is unlikely to help you achieve any positive goals in your interactions with them.

7. A great deal of your anger involves your defense against loss of self-esteem when people criticize you, disagree with you or fail to behave as you want them to. Such anger is always inappropriate because only your own negative distorted thoughts can cause you to lose self-esteem. When you blame others for your feelings or worthlessness, you are always fooling yourself.

8. Frustration results from unmet expectations. Since the event that disappointed you was a part of "reality," it was "realistic." This, your frustration always results from your unrealistic expectation. You may try to bring reality in line with your expectations, but this is not always practical, especially when those expectations are in conflict with what others view as human nature. The simplest solution is to change your unrealistic expectations. Some example of unrealistic expectations are:

   a. If I want something (love, happiness, a promotions, etc.), I deserve it.
   b. If I work hard at something, I should be successful.
   c. Other people should try to live up to my standards and believe in my concept of "fairness."
   d. I should be able to solve any problem quickly and easily.
   e. If I am a good partner, my partner is bound to love me.
   f. People should think and act the way I do.
   g. If I'm nice to someone, they should reciprocate.

9. It is just childish pouting to insist that you have the right to be angry. Of course you do. The crucial issue is—is it to your advantage to feel angry or rageful? How will it benefit you or the world?

10. You rarely need your anger to feel human. In fact, when you rid yourself of it, you will feel greater zest, joy, peace, and productivity.

*Can you **prepare** yourself in advance of a crisis? Consider the coming crisis. Use a "proactive" self-regulation strategy (this is useful even when no crisis is expected).

*What are your **warning signals**—that tell you that you are getting upset? If you feel that you have no warning signals we suggest that you resort to regular use of a "proactive" strategy.

[This is the place to practice emotional regulation skills—the first line of defense. However there are some times when the first line of defense isn't sufficient. Distress tolerance skills provide ways to tolerate those inevitable periods of very diminished energy, depleted optimism, emotional and/or physical pain.]

*Consider that a crisis can cause **temporary attention deficit disorder (ADD).**

[Review the ADD tools:

1. select signals (Sunrise, Sunset, meal time, going to the bathroom etc.);
2. make a task list (list things that are bothering you—jobs you should do etc.);
3. decide which is the first one of these things you need to do something about;
4. decide what is the best first step;
5. contract with yourself to spend one minute on that task when the next signal occurs.]

***Now—think over and select the one or two best strategies or tools that have been considered today.

*NOW, FOR THE LONG-TERM: Consider developing a document that can help you get through difficult times. (One client has selected *"this too will pass"*; another client has selected *"the sun will shine again, and the warmth and the light of the sun are within me always"*; another client has selected *"my sons love and respect me."* Some clients have selected one or two strategies from each of the four days of this program, and put them on a card to carry in their wallet.)

APPENDIX 5

PANIC PROTOCOL

A Six Session Program

The Psychology Section at the VA Medical Center, White River Junction, VT, developed this protocol from the following sources:

1. Mark Hegel's format, an unpublished document from Dartmouth Hitchcock Behavioral Medicine Unit
2. Barlow's format described in <u>Anxiety and Its Disorders</u>, Guilford Press, New York, 1988.
3. The format of Dattilio and Berchick described in <u>The Comprehensive Case Book of Cognitive Therapy</u>, Freeman and Dattilio, Eds., Plenum Press, New York, 1992

PANIC PROTOCOL: A Six Session Program

CONTENTS:

Sessions one through six.

Appendix A: Hierarchy Development

Appendix B: Coping Statement Development

Appendix C: Panic Log

Appendix D: Interoceptive Exposure Record

Appendix E: Interoceptive Exposure Practice Record Form

Session One (90 minutes)

1. Take a Panic Attack history

2. Do a "functional analysis" of specific episodes to determine:
   a. Antecedents
   b. Consequences
   c. Incentives

3. Develop a model of the patient's usual symptoms, by asking what goes on during a panic attack. Document details, including antecedents and consequences of:
    a. First panic attack
    b. Worst panic attack
    c. Most recent panic attack
    d. Worst Imaginable panic attack

4. Explore the "Hierarchy" of panic attack severity. Here the focus is on interoceptive sensations/correlates. (See Appendix A: Hierarchy Development for specific suggestions.)

5. Teach/refresh relaxation exercises. (Transcripts of several relaxation formats are available from the author).
    a. Make a tape of relaxation exercises for the patient.
    b. Urge daily relaxation practice.

Note: During this session relaxation exercises may be done while monitoring psychophysiological variables, but this is not mandatory.

6. Assign record keeping: Panic Log (Appendix C)

Session Two (90 minutes)

Starting with Session Two make an audiotape of each session. Give the tape to the client to take home and review, then recycle the tape.

1. Review the Panic Log

2. Present psychoeducational material. The purpose here is to teach the client about program objectives, with specific emphasis on learning to tolerate, and perhaps control the interoceptive/subjective feelings, sensations, etc. that occur during a panic attack.

3. Present and discuss the interoceptive and stimulus/situation hierarchy developed on day one. (If psychophysiological monitoring is being done, use it now to evaluate the client's use of the relaxation exercise.)

4. Discuss the client's practice of relaxation.

5. Refine the relaxation tape, if necessary, using feedback from the client regarding what works best.

6. Begin exploration/development of a personalized coping statement (see Appendix B: Coping Statement, for suggestions).

7. Give the client a new panic log.

8. Describe the next session and the purpose of the interoceptive exposure hierarchy.

Session Three (60 minutes)

1. Review the Panic Log.

2. Review briefly the relaxation practice.

3. Review/refine the coping statement.

4. Using the Interoceptive Exposure Record (Appendix D) as a guide, complete the interoceptive exposure test session. Go through each of the 9 separate exposures (unless contraindicated). Help the client use a brief relaxation and a coping statement between each segment of the interoceptive testing format. Complete the Exposure record for each test, carefully recording the client's reactions on the record sheet.

5. Make note of each exposure that leads to an anxiety/panic response, and on the basis of these assign one exercise, or a simple composite of exercises as homework.

6. Review with the client the interoceptive homework assignment.

7. Give the client an Exposure Practice Record and a new Panic Log.

Session Four (60 minutes)

1. Review the Panic Log.

2. Review the client's homework (interoceptive exposure practice record) and discuss the client's experience of being able to use the relaxation routine and coping statement to calm down quickly after the interoceptive exposure trial.

3. Examine specific stimuli and interoceptive events leading to escalation of panic/anxiety and help the client link these stimuli (internal and external) to automatic thoughts.

4. Help the client understand the escalation pattern:
    Stimuli > Automatic Thoughts > Catastrophic Expectations

5. Explain how this cascade can be interrupted by use of cognitive/covert coping statements.

6. Refine and practice coping statements with the client.

7. Have client, in your office, do the interceptive exposure homework assignment and use the rapid relaxation and coping statement. (If psychophysiological monitoring is being done, it should be used now. The rise and fall of skin conductance is particularly important to monitor.)

8. Use the following format:
    a. One minute relaxation,
    b. 2 minutes exposure to the interoceptive homework stimulus (preferably while the therapist describes an appropriate external stimulus situation.)
    c. 2 minutes relaxation with use of coping statement.

9. Discuss observations.

10. Give the client a new Exposure Practice Record and new Panic Log.

11. If possible, negotiate with the client to experiment with exposure to an external stimulus situation from the stimulus/situation elements in the hierarchy.

Session Five (60 minutes)

1. Review the Panic Log.

2. Review the Exposure Practice Record.

3. Re-review and update both the external and interoceptive hierarchies. Use the same exposure format as was used on day four; include new external stimulus hierarchy elements if appropriate.

4. Give the client a new Exposure Practice Record and new Panic Log.

5. Assign exposure to an external stimulus situation on the hierarchy if appropriate.

Session Six (60 minutes)

1. Review the Panic Log; Review the Exposure Practice Record.

2. Replicate the steps from day five

3. End this session by giving the client 4 weeks of Panic Logs.

4. Schedule a follow-up session in one month.

Appendix A

HIERARCHY DEVELOPMENT:
Interoceptive Focus

The development of this hierarchy focuses on interoceptive sensation: those sensations arising within the body, especially within the viscera.

Begin the hierarchy development with the client by asking a series of questions:

1. "What physical sensations do you notice in the *earliest stages* of a panic attack?"
2. "What physical sensations do you notice when you have a *slight or small* panic sensation?"

(The objective is to learn about the physical sensations in the lower third of the range of panic attack severity.)

Next ask:

3. "What physical sensations do you notice in the *middle* stages of a panic attack?"
4. "What physical sensations do you notice when you have a *medium size or moderately severe* panic attack?"

Next ask:

5. "What physical sensations do you notice in the *final* stages of a panic attack?"

6. "What physical sensations do you notice when you have a *severe* panic attack?"

If the client is having problems in coming up with specific physical sensations you could say:

"Some people notice perspiration or dizziness in early stages, and notice their heart pounding in the middle stages; in the final stages of a severe attack some people report feeling a dry mouth, sweating palms, hot and flushed face, fast breathing, tension or weakness throughout the whole body, severe dizziness and tunnel vision."

"Do you notice any of these sensation in the early part of a mild attack?"

Continue with suggestions of sensations to fill out the three stages and/or three levels of severity.)

When you have sketched out the three levels of the interoceptive hierarchy, begin asking questions and noting answers about the following correlates of each level.

(Suggestion: write out the physical sensation hierarchy on the left side of a long piece of paper, and write the other details beside the appropriate hierarchy levels or elements.)

I.   SITUATION

Ask:

"What *situation* might make you feel the beginnings of a low level panic attack?"

Go on to ask the same sort of question about the "middle level panic attack" and the "most severe panic attack." Be sure to ask questions about what situations

a.   led up to;
b.   coincided with;
c.   followed

the *most recent, the first, the worst,* and the *most memorable* panic attacks. If the client needs help, consider suggesting situations such as being in a store, being in a crowd of people, feeling trapped, feeling isolated, having someone ask you a question.

II. PEOPLE

Ask:

"Which *people* might be present, or responsible, when you have a mild or low level panic attack?"

Go on to ask the same sort of questions about the "middle" and "most severe" panic attack.

III. EMOTIONS

Ask:

"What emotions would you fell at the earliest stages of a low level panic attack? Might you feel lonely, isolated, humiliated, or frustrated or bored?"

Go on to ask the same sort of questions about the "middle" and "most severe" panic attacks; consider suggesting emotions such as loneliness, vulnerability, sadness, depression, shame, guilt, disgust, fear, rage, terror, and panic, as you go up the hierarchy.

IV. THOUGHTS

Ask:

"What *thoughts* would you think at the earliest stages of a low level panic attack? Might you think 'I might have an attack, I might faint, I'm confused' or 'they're looking at me'?"

Go on to ask the same sort of question about the middle and severe attacks; consider suggesting thoughts such as "they are noticing that I'm losing it," "I've lost it," "get out of here before it's too late."

V. BEHAVIORS

Ask:

"What *behaviors* might you do in the earliest stages of a low level panic attack?
Might you look for an escape route? Might you lean against a wall? Might you clench your fists?"

Go on to ask the same sort of question about the middle and severe attacks; consider suggesting behaviors such as pacing, sitting, putting your head in your hands, running out the door, lying down, calling out for help.

Appendix B

COPING STATEMENT

DEVELOPMENT

(This feature is included to give the client a document or motto that is specifically tailored to be calming/comforting to him/her.)

The development of a coping statement is often difficult. The client may have a hard time thinking of a possible coping statement, and it helps to suggest several.

Consider the following:

"I can handle this"

"I will use my breathing exercises"

"Easy does it"

"I'm not going to let it get to me"

"I'll stay cool"

"Keep it simple—keep my eye on the prize"

"Take it one step at a time"

"I can keep from getting upset"

"I will just say 'I'm feeling a little upset'"

"I can feel myself getting upset—then I notice that I can relax quickly"

"I can get upset and still think clearly"

"Feeling upset can help me—because it can signal me to relax and focus my mind"

"When other people are angry or irritable I can stay calm and help them calm down"

"I'm the man with the plan—I can make a simple plan to solve this"

"I can keep my sense of humor—this may seem funny later"

"I can speak softly, I can stay calm"

Appendix C

PANIC LOG

NAME:

DATE STARTED:

Date, Time, Duration of the Panic Attack	Situation In which Panic Attack Occurred and Severity (rated from 1 - 10)	Description of the Panic Attack; Symptoms and Sensations	Your response to the Panic Attack: What did you do?	Did you do the Homework?

Appendix D

INTEROCEPTIVE EXPOSURE RECORD
(For Use In Session)

CLIENT NAME:
CLINICIAN:
DATE:
(Instructions: Allow at least one minute of recovery between tasks; Use of a timer is recommended. Select and adjust tasks to match the client's medical condition and general fitness; Also, select tasks to match clients description of subjective sensations during panic attack.)

EXERCISE	SENSATIONS	INTENSITY OF SENSATION (0–10)	INTENSITY OF ANXIETY (0–10)	SIMILARITY TO NATURAL PANIC (0–10)
Shake head from side to side. 30 sec				
Place head between legs for 30 sec then lift head				
Run on spot (or step-up) 1 minute				
Hold breath. 30 seconds				
Spin in chair. 1 minute				
Complete body muscle tension 1 minute				
Hyperventilate 1 minute				
Breathe through straw. 2 minutes				
Stare at bright light (1 minute) then read.				

Appendix E

INTEROCEPTIVE EXPOSURE PRACTICE RECORD FORM
(For Homework)

CLIENT NAME:

DATE:

CLINICIAN:

DESCRIPTION OF EXERCISE: _____

Level of Anxiety/Intensity of Sensations

0-----1-----2-----3-----4-----5-----6-----7-----8-----9-----10

Date	Trial #	Alone? (Y or N)	Anxiety Before	Maximum Anxiety	Maximum Intensity of Sensations

References

Abel, G. G., Becker, J. V., Cunningham-Rathner, N., Rouleau, J. L. & Murphy, W. D. (1987). Self-reported sex crimes of non-incarcerated paraphiliacs. *Journal of Interpersonal Violence*, 2, 3–25.

Adler, A. (1979). *Superiority and social interest.* (Ansbacher, H. L. & Ansbacher, R. R., eds. and trans.) (3rd rev. ed.). New York: W.W. Norton.

Allport, G. W. (1937). *Personality: A psychological interpretation.* New York: Holt, Rinehart & Winston.

Almy, T. P. & Corson, J. A. (in press). Psychophysiologic observations. In D. A. Drossman (ed.), *The Patient with Gastrointestinal Complaints.* New York: Grune & Stratton.

——— (1978). The stress interview: Unfinished business. *Journal of Human Stress*, 4, 3–8.

Ansbacher, H. L. & Ansbacher, R. R. (1956). *The individual psychology of Alfred Adler.* New York: Basic Books.

Arambula, P., Peper, E., Kawakami, M., & Hughes G. K. (2001). The Physiological correlates of Kundalini Yoga Meditation: A study of a yoga master. *Applied Psychophysiology and Biofeedback*, 26,127–140.

Arena, J. G., Goldberg, S. J., Saul, D. L., & Hobbs, S. H. (1989). Temporal stability of psychophysiological response profiles: Analysis of individual response stereotypy and stimulus response specificity. *Behavior Therapy*, 20, 609–618.

Atthowe, J. M., Jr. (1973). Token economies come of age: *Behavior Therapy*, 4, 646–654.

Bandura, A. (1969). *Principles of behavior modification.* New York: Holt, Rinehart and Winston.

————— (1977). Social learning theory. Englewood Cliffs, NJ: Prentice-Hall.

————— (1978). The self system in reciprocal determinism. *American Psychologist*, 33, 344–358.

————— (1982). The self and mechanisms of agency. In J. Suls (ed.), *Psychological perspectives on the self.* (Vol. 1, pp. 3–39). Hillsdale, NJ: Lawrence Erlbaum.

————— (1982). Self-efficacy mechanism in human agency. *American Psychologist,* 37, 122–147.

Bannister, R. (1982). Autonomic failure. New York: Oxford.

Barkley, R. A. (1998). *Attention-deficit hyperactivity disorder: A handbook for diagnosis and treatment* (2nd edition). New York: Guilford.

Barlow, D. H., Craske, M. G., Cerny, J. A., & Klosko, J. S. (1989). Behavioral treatment of panic disorder. *Behavior Therapy*, 20, 261–282.

Bauer, W. D., & Twentyman, C. T. (1985). Abusing, neglectful and comparison mothers' responses to child-related and non-child-related stressors. *Journal of Consulting and Clinical Psychology*, 53 (3), 335–343.

Benson, B. A., Johnson Rice, C., & Miranti, S. V. (1986). Effects of anger management training with mentally retarded adults in group treatment. *Journal of Consulting and Clinical Psychology*, 54 (5), 728–729.

Benson, H., Beary, J. F., & Carol, M. P. (1974). The relaxation response. *Psychiatry*, 37, 37–46.

Berman, P. A., & Johnson, H. J. (1985). A psychophysiological assessment battery. *Biofeedback and Self-Regulation*, 10, 203–221.

Bermudez, J. L., Marcel, A., & Eilan, N. (eds.) (1995). The body and the self. Cambridge, MA: The MIT Press.

Bindra, D. (1959). *Motivation: A systematic reinterpretation.* New York: Ronald Press.

————— (1974). A motivational view of learning, performance, and behavior modification. *Psychological Review*, 81,199–213.

Bion, W. R. (1961). *Experiences in groups and other papers.* New York: Routledge.

Block, J. (1971). *Lives through time.* Berkeley, CA: Bancroft Books.

Blumer, D., & Migeon, C. (1975). Hormone and hormonal agents in the treatment of aggression. *Journal of Nervous and Mental Disease*, 160 (2), 127–137.

Bouchard, C., & Corson, J. A. (1976). Heart rate regulation with success and failure signals. *Psychophysiology*, 13, 69–74.

Bradford, J. W. (1998). Treatment of men with paraphilia. *New England Journal of Medicine*, 338, 464–465

Bradley, S. J. (2000). *Affect regulation and the development of psychopathology.* New York: Guilford Press.

Brener, J. (1977). Sensory and perceptual determinants of voluntary visceral control. In Schwartz, G. E., & Beatty, J., (eds.) *Biofeedback theory and research.* New York, Academic Press.

Brett, E. A., & Ostroff, R. (1985). Imagery and post-traumatic stress disorder: An overview. *The American Journal of Psychiatry*, 141 (4), 417–424.

Brooks, C. McC. (1979). Present interests in and concepts of autonomic nervous system function. *Journal of the Autonomic Nervous System*, I (1) 1–12.

——— & Lange, G. (1982). Patterns of reflex action, their autonomic components, and their behavioral significance. *The Pavlovian Journal of Biological Science*, 17, 55–61.

Buros, O. K. (1974). *Tests in print II.* Highland Park, NJ: Gryphon.

Cacioppo, J. T., Tassinary L. G., & Bernston G.G. (eds.). (2000). *Handbook of Psychophysiology.* New York: Cambridge University Press.

Cattell, R. B. (1965). *The scientific analysis of personality.* Baltimore: Penguin.

Cheshire, N. & Thomae, H. (eds.). (1987). *Self, Symptoms and Psychotherapy.* New York: John Wiley & Sons.

Christopherson, E. R. (1980). The pediatrician and parental discipline. Pediatrics, 66, 641–642.

———, Kuehn, B. S., Grinstead J. D., et al. (1976). A family training program for abuse and neglect families. *Journal of Pediatric Psychology*, 1, 90–94.

Clark, D. M. (1986). A cognitive approach to panic. *Behavior Research & Therapy*, 24 (4), 461–470.

Cleghorn, R. A., & Pattee, C. J. (1954). Psychologic changes in 3 cases of Addison's Disease during treatment with cortisone. *Journal of Clinical Endocrinology & Metabolism*, 14, 344–352.

Cochran, S. V., & Rabinowitz, F. E. (2002). Recommendations for clinicians concerning psychotherapy with men. *Clinicians Research Digest*; supplemental bulletin 26; June 2002.

——— (2003). Gender-sensitive recommendations for assessment and treatment of depression in men. *Professional Psychology: Research and Practice*, 34, 132–140.

Coleman, J. S. (1966). *Equality of educational opportunity.* U.S. Government Printing Office, Washington, D.C.

Cohen, M. J., Rickles, W. H., & McArthur, D. L. (1978). Evidence for physiological response stereotypy in migraine headache. *Psychosomatic Medicine*, 40, 344–354.

Corson, J. A. (1964). The effect of human presence on the extinction performance of a cat. *Psychonomic Science*, 1, 413–414.

———— & Heseltine, G. F. (1971). A systems approach to delivery of mental health treatment. *The Journal of Biomedical Systems*, 2 (8), 25–31.

————, Bouchard, C., Scherer, M. W., et al. (1973). Instrumental control of autonomic responses with the use of a cognitive strategy. *Canadian Psychiatric Association Journal*, 18, 21–24.

———— (1976). Families as mutual control systems: Optimization by systematization of reinforcement. In E. J. Mash, L. A. Hamerlynck, & L. C. Handy, (eds.), *Behavior modification and families* (pp. 317–330). New York: Brunner/Mazel.

————, Grant, J. L. Moulton, D. P., Green, R. L., & Dunkel, P. T. (1979). Use of biofeedback in weaning paralyzed patients from respirators. *Chest*, 76, 543–545.

————, Schneider, M. J., Biondi C. G., & Myers, H. K. (1980). Psychophysiological assessment: Toward a general strategy. *American Journal of Clinical Biofeedback,* 3, 52–67.

———— & Schneider, M. J. (1984). The Dartmouth Pain Questionnaire. *Pain*, 19, 59–69.

———— (1989). *Stress, self-concept, and violence.* New York: AMS Press.

———— (1995). Clinical psychology: the state-of-the-art. *Journal of Pain and Symptom Management*, 10 (6), 487–489.

Corrigan, P.W. (2001). Getting ahead of the data: A threat to some behavior therapies. *The Behavior Therapist*, 24,189–193.

Craske, M. G. & Barlow, D. H. (1990). *Therapist's guide for mastery over your anxiety and panic.* San Antonio, Texas: The Psychological Corporation/Harcourt Brace & Co.

———— (1994). *Mastery of your anxiety and panic II, Client Workbook.* San Antonio, Texas: The Psychological Corporation/Harcourt Brace & Co.

Csikszentmihalyi, M. (1993). *The Evolving Self.* New York: Harper Collins.

Deffenbacher, J. L., Demm, P. M., & Brandon, A. D. (1986). High general anger: Correlates and treatment. *Behavior Research & Therapy*, 24 (4), 481–489.

Delis, D. C., Kaplan, E., & Kramer, J. H. (2001). *Delis-Kaplan executive function system.* San Antonio: The Psychological Corporation.

Demos, E. V. (ed.). (1995). *Exploring affect: The selected writings of Sylvan E. Tompkins.* New York: Cambridge University Press.

Denicola, J., & Sandler, J. (1980). Training abusive parents in child management and self-control skills. *Behavior Therapy*, II, 263–270.

DeRubeis, R. J., & Crits-Christoph, P. (1998). Empirically supported individual and group psychological treatments for adult mental disorders. *Journal of Consulting and Clinical Psychology*, 66, 37–52.

Detrick, D. W. & Detrick, S. P. (eds.). (1989). *Self Psychology: Comparisons and Contrasts*. Hillsdale, New Jersey: the Analytic Press.

Drabman, R. S., & Jarvie, G. (1977). Counseling parents of children with behavior problems: The use of extinction and time-out techniques. *Pediatrics*, 59, 78–85.

Elliott F. A. (1982). Neurological findings in adult minimal brain dysfunction and the dyscontrol syndrome. *Journal of Nervous and Mental Disease*, 170, 680–687.

Ekman, P., Levenson, R. W., & Friesen, W. V. (1983). Autonomic nervous system activity distinguishes among emotions. *Science*, 221, 1208–1210.

Engel, G. L. (1980). The clinical application of the biopsychosocial model. *American Journal of Psychiatry*, 137 (5), 535–544.

Epstein, N. (1980). Social consequences of assertion, aggression, passive aggression, and submission: Situational and dispositional determinants. *Behavior Therapy*, 11, 662–669.

Epstein, S. (1973). The self-concept revisited, or a theory of a theory. *American Psychologist*, 28, 404–416.

———— (1980). The self-concept: A review and the proposal of an integrated theory of personality. In E. Staub (ed.), *Personality: Basic aspects and current research*. Englewood Cliffs, NJ: Prentice-Hall.

Eron, L. D. (1987). The development of aggressive behavior from the perspective of a developing behaviorism. *American Psychologist*, 42 (5), 435–442.

Everly, G., & Sobelman, S. A. (1987). *Assessment of the human stress response*. New York: AMS Press.

Fahrenberg, J., Foerster, F., Schneider, H. J., Muller, W., & Myrtek, M. (1986). Predictability of individual differences in activation processes in a field setting based on laboratory measures. *Psychophysiology*, 23 (3), 323–332.

Feallock, R., & Miller, L. K. (1976). The design and evaluation of a worksharing system for experimental group living. *Journal of Applied Behavior Analysis*, 9, 277–288.

Feldman, R. G., & Paul, N. L. (1976). Identity of emotional triggers in epilepsy. *Journal of Nervous and Mental Disease*, 162 (5), 345–353.

Ferguson, G. A. (1959). *Statistical analysis in psychology and education*. New York: McGraw Hill.

Feshbach, S. (1970). Aggression. In P. H. Mussen (ed.), *Carmichael's manual of child psychology (Vol. 2)*. New York: Wiley.

Firestone, P., Bradford, J., Greenberg, D., Larose, M., & Curry, S. (1998). Homicidal and non-homicidal child molesters: Psychological, phallometric, and criminal features. *Sexual Abuse: Journal of Research & Treatment*, 10, 305–323.

Fisch, B. J. (ed.). (1991). *Spehlmann's EEG primer (2nd ed.)*. New York: Elsevier.

Fitzgerald, H. E., & Brackbill, Y. (1976). Classical conditioning in infancy: Development and constraints. *Psychological Bulletin*, 83, 353–376.

Flor, H., Turk, D. C., & Birbaumer, M (1985). Assessment of stress-related psychophysiological reactions in chronic back pain patients. *Journal of Consulting and Clinical Psychology*, 53, 354–364.

Fowles, D. C. (1980). The three arousal model: Implications of Gray's two-factor learning theory for heart rate, electrodermal activity, and psychopathy. *Psychophysiology*, 17 (2), 87–103.

Foy, D. W., Eisler, R. M., & Pinkston, S. (1975). Modeled assertion in a case of explosive rage. *Journal of Behavior Therapy and Experimental Psychiatry*, 6, 135–137.

Fransella, F. (1985). In Button, E. *Personal construct theory and mental-health* (p. 285). Cambridge, MA: Brookline Books.

Freud, S. (1930). *Civilization and its discontents*. Standard Edition, London: Hogarth Press, 21, 59. [as cited by Gaylin (1984)].

Frisch, M. B. (1992.). Use of the quality of life inventory in problem assessment and treatment planning for cognitive therapy of depression. In A. Freeman and F. M. Dattilio (eds.), *Comprehensive Casebook of Cognitive Therapy*. New York: Plenum Press, 27–52.

Frodi, A. M., & Lamb, M. E. (1980). Child abusers' responses to infant smiles and cries. *Child Development*, 51, 238–241.

Garbutt, J. C., & Loosen, P. T. (1983). Is carbamazepine helpful in paroxysmal behavior disorders? *American Journal of Psychiatry*, 140 (10), 1363–1364.

Gaylin, W. (1984). *The rage within*. New York: Simon and Schuster.

Gazzaniga, M. S. (1998). *The mind's past*. Berkeley: University of California Press.

Gendreau, P., & Ross, R. R. (1987). Revivification of rehabilitation: Evidence from the 1980's. *Justice Quarterly*, 4 (3), 349–407.

Gergin K. J. (1991). *The Saturated Self*. New York: Basic Books.

Gilligan, J. (1996). *Violence*. New York: G. P. Putnam and Sons.

Goldfried, M., Decenteceo, E., & Weinberg, L. (1974). Systematic rational restructuring as a self-control technique. *Behavior Therapy*, 5, 247–254.

Goleman, D. (1985). *Vital lies, simple truths*. New York: Simon & Schuster.

Goodwin, S.E., & Mahoney, M.J. (1975). Modification of aggression through modeling: An experimental probe. *Journal of Behavior Therapy & Experimental Psychiatry*, 6, 200–202.

Greendyke, R. M., Kanter, D. R., Schuster, D. B., Verstreate, S., & Wootton, J. (1986). Propranolol treatment of assaultive patients with organic brain disease. A double-blind crossover, placebo-controlled study. *Journal of Nervous and Mental Disease*, 174 (5), 290–294.

Grossman, L. S., Martis, B., & Fichtner, C. G. (1999). Are sex offenders treatable? *Psychiatric Services*. 50, 349–361.

Hammond, D. C., Sterman, M. B., LaVaque, T. J., Moore, N.C., & Lubar, J. The efficacy of neurofeedback. *The Behavior Therapist*, 25, 90–91.

Hannon, L., DeFronzo, J., & Prochnow, J. (2001). Moral commitment and the effects of social influences on violent delinquency. *Violence and Victims*, 16 (4), 427–439.

Hanson, R. K. & Bussiere M. T. (1998). Predicting relapse: A meta-analysis of sexual offender recidivism studies. *Journal of Consulting and Clinical Psychology*, 66, 348–362.

Harris, T. A. (1967). *I'm OK—You're OK. A practical guide to transactional analysis*. New York: Harper & Row.

Harvey, J. R., Karan, O. C., Bhargava, D., & Morehouse, N. (1978). Relaxation training and cognitive behavioral procedures to reduce violent temper outbursts in a moderately retarded woman. *Journal of Behavior Therapy & Experimental Psychiatry*, 9, 347–351.

Hatch, J. P., Fisher, J. G., & Rugh, J. D. (1987). *Biofeedback: Studies in clinical efficacy*. New York: Plenum.

Hays, J. R., Roberts, T. K., & Solway, K. S. (eds.). (1981). *Violence and the Violent Individual*. New York: Spectrum.

Hazaleus, S. L., & Deffenbacher, J. L. (1986). Relaxation and cognitive treatments of anger. *Journal of Consulting and Clinical Psychology*, 54, 222–226.

Heath, L., Kruttschnitt, C., & Ward, D. (1986). Television and violent criminal behavior: Beyond the booboo doll. *Violence and Victims*, 1 (3), 177–190.

Hebb, D. O. (1949). *The organization of behavior*. New York: Wiley.

———— (1960). The American revolution. *American Psychologist*, 15, 735–745.

———— (1980). *Essay on mind*. Hillsdale, NJ: Laurence Erlbaum Associates.

———— (1972). *Textbook of psychology*. Philadelphia, PA: W.B. Saunders Co.

Higgins, E. T., Bond, R. N., Klein, R., & Strauman, T. J. (1986). Self-discrepancies and emotional vulnerability: how magnitude, accessibility, and type of discrepancy influence affect. *Journal of Personality and Social Psychology*, 51 (1), 5–15.

Holmes, T. H., & Rahe, R. H. (1967). The social readjustment rating scale. *Journal of Psychosomatic Research*, 11, 213–218.

Holden, C. (1987). The genetics of personality. *Science*, 237, 598–601.

Horowitz, M. J. (1981). Self-righteous rage and the attribution of blame. *Archives of General Psychiatry*, 38, 1233–1238.

Houtler, B. D., & Rosenberg, H. (1985). The retrospective baseline in single case experiments. *The Behavior Therapist*, 8, 97–98.

Hoyer, J., Kunst, H., & Schmidt A. (2001). Social phobia as a comorbid condition in sex offenders with paraphilia or impulse control disorder. *Journal of Nervous and Mental Disease*, 189, 463–470.

Hughes, J. R., & Hermann, B. P. (1984). Evidence of psychopathology in patients with rhythmic midtemporal discharges. *Biological Psychiatry*, 19, 1623–1634.

Hunt, J. MCV. (1972). Early childhood education and social class. *Canadian Psychologist*, 13, 305–328.

Infantino, J. A., Jr., & Musingo, S. Y. (1985). Assaults and injuries among staff with and without training in aggression control techniques. *Hospital and Community Psychiatry*, 36 (12), 1312–1314.

Itil, T. M., & Wadud, A. (1975). Treatment of human aggression with major tranquilizers, antidepressants and newer psychotropic drugs. *Journal of Nervous and Mental Disease*, 160 (2), 83–99.

James, W. (1892). *Psychology: Briefer course*. New York: Holt.

———— (1907). *Pragmatism: A new name for some old ways of thinking*. New York: Longmans, Green.

Kazdin, A. E., & Bootzin, R. R. (1972). The token economy: An evaluative review. *Journal of Applied Behavior Analysis*, 5, 343–372.

Keller, S. (1963). The social world of the urban slum child: Some early findings. *American Journal of Orthopsychiatry*, 33, 823–831.

Kelley, P. (2002). A narrative therapy approach to brief treatment. *Journal of Brief Therapy*, 1, 91–100.

Kelly, G. A. (1955). *The psychology of personal constructs*. New York: Norton.

Kindlon, D. & Thompson, M. G. (1999). *Raising Cain: Protecting the emotional life of boys*. New York: Ballantine Books.

Kinkade, K. (1973). *A Walden-Two experiment: The first five years of Twin Oaks community*. New York: William Morrow.

Kolata, G. (1987). What babies know and noises parents make. *Science*, 237, 726.

Kolb, L. C. (1987). A neuropsychological hypothesis explaining posttraumatic stress disorders. *American Journal of Psychiatry*, 144 (8), 989–995.

Kosslyn, S. M., Cacioppo,J. T., Davidson, R. J., Hugdahl, K., Lovallo, W. R., Spiegel, D., & Rose, R. (2002). Bridging psychology and biology. *American Psychologist*, 57, 341–351.

Lane, R. D., & Schwartz, G. E. (1987). Induction of lateralized sympathetic input to the heart by the CNS during emotional arousal: A possible neurophysiologic trigger of sudden cardiac death. *Psychosomatic Medicine*, 49 (3), 274–284.

Lang, P. J. (1979). A bio-informational theory of emotional imagery. *Psychophysiology*, 16 (6), 495–512.

Lanyon, R. I. (2001). Psychological assessment procedures in sex offending. *Professional Psychology: Research and Practice*, 32, 253–260.

Lazarus, A. A. (1987). The multimodal approach with adult outpatients. In N. S. Jacobson (ed.), *Psychotherapists in Clinical Practice*. New York: Guilford Publications Inc.

LeDoux, J. (1996). *The emotional brain: The mysterious underpinnings of emotional life*. New York: Simon & Schuster.

Levine, L., Garcia Coll, C. T., & Oh, W. (1985). Determinants of mother-infant interaction in adolescent mothers. *Pediatrics*, 75 (1), 23–29.

Lewinsohn, P. M., Weinstein, M. S., & Shaw, D. A. (1968). Depression: A clinical-research approach. In R. D. Rubin & C. M. Franks (eds.). *Advances in Behavior Therapy*. New York: Academic Press.

Lindon, J. A. (1991). *Bulletin of the Menninger Clinic*, 55,1–21.

Linehan, M. M. (1993). Skills training manual for treating borderline personality disorder. New York: Guilford press.

Lion, J. R., Madden, D. J., & Christopher, R. L. (1976). A violence clinic: Three years' experience. *American Journal of Psychiatry*, 133 (4), 432–435.

Long, B. H., & Henderson, E. H. (1967). Social schemata of school beginners: Some demographic correlates. *Proceedings of the 75th Annual Convention of the American Psychological Association*, Washington, D.C.: American Psychological Association, 329–330.

Lorr, M., & Wunderlich, R. A. (1986). Two objective measures of self-esteem. *Journal of Personality Assessment*, 50 (1), 18–23.

Luiselli, J. K. (1984). Treatment of an assaultive, sensory-impaired adolescent through a multicomponent behavioral program. *Journal of Behavior Therapy and Experimental Psychiatry*, 15 (1), 71–78.

MacLean, P. D. (1986). Ictal symptoms relating to the nature of affects and their cerebral substrate. In R. Plutchik, & H. Kellerman, (eds.)., *Biological foundations of emotion* (pp. 61–90). New York: Academic Press.

Mahalik, J. R., Good, G. E., & Englar-Carlson, M. (2003). Masculinity scripts, presenting concerns, and help seeking: implications for practice and training. *Professional Psychology: Research and Practice*, 34 (1), 123–131.

Maitland, S. C. (1966). *The perspective, frustration-failure and delay of gratification in middle-class and lower-class children from organized and disorganized families.* Unpublished doctoral dissertation, Minneapolis: University of Minnesota.

Malta, L. S., Blanchard, E. B., Freidenberg, B. M., Galovski, T. E., Karl, A., & Holzapfel, S. R. (2001). Psychophysiological reactivity of aggressive drivers: An exploratory study. *Applied Psychophysiology and Biofeedback*, 26, 95–116.

Mandelzys, N., Lane, E. B., & Marceau, R. (1981). The relationship of violence to alpha levels in a biofeedback training paradigm. *Journal of Clinical Psychology*, 37 (1), 202–209.

Mann, J. (1973). Time-limited psychotherapy. New York: McGraw-Hill.

———— & Goldman, R. (1982). *A casebook in time-limited psychotherapy.* New York: McGraw-Hill.

Markus, H., & Nurius, P. (1986). Possible selves. *American Psychologist*, 41 (9), 954–969.

———— (1986). Possible selves: The interface between motivation and the self-concept. In K. Yardley & T. Honess, (eds.). *Self and identity: Psychosocial perspectives* (pp. 157–172). New York: Wiley.

Marshall, W. L., Jones, R., Ward, T., Johnston, P., & Barbaree, H. E. (1991). Treatment outcome with sex offenders. *Clinical Psychology Review*, 11, 465–485.

———— & Pithers, W. D. (1994). A reconsideration of treatment outcome with sex offenders. *Criminal Justice and Behavior*, 21, 10–27.

———— (1996). Assessment, treatment, and theorizing about sex offenders. Criminal Justice and Behavior, 23, 162–169.

Masters, J. C., Burish, T. G., Hollon, S. D., & Rimm, D. C. (1987). *Behavior therapy: Techniques and empirical findings* (3rd ed.). New York: Harcourt, Brace, Jovanovich.

McGrady, A. V., Bush, E. G. & Grubb, B. P. (1997). Outcome of biofeedback assisted relaxation for neurocardiogenic syncope and headache: a clinical replication series. *Applied Psychophysiology and Biofeedback*, 22, 63–72.

McGrath, R. J. Cumming, G. Livingston, J. A. & & Hoke, S. E. (2003). Outcome of a treatment program for adult sex offenders. Journal of Interpersonal Violence, 18 (1), 3-17.

McNiel, D. E., Eisner, J. P., & Binder, R. L. The relationship between aggressive attributional style and violence by psychiatric patients. *Journal of Consulting and Clinical Psychology*, 71 (2), 399–403.

Megargee, E. I. (1966). Undercontrolled and overcontrolled personality types in extreme antisocial aggression. *Psychological Monographs*, 3, (Whole No. 611).

Meichenbaum, D. (1974). *Cognitive behavior modification*. Morristown, NJ: General Learning Press.

———— (1977). *Cognitive behavior modification: An integrative approach*. New York: Plenum Press.

———— (1980). Stability of Personality: Change and psychotherapy. In E. Staub (ed.), *Personality: Basic aspects and current research*. Englewood Cliffs, NJ: Prentice-Hall.

———— & Fitzpatrick, D. (1994). A constructivist narrative perspective on stress and coping. Stress inoculation application. In L. Goldberger and S. Breznitz (eds.) *Handbook of stress: Theoretical and clinic aspects*. New York: Free Press.

———— (2000). Treating patients with PTSD: A constructive narrative approach. *National Center—PTSD Clinical Quarterly*, 9, 55–59.

Metcalfe, J., & Jacobs, W. J. (1996). A "hot system/cool system" view of memory under stress. *PTSD Research Quarterly*, 7 (2), 1–6.

Miller, A. (1984). *For your own good* (2nd ed.). New York: Farrar, Straus & Giroux.

Miller, W. R., & Seligman, M. E. P. (1976). Learned helplessness, depression and the perception of reinforcement. *Behavior Research and Therapy*, 14, 7–17.

Mischel, W. (1976). *Introduction to personality* (2nd ed.). New York: Holt, Rinehart and Winston.

———— & Metzner, R. (1962). Preference for delayed reward as a function of age, intelligence and length of delay interval. *Journal of Abnormal and Social Psychology*, 64, 245–431.

Monroe, R. R. (1975). Anticonvulsants in the treatment of aggression. *Journal of Nervous and Mental Disease*, 160 (2), 119–126.

Moos, R. (1973). Conceptualizations of human environments. *American Psychologist*, 28, 652–665.

———— (1976). *The human context: Environmental determinants of behavior*. New York: Wiley.

Moos, R. H. (1969). Sources of variance in responses to questionnaires and in behavior. *Journal of Abnormal Psychology*, 74, 405–412.

———— & Insel, P. M. (eds.). (1974*). Issues in social ecology*. Palo Alto, CA: National Press Books.

Murray, H. A. (with collaborators) (1938). *Explorations in personality*. New York: Oxford University Press.

Newmark, C. S. (ed.). (1985). *Major psychological assessment instruments*. Boston: Allyn & Bacon.

Novaco, R. W. (1975). *Anger control: The development and evaluation of an experimental treatment.* Lexington, MA: Heath.

——— (1976). The functions and regulation of the arousal of anger. *American Journal of Psychiatry*, 133,1124–1128.

Nurius, P. S., and Berlin, S. (1994). Treatment of negative self-concept and depression. In Granvold, D. K. (ed.), *Cognitive and Behavioral Treatment.* Belmont, California: Brooks/Cole Publishing Company (a division of Wadsworth Inc.).

O'Brian, P. (1991). *The nutmeg of consolation.* New York: W.W. Norton.

Otto, M. W., Pollack, M. H., & Maki, K. M. (2000). Empirically supported treatments for panic disorder: costs, benefits, and stepped care. *Journal of Consulting and Clinical Psychology*, 68 (4), 556–563.

Pennebaker, J. W. (1997). *Opening up: The healing power of expressing emotion.* New York: Guilford Press.

——— (1999). The effects of traumatic disclosure on physical and mental health: The values of writing and talking about upsetting events. *International Journal of Emergency Mental Health*, 1, 9–18.

Peper, E. & Tibbets, V. (1992). Fifteen-month follow-up with asthmatics utilizing EMG/incentive inspirometer feedback. *Biofeedback and Self-Regulation*, 17 (2), 143–151.

Peterson, C., & Seligman, M. E. P. (1984). Causal explanations as a risk factor for depression: Theory and evidence. *Psychological Review*, 91, 347–374.

Plaud, J. J. & Martini, J. R. (1999). The respondent conditioning of male sexual arousal. *Behavior Modification*, 23, 254–268.

Plutchik, R. (2001) The nature of emotions. *American Scientist*, 89, 344–350.

Rachman, S., & Lopatka, C. (1986). Match and mismatch in the prediction of fear – I. *Behavior Research & Therapy*, 24, (3), 387–393.

——— (1986). Match and mismatch of fear in Gray's theory – II. *Behavior Research & Therapy*, 24, (4), 395–401.

Ratey, J. J., Morrill, R., & Oxenkrug, G. (1983). Use of propranolol for provoked and unprovoked episodes of rage. *American Journal of Psychiatry*, 140 (10), 1356–1357.

Raymond, N. C., Coleman, E., Ohlerking, F. Christenson, G. A., & Miner, M. (1999). Psychiatric comorbidity in pedophilic sex offenders. *American Journal of Psychiatry*, 156, 786–788.

Rehm, L. P., & Plakosh, P. (1975). Preference for immediate reinforcement in depression. *Journal of Behavior Therapy & Experimental Psychiatry*, 6, 101–103.

Reiss, A. J., Jr., & Roth, J. A. (eds.). (1993). *Understanding and preventing violence, National Academy of Sciences Panel on the Understanding and Prevention of Violent Behavior.* Washington DC: National Academy Press.

Rhodes, R. (1999). *Why they kill.* New York: Alfred A. Knopf.

Riley, T., & Niedermeyer, E. (1977). Rage attacks and episodic violent behavior: Electroencephalographic findings and general considerations. *Clinical Electroencephalography,* 9, 131–139.

Rimm, D. C., de Groot, J. C., Board, P., Heiman, J., & Dillow, P. V. (1971). Systematic desensitization of an anger response. *Behavior Research & Therapy,* 9, 273–280.

————— & Masters, J. C. (1979). *Behavior therapy: Techniques and empirical findings* (2nd ed.). New York: Academic Press.

Roth, L. H. (ed.). (1987). *Clinical treatment of the violent person.* New York: Guilford.

Roy, A. (1977). Hysterical fits previously diagnosed as epilepsy. *Psychological Medicine,* 7, 271–273.

Russell, J. A., Weiss, A., & Mendelson, G. A. (1989). Affect grid: single-item scale of pleasure and arousal. *Journal of Personality and Social Psychology,* 57 (3), 493–502.

Rychlak, J. F. (1977). *The psychology of rigorous humanism.* New York: Wiley.

Ryle, A., & Marlowe, M. J. (1995). Cognitive analytic therapy of borderline personality disorder: Theory and practice and the clinical and research uses of the self-states sequential diagram. *International Journal of Short-Term Psychotherapy,* 10, 21–34.

Salkovskis, P. M., & Clark, D. M. (1990). Affective responses to hyperventilation: A test of the cognitive model of panic. *Behavior Research & Therapy,* 28, 51–61.

Samenow, S. E. (1984). *Inside the criminal mind.* New York: Times Books.

Sandler, J., Van Dercar, C., & Milhoan, M. (1978). Training child abusers in the use of positive reinforcement practices. *Behavior Research & Therapy,* 16,169–175.

Sanders, W. (1978). Systematic densensitization in the treatment of child abuse. *American Journal of Psychiatry,* 135, 483–484.

Schatzman, M. (1973). *Soul murder: Persecution in the family.* New York: Penguin.

Schretlen, D. (1996). *Brief Test of Attention: Professional Manual.* Odessa, Florida: Psychological Assessment Resources Inc.

Schore, A. N. (1994). *Affect regulation and the origin of the self.* Hillsdale, NJ: Lawrence Erlbaum Associates.

Schwartz, M. S. (1995). *Biofeedback, a practitioner's guide* (second edition). New York, NY: The Guilford Press.

Seligman, M. E. P. (1975*). Helplessness: On depression, development and death*. San Francisco: W. H. Freeman.

Selye, H. (1974). *Stress without distress*. Philadelphia: Lippincott.

———— (1976*). The stress of life*. New York: McGraw-Hill.

———— (1978, March). On the real benefits of eustress. *Psychology Today*, 60–64.

Shefler, G., Dasberg, H., & Gershon, B. (1995). A randomized controlled outcome and follow-up study of Mann's time-limited psychotherapy. *Journal of Consulting and Clinical Psychology*. 63, 585–593.

Skinner, B. F. (1948). *Walden two*. New York: Macmillan.

———— (1961, Summer). The design of cultures. *Daedalus*, 534–546.

———— (1971). *Beyond freedom and dignity*. New York: Knopf.

Smith, J. S. (1980). Episodic rage. In M. Girgis & L.G. Kiloh (eds.), *Limbic epilepsy and the dyscontrol syndrome*. Amsterdam: Elsevier.

Staub, E. (ed.). (1980). *Personality: Basic aspects and current research*. Englewood Cliffs, NJ: Prentice-Hall.

Steen, M. T. (1966). *The effects of immediate and delayed reinforcement on the achievement behavior of Mexican-American children of low socioeconomic status*. Unpublished doctoral dissertation, Stanford University, California.

Sterman, M. B. (2000). Basic concepts and clinical findings in the treatment of seizure disorders with EEG operant conditioning. *Clinical Encephalography*, 31, 45–55.

Stern, R. M., Ray, W. J., & Quigley, K. S. (2001). *Psychophysiological recording* (second edition). Oxford: Oxford University press.

Stone, J. L., McDaniel, K. D., Hughes, J. R., & Hermann, B. P. (1986). Episodic dyscontrol disorder and paroxysmal EEG abnormalities: Successful treatment with carbamazepine. *Biological Psychiatry*, 21, 208–212.

Strauman, T. J. (1990). Self-guides and emotionally significant childhood memories: a study of retrieval insufficiency and incidental negative emotional content. *Journal of Personality and Social Psychology*, 59, (5), 869–880.

Stringer, A. Y., & Josef, N. C. (1983). Methylphenidate in the treatment of aggression in two patients with antisocial personality disorder. *American Journal of Psychiatry*, 140 (10), 1365–1366.

Stroebel, C. (1982). *QR the quieting reflex*. New York: Berkley Books.

Sweetland, R. C., & Keyser, D. J. (1983). *Tests*. Kansas City: Test Corporation of America.

Tardiff, K. (1987). Violence and the violent patient. In R. E. Hales & A. J. Frances (eds.), *Psychiatry update: The American Psychiatric Association Annual Review*, 6, 447–566.

Terrel, G., Jr., Durkin, K., & Weisley, M. (1959). Social class and the nature of the incentive in discrimination learning. *Journal of Abnormal & Social Psychology*, 59, 270–272.

Tesser, A., Felson, R. B. & Suls, J. M. (2000). *Psychological perspectives on self and identity*. Washington, DC: American Psychological Association.

Tharp, R. G., & Gallimore, R. (1976). Basketball's John Wooden: What a coach can teach a teacher. *Psychology Today*, 9, 74–78.

Tsao, J.C.I., Mystkowski, J.L., Zucker, B.G., & Craske, M.G. Effects of cognitive-behavioral therapy for panic disorder on co-morbid conditions: replication and extension. *Behavior Therapy*, 33, 493–509.

Tyler, L. E. (1965). *The psychology of human differences* (3rd ed.). Englewood Cliffs, NJ. Prentice-Hall.

Ulman, R. B., & Brothers, D. (1988). *The Shattered Self*. Hinsdale, NJ: The Analytic Press.

Van der Kolk, B. A., & Greenberg, M. S. (1987). The psychobiology of the trauma response: Hyperarousal, constriction, and addiction to traumatic re-exposure. In B.A. Van der Kolk (ed.), *Psychological Trauma* (pp. 63–87). Washington, DC: American Psychiatric Press.

Walsh, P. C. (ed.). (1998). *Campbell's Urology* (7th ed.). Philadelphia: Saunders.

Waltz, J., Babcock, J. C., Jacobson, N. S., & Gottman, J. M. (2000). Testing a typology of batterers. *Journal of Consulting and Clinical Psychology*, 68 (4), 658–669.

Watson, D. L., & Tharp, R. G. (2002). *Self directed behavior* (8th ed.). Belmont, California: Wadsworth/Thompson Learning.

Wallace, J. (1966). An abilities conception of personality: Some implications for personality measurement. *American Psychologist*, 21, 132–138.

Wallin, B. G., & Fagius, J. (1986). The sympathetic nervous system in man—aspects derived from microelectrode recordings. *Trends in Neuroscience*, 63–73.

Weilburg, J. B., Bear, D. M., & Sachs, G. (1987). Three patients with concomitant panic attacks and seizure disorder: Possible clues to the neurology of anxiety. *American Journal of Psychiatry*, 144 (8), 1053–1056.

Weinrott, M. R., Riggan, M., & Frothingham, S. (1997). Reducing deviant arousal in juvenile sex offenders using vicarious sensitization. *Journal of Interpersonal Violence*, 12, 704–728.

Wenger, M. A., Averill, J. R., & Smith, B. (1968). Autonomic activity during sexual arousal. *Psychophysiology*, 4, 468–478.

White, M. A. (1975). Natural rates of teacher approval and disapproval in the classroom. *Journal of Applied Behavior Analysis*, 8, 367–372.

White, M. & Epston, D. (1990). *Narrative means to therapeutic ends*. New York: W.W. Norton.

White, R. W. (1952). *Lives in progress*. New York: The Dryden Press.

Willerman, L., Turner, R. G., & Peterson, M. A. (1976). A comparison of the predictive validity of typical and maximal personality measures. *Journal of Research in Personality*, 10, 482–492.

Wilson, S. J., Lipsey, M. W., & Derzon, J. H. (2003). The effects of school-based intervention programs on aggressive behavior: a meta-analysis. *Journal of Consulting and Clinical Psychology*, 71, 136–149.

Wong, S. E., Slama, K. M., & Liberman, R. P. (1987). Behavioral analysis and therapy for aggressive psychiatric and developmentally disabled patients. In L. H. Roth (ed.). *Clinical treatment of the violent person*. New York: Guilford.

Yalom, I. D. (1995). *The theory and practice of group psychotherapy* (4th ed.). New York: Basic Books.

——— (2002*). The gift of therapy*. New York: Harper Collins.

Yudofsky, S. C., Silver, J. M., Jackson, W., Endicott, J., & Williams, D. (1986). The overt aggression scale for the objective rating of verbal and physical aggression. *American Journal of Psychiatry*, 143 (1), 35–39.

Zigler, E., & DeLabry, J. (1962). Concept-switching in middle-class, lower-class and retarded children. *Journal of Abnormal and Social Psychology*, 65, 267–273.

Index